Surveying

Surveying the People

The interpretation and use of document sources for the study of population in the later seventeenth century

---

Edited by

KEVIN SCHURER
and
TOM ARKELL

A LOCAL POPULATION STUDIES SUPPLEMENT

First published in 1992 by
LEOPARD'S HEAD PRESS LIMITED
2a Polstead Road, Oxford OX2 6TN

© Local Population Studies
Tawney House, Matlock, Derbyshire, DE4 3BT

ISBN 0 904920 24 0

Whilst copyright in the volume as a whole is vested in Local Population Studies, copyright in the individual contributions belongs to the respective authors and no article may be reproduced in any form or by any means without the prior permission, in writing, of the editors, author and publisher.

The publication of this volume has been assisted by a grant from the Marc Fitch Fund, which is gratefully acknowledged.

Printed in Great Britain by
Blackmore Press, Longmead, Shaftesbury, Dorset

Contents

List of Contributors

James Alexander, *Research Assistant, Business History Unit, London School of Economics*

Tom Arkell, *Associate Fellow and former Senior Lecturer in Arts Education, University of Warwick*

Jeremy Boulton, *Lecturer in History, University of Newcastle*

Sheila Cooper, *Assistant Professor of History, University of Indiana*

Chris Husbands, *Lecturer in History Education, University of East Anglia*

Peter Jackson, *Lecturer in History, University of Brighton*

Peter Laslett, *Advising Director, ESRC Cambridge Group for the History of Population and Social Structure and Fellow, Trinity College, University of Cambridge*

Kevin Schurer, *Senior Research Associate, ESRC Cambridge Group for the History of Population and Social Structure*

Anne Whiteman, *Emeritus Fellow in Modern History, Lady Margaret Hall, University of Oxford*

List of Tables

List of Figures

List of Illustrations

Preface

Like many other publications before it, this book has been a long time in the making. In one form or another it has been in existence almost as many years as it has chapters. As such it has acquired a history of its own. Its life started as a result of a discussion during an editorial board meeting of the *Local Population Studies* journal. In line with the traditional mid-way stance of the journal, standing as it does like a bridge between the professional and amateur researching the patterns and behaviour of populations in the past, it was seen as a good idea for the journal to publish a series of articles which highlighted both the potential of various key sources for the study of historical demography and social structure in the seventeenth century and the problems of interpretation associated with these documents. As a consequence a number of likely contributors were contacted in order to judge their response to the suggestion. As the initial idea developed and began to take shape, it gradually became evident that the proposed work would have a greater attraction and strength as a single collected volume, rather than a series of disparate essays. Thus, the notion of the present book was born.

However, after the first drafts of many of the chapters had been gathered in, it became painfully clear that one of the central problems of using the four key sources identified for research – the Hearth tax, Compton census, Poll taxes and Marriage Duty assessments (particularly the latter two) – was that no general text detailing their legislative and administrative framework existed in a form that was easily accessible for many of those within the academic network, let alone those outside of it. This realisation resulted in a subsequent shift in emphasis in the proposed format and structure of the book – from one in which the potential and problems of the identified sources was illustrated solely by examples of their use, to one which required a balance between the worked example approach and the detailed, rather descriptive review of the processes which led to the creation of the sources in question. We would like to think that the text that follows achieves this much needed balance. Due to the strong connections between the Poll taxes and the Marriage Duty assessments it was decided to bracket these two sources together in detailing their background. As a consequence, the chapters dealing with these two sources form the second part of this volume, while those which relate to the Compton census and the Hearth taxes form the first. Brief introductions, with appropriate examples, which discuss the key features of the documents in terms of form and structure are provided for both parts.

As one might expect in the case of any volume with a long and changing history, there are many individuals whose endeavours require recognition. The list that follows is not necessarily placed in order of indebtedness, yet we agree that the first mention must go to Richard Wall. In his capacity as editor of *Local Population Studies* it was upon Richard's shoulders that the burden of collating the volume first fell. Unfortunately, the pressure of other duties intervened to ensure that he would not be in a position to finish the work he had started. That we are indebted to his careful guiding throughout the initial stages of editorial work goes without saying. In many respects his contribution during the nascent period of this volume warrants the inclusion of his name as editor alongside ours. Yet despite this, from his own choosing, he remains in the background, as the third man.

We must also convey our thanks to the other members of the editorial board team of *Local Population Studies*, both past and present – Christopher Charlton, Michael Drake, Terry Gwynne, May Pickles, Roger Schofield, Malcolm Smith and Geoffrey Stevenson. Collectively they have given much needed support and encouragement, and individually they have each contributed valuable advice, comments and suggestions concerning not only the detailed content but also the overall structure and format of the volume.

The authors of the individual chapters of the volume also deserve a special mention of gratitude. They are to be thanked not only for their contributions, but also, given the prolonged preparation of the volume, for their patience and understanding. We would also like to express our thanks to Jeremy Boulton who not only contributed a chapter of his own, but in addition read through the drafts of other chapters and provided important and helpful suggestions. Our special thanks are extended to Anne Whiteman who, in addition to offering a chapter of her own, provided much help in the preparation of the final text of this volume. It goes without saying, however, that any errors or oversights are ours alone.

A book which draws so heavily on sources cannot easily avoid a discussion of the availability and physical appearance of the documents in question. To this end we have decided to include in the volume a number of illustrations of relevant documents. This would not have been possible without the permission of many record offices and repositories, all of whom we thank most sincerely – the Public Record Office, Warwickshire Record Office, Norfolk Record Office and Borough Council of King's Lynn and West Norfolk, Southampton City Records Office, Bristol Record Office, Northamptonshire Record Office, the William Salt Library and the Corporation of London Records Office.

Lastly, a special message of thanks has to go to Ruth. When she first started work on this volume she was Ruth Omoregie; now as a result of marriage, she is Ruth Bridgen. Not only did Ruth type virtually every word in this volume, she edited and re-edited the text each time we waved our editorial pens into action. Moreover, she chased us when we needed chasing and consoled us when we needed consolation. We thank her for all her efforts.

1

Introduction

TOM ARKELL & KEVIN SCHURER

Historical demographers with an interest in the later seventeenth century have long been aware that, in addition to parish registers, a rich variety of sources is available for the study of the population of England and Wales in this period compared with others. Some of these sources, such as the Hearth taxes and the Compton census, are much better known than others, but so far the collective potential of these sources for illuminating important aspects of later seventeenth-century society seems to have been largely unfulfilled. In part this derives from the patchiness of the surviving records and from uncertainties over their reliability as well as from fundamental ignorance about the main variations in their formats and their administration. As a consequence this volume has been planned with the intention of shedding much-needed light on the nature and some potential uses of these four principal sources – the Hearth taxes, the Compton census, the Poll taxes and the Marriage Duty assessments.

A proper understanding of these documents requires some knowledge of the political instability and financial problems experienced by the governments of later Stuart England and Wales, as well as of the improving levels of popular numeracy and of the emergence of the new science of political arithmetic during this period. The determination of the landed classes and of the established church in post-Restoration England to re-establish and maintain their economic superiority, spiritual power and social control led to the drawing up of a great variety of nominal lists throughout the country by parochial officers, clerks and parsons, the vast majority of which have since disappeared.[1] Their various purposes included listing the payers, defaulters and the exempt for taxation purposes, the able-bodied males for military purposes, and the regular recording of communicants or at least

1 The impact of this whole process on one county is described with great clarity and insight in Coleby, *Central government*, pp.87-155.

those of age to communicate for obvious religious purposes.[2] Enumerations of whole communities were required for the assessments for the Marriage Duty Act from 1695 and they were also undertaken on other isolated occasions.[3] However, though many people were experienced in the compilation of such full or partial lists, one must be wary of assuming that all are of equal value or reliability.

Recently Keith Thomas has described how society as a whole became increasingly numerate at this time.[4] Arabic numerals generally replaced Roman ones in the calculations required for the keeping of trade and administrative records, while the provision of a nought or zero made it much easier for people to undertake addition, subtraction and multiplication, as well as making possible the use of decimals. But in the age of pocket calculators it is easy to forget how tedious these calculations still were and how cumbersome the contemporary methods of division remained. Nonetheless, these developments were, in part, a response to the growing demand for officials competent in arithmetical skills. This new science of investigating society and its economy through numerical analysis – 'political arithmetick' as it was known among contemporaries – which became established as one of the main forms of intellectual activity by the end of the seventeenth century, is discussed at some length in the contribution by Peter Laslett that follows. In it he demonstrates how much is owed to the pioneering labours of John Graunt and in particular Gregory King. Even without considering the base from which the work of King started, his intellectual achievements are breathtakingly remarkable and have provided countless modern scholars with a proliferation of insights into the economic, social and demographic

[2] For the latter see the comprehensive guide to the Easter Books in Wright, 'Guide' pp.18-31 and 'Guide', part II, pp.13-27.

[3] Some confusion currently surrounds the date of the inception of the Marriage Duty Act. This is frequently given as 1694, following Glass, 'Introduction', p.ix. Although 1694 is the date recorded at the top of the pages in the appropriate section of the *Statutes of the realm*, this date is of course in the Old Style and refers to when the relevant parliamentary session began. This was actually in 1694-5, which modern convention now records consistently as 1695. In addition, the Marriage Duty Act itself was not approved by parliament until April 1695 for implementation from 1 May 1695 so that to continue to ascribe it to 1694 would appear to be unacceptably pedantic.

[4] Thomas, 'Numeracy', pp.103-32.

structure of pre-industrial England.[5] But often the very precision of King's calculations has engendered niggling doubts about the degree of their accuracy, a question which is directly confronted in the chapter by Laslett.

Sir William Petty, who appears to have coined the term 'political arithmetick', concluded that the results of the Compton census were compatible with the 'accounts' of the recent Poll taxes and Hearth taxes.[6] King, however, was convinced that Petty's demographic calculations were disastrously wrong. This he set out to prove by using such statistics as the total number of houses in the country which Davenant had earlier compiled from what he claimed to be the Hearth tax of 1690,[7] as well as the yields from the Poll taxes of 1689 and 1692 and a selection of the earliest available Marriage Duty assessments from 1695.[8] The main result of these labours is his well-known 'Scheme of the Income and Expence', for England in 1688, reproduced as Table 1 in the chapter by Peter Laslett. It can be seen therefore that these sources have a long and honourable pedigree for scholars devoted to unravelling the secrets of the demographic and social structure of later Stuart England. Equally challenging opportunities exist in the application of the new techniques of historical demography in order to elaborate and refine further the impressive achievements of the seventeenth-century pioneers. This work, however, cannot be undertaken without detailed knowledge of the surviving documents, especially since it is clear that what survives was not compiled in a consistent and reliable format, like later enumerations of the country's population such as the nineteenth-century census schedules.

A very detailed introduction to the intricacies of the Compton census has already been provided by Anne Whiteman as an

[5] During the last sixty years or so King's estimates have been well publicised, being reprinted in somewhat abbreviated form in, for example, George, *England in transition*, pp.216-7; Clark, *Wealth of England*, pp.192-3; Wilson, *England's apprenticeship*, p.239 and Laslett, *World we have lost – further explored*, pp.32-3.

[6] Whiteman, 'The census that never was', p.8.

[7] However, he clearly had his dates confused since the Hearth taxes were abolished in 1689. See chapters 3 and 8 by Tom Arkell.

[8] The extent of King's use of these sources has still not been fully explored, but a preliminary discussion is contained in Arkell, 'Poverty', pp.24-9. See also the chapter by Laslett that follows and that by Arkell (chapter 8).

accompaniment to her *Critical edition* of its content.[9] Her contribution to this volume both serves to alert readers to the value of her work on the Compton returns as well as providing them with a succinct summary of the main problems identified in her research for the *Critical edition*. Unfortunately, no comparable comprehensive companions exist for the other sources that are considered here and so, for these, substantial editorial contributions have been included, describing the administration of the Hearth tax, Poll taxes and Marriage Duty Act.[10] Together with the sections which describe the key features of these documents, they have been designed as introductions or background information to the chapters which follow them, using the sources they describe. In addition, Laslett's opening chapter places the compilation of the four sources in the context of the developing fascination contemporaries had with analysing the society in which they lived.

In this respect, the individual chapters of this volume can be seen to fall into one of two categories. The first is that which has already been identified, those which set out in some detail the legislation and administrative processes which surround the generation of the sources in question (chapters 3, 5 and 8), and the brief introductions which, with reference to appropriate examples, discuss key features regarding the form and structure of the documents. The second category of chapter is that which, by example, provides pointers to some of the ways in which the four sources may be used. Clearly these chapters are not in any way exhaustive in terms of the variety of research uses to which these sources can be put, nor are they intended to be. Rather, focusing on aspects of demography and social structure, they concentrate on particular issues of historical inquiry upon which light can be thrown by the analysis and interpretation of these sources of information. From a straightforward demographic point of view, the estimation of population totals using a combination of the Hearth tax and Compton census returns forms the basis of chapter 6 by Tom Arkell, while the reliability of parish register information in London is the main concern of the contribution of Jeremy Boulton. In addition to the religious aspects of non-conformity at the time of the Compton census, the problems of registration also feature in the chapter by Peter Jackson.

9 Whiteman, *Critical edition*.

10 Chapters 3 and 8.

Occupational structure, hierarchies of social class and the distribution of wealth form the focus of the study of the Hearth tax returns by Chris Husbands, as well as that by James Alexander investigating the Poll tax returns for the City of London. The final theme examined by the second category of chapters is household and family structure. The chapter by Kevin Schurer utilizes a collection of Marriage Duty assessments to investigate the possible existence of regional variations in the characteristics of households, while Sheila Cooper, using instead a number of sequential Poll tax lists, provides a micro-study of the structure and form of families and households in the Norfolk town of King's Lynn. Unfortunately, as yet there is no full and reliable guide to the extent, state, quality and location of all these surviving records, nor to those which have been transcribed, published or microfilmed and lodged in a local record office or library.[11]

It is the case that the surviving records from the Hearth taxes and the Compton census cover so much more of the country than the other two sources discussed in this volume that together they provide potential material for estimating the size and distribution of much of the nation's population in the 1660s and 1670s – or at least of its households or adults. This has most clearly been demonstrated by Anne Whiteman in her impressive *Critical edition*.[12] In contrast the extant Poll tax and Marriage Duty assessment documents are much more patchy, with the result that a profound sense of frustration is often caused by the realisation that most of these records no longer exist, especially for rural areas. Nonetheless, as indicated above, the most detailed of these lists still contain much untapped information about the nature of later seventeenth-century urban society, as is illustrated in the chapters by Alexander, Cooper and Schurer. What is clear is that, due in part to the inadequate cataloguing of later seventeenth-century taxation records within the various repositories in which they are held, it is undoubtedly the case that the discovery of important documents still awaits the diligent archive sleuth.[13] With this in mind, may we wish all those who care to enter the chase, not only happy but fruitful hunting.

11 However, Gibson's slim volume on *The Hearth tax* comes closest to meeting these requirements and is recommended as a starting point.

12 Whiteman, *Critical edition*, pp.xcvii-cxxii.

13 See Medlycott, 'Survey'.

2

Natural and political observations on the population of late seventeenth-century England: reflections on the work of Gregory King and John Graunt

PETER LASLETT

Introduction

It could be said that the English people who lived between the 1660s and the 1730s made up the most important population which has ever occupied our country, at least from an intellectual point of view.[1] Not only did they have amongst them a set of individuals whose activities help to justify the expression 'the century of English genius', names like Newton, Boyle and Locke, Milton, Wren and Pope;[2] they also took the actions and adopted the attitudes which were soon to give rise to the earliest industrial revolution. A further reason for their salience in history is the most significant for this collection of essays. The first demographers and the first students of social structure appeared amongst the inhabitants of late seventeenth-century England, making its population the earliest ever studied in a scientific fashion.

It is a singular fact that the first two expositions of demographic and social structural analysis in English history should have been headed in an identical way, with the phrase, *Natural and Political Observations*, although they were composed a generation apart. The reason is quite straightforward. Gregory King, who wrote, but never published, several versions of the second of these two works in the mid 1690s, admired the first of them so much

1 This chapter is an adaptation and revision of my 'Introduction' in Laslett, *Earliest Classics*. Besides a reproduction of King's 'Notebook', known as the *Burns Journal*, it contains reproductions of Chalmers' 1804 printing of King's *Observations*, and of the first edition of those of Graunt.

2 Robert Boyle was actually born in Ireland in 1627. However since all his work was carried out in England it is appropriate that he be included in this list.

that he seems deliberately to have imitated the key words of its title. Written out in full, then, the title of the first was *Natural and Political Observations made Upon the Bills of Mortality*, published in 1662 by John Graunt, reprinted several times in his lifetime, and often since.[3] The second was *Natural and Political Observations and Conclusions Upon the State and Condition of England* written by King in about 1696, but left by him in manuscript in various versions.

Our primary interest in these two works is how they can help us to study the inhabitants of the English part of the British Isles in the later seventeenth century; to discover, for example, how many of these inhabitants there were; whether their numbers were rising or falling, and by how much; how many lived in the country and how many in the towns, how many in the cities; how large their families and households were; how the population was arranged for the purposes of production; how the society as a whole was adapted to its environment and to its productive capacities, and so on and so on. We must exercise our critical insight when it comes to the exactness of the figures, as we shall see. But I hope we shall not stop there in our consideration of English people during the interlude which interests us. For the careers of the two great originators whom I have named, Graunt and King, and who, along with Sir William Petty, were the founders of our study as demographers and historical sociologists, can be used to make suggestions about the circumstances under which advances like theirs ever get made.

Before we get to these issues, however, we must establish who these two men were, what they did and why they are agreed on all sides to have been so important.

John Graunt (1620-1674)

Graunt's little book, *Natural and Political Observations made Upon the Bills of Mortality*, appeared as we have seen in 1662. It was believed by its author to be readable within a couple of hours; two very diverting and illuminating hours they would have been, to be sure. It is now universally recognised as a work of

3 Graunt, *Natural and Political Observations*. The original edition of 1662 is reproduced in Laslett, *Earliest Classics*. A further edition of Graunt's book was published later in 1662. The plague of 1665 called forth a third edition in the early summer and a fourth in November (printed at Oxford) of that year. The fifth edition 'much larger', was posthumously printed in 1676.

genius, and most competent authorities attribute to it the origin both of statistics and of demography.

It may seem extravagant to class this essay with Harvey's *De Motu Cordis* (1654), Newton's *Principia* (1687) or Locke's *Essay on Human Understanding* (1690). But to the social scientists of our own day, the man who was the first to collect medical and vital statistics, to apply mathematics, if only very elementary mathematics, to social facts, to recognise urbanisation as a major effect on behaviour and on social structure, must be considered as ranking among the great natural scientists of the early years of the Royal Society.

By express royal injunction of Charles II Graunt was, in fact, created a member of that body, and his *Observations* have a real advantage for us over most of the books which were produced by its members, because they are interesting reading even now, as well as of extraordinary intellectual calibre. Graunt, moreover, was a particularly interesting man. Perhaps the only practising tradesman amongst the whole company of the early English scientists, a captain in the city militia, he was a mild, merciful, engaging personality.

Maybe this is why he has been the subject of so much commentary, both scientific and biographical, during the last three quarters of a century, and why we may accordingly safely leave his significance, and his reputation, to others. Many have checked, re-checked and extended the woefully small stock of personal facts which we have about this London draper and haberdasher who became a friend of the great Sir William Petty, but wrote nothing of note apart from the *Observations*. These scholars have substantiated Graunt's demographic claims and have enlarged on the effectiveness of his theories and his models. They have underlined his critical insight and appreciated his scientific reticence and cautiousness. They have substantiated his claim (not advanced by him on his own behalf, for Graunt was a genuinely modest writer) to be the originator of the conception of the life table and so also of the notion of the expectation of life.[4]

[4] For a discussion of the life and work of John Graunt see Hull, *Economic writings*; Lansdowne, *Petty-Southwell Correspondence*; Willcox, *Natural and Political Observations*; Greenwood, *Medical statistics*; Sutherland, *John Graunt* and, in particular, Glass, 'John Graunt'.

Finally they have, in my opinion anyway, established without possibility of further doubt that John Graunt himself, not Sir William Petty, was the original and major, if not the only begetter, of the astringent little piece of writing which has nearly always gone under Graunt's name. Petty must undoubtedly be freely credited with a part of the original composition and of the minor revisions which can be found in the later editions.[5] Though it is a little puzzling that Graunt's successor in the study of the life-table, Edmund Halley of the comet, could have attributed the whole authorship to Petty, it is more understandable that Petty's noble descendant, Lord Lansdowne, should argue in defence of that attribution a generation or two ago.[6] But the following pronouncement made by Willcox now seems unlikely ever to be overset and it is the judgement of the outstanding American statistician of his generation:

> 'To the trained reader Graunt writes statistical music: Petty is like a child playing with a new musical toy which occasionally yields a bit of harmony'.[7]

John Graunt was on the very edge of the in-group of his times, of those in and around the Royal Society, the late seventeenth-century scientific and social establishment. He is not counted as the founder of any great aristocratic house, as was the brilliantly self-aggrandising and successful William Petty. Indeed Graunt died a bankrupt and, what was even worse, a fervent Roman Catholic with a daughter in a Belgian nunnery.

'To what purpose tends all this laborious bustling and groping',[8] he asks of his own lengthy lists of figures, his cautious consistency checks, and his critical discussion of his data. We may reply with a further quotation from Willcox and accept his assessment of Graunt's *Natural and Political Observations*:

> 'Graunt is memorable mainly because he discovered the numerical regularity of deaths and births, of the ratios of the sexes at death and birth, and of the proportion of deaths from certain causes to all deaths in successive

5 In addition, Petty is commonly credited with having carried out a major revision to the fifth edition of 1676, the first to be published after Graunt's death.

6 See Lansdowne, *Petty-Southwell Correspondence*.

7 Willcox, *Natural and Political Observations*, p.x.

8 Graunt, *Natural and Political Observations*, p.71. The word 'Buzzling' appears where 'bustling' seems to be meant.

> years and in different areas; or in general terms, the uniformity and predictability of many important biological phenomena taken in the mass. In doing so, he opened the way both for the later discovery of uniformities in many social or volitional phenomena like marriage, suicide and crime, and for a study of these uniformities, their nature and their limits; thus he, more than any other man, was the founder of statistics'.[9]

In our situation, in our day, we must add to this highly professional judgement John Graunt's genius with the evidence. There were the London Bills of Mortality in the first place which he was the first to recognise as important and from which he squeezed out such illuminating conclusions.

These included, for example, analyses of the causes of 229,250 deaths in London between 1629 and 1658. Then there were the parish registers and his demonstration from them of the widespread under-registration of baptisms in the 1650s. Petty in fact preceded Graunt in the use of the parish registers, yet in the 1660s both seem to have worked on those for Romsey in Hampshire, Petty's native town, as well as those of various London parishes. They did this in much the same way as so many local historians of population and social structure have done in association with the Cambridge Group for the History of Population and Social Structure. However, it was to be 300 years before our contemporary interest in such exercises came into being, and very few historical demographers and historical sociologists can have realised where and when it all began. An important part of what we now do, and perhaps the most interesting part, consists in recognizing how such unlikely materials can be used, and wringing absolutely everything possible out of them. We can all identify ourselves with John Graunt.

Gregory King (1648-1712)

The interrelationship between Petty, Graunt and King is quite intriguing. For the intellectual historian it is one more example of what happens when you try to trace back a subject to its beginnings. Uncomfortably often you find yourself at the very dawn itself faced not with one individual, but with several, and

[9] Willcox, *Natural and Political Observations*, p.xiii.

with obstinate problems as to who first thought what, and when, or whether the earliest traceable idea was really continuous with what followed.

In the case of these three, there can be no doubt of the priority in time of Sir William Petty (1623-87) in respect of that which he, and posterity, have delighted to call 'political arithmetic', often spelt with a final k, arithmetick, so as to catch its individuality. Charles Davenant, who in his turn had a literary relationship with Gregory King which intrigues and baffles the enquirer, asserts as much in one of the books in which he made extensive use of extracts from King's manuscripts. Under the title *Of the use of political arithmetick*, Petty is declared to have been the originator of the subject, the man who 'brought it into rules and method'.

Petty, as we have seen, preceded Graunt without actually being able to compose anything quite of the order of Graunt's famous publication, and as clearly anticipated social structural analysis along the lines of what King was to do. In spite of its outstanding originality, however, Petty's work in this direction was slighter, somewhat less systematic and less accurate and appropriate than King's. It is discernibly biased in favour of his adopted country, Ireland, as Davenant insists. Davenant claims of King on the other hand, that 'nothing escapes the comprehensive industry of that gentleman ... [that] wonderful genius and master in the art of computing'.[10]

Whatever we may think about priority, and the issue is perhaps left undecided here, there can be no doubt of the singularity of Gregory King as a writer. For he never published anything of his own. All that he collected, discovered, calculated or composed as a student of the structure of pre-industrial society has had to be taken from Davenant's printing of extracts from his materials, or from King's surviving manuscripts.[11]

10 Laslett, 'English social realism', p.354, fn. 8. The quotation from Davenant comes from his *Discourse on the public revenues and trade of England*, 1699. For an account of these men, see the forthcoming publication of the lectures given for the Mattioli foundation in Milan in 1986 by Sir Richard Stone. In 1987 and 1989 Stone analyzed the treatment of consumer behaviour and of public finance by Petty, King and Davenant, paying particular attention to Petty's entrepreneurial qualities: see *Some seventeenth century econometrics*.

11 For King's failure to publish, see Laslett, 'English social realism'.

Table 1 Gregory King's Scheme of the income and expense of the several families of England calculated for the year 1688

Number of Families	Ranks, Degrees, Titles and Qualification	Heads per Family	Number of Persons
160	Temporal Lords	40	6,400
26	Spiritual Lords	20	520
800	Baronets	16	12,800
660	Knights	13	7,800
3,000	Esquires	10	30,000
12,000	Gentlemen	8	96,000
5,000	Persons in greater Offices and Places	8	40,000
5,000	Persons in lesser Offices and Places	6	30,000
2,000	Eminent Merchants and Traders by Sea	8	16,000
8,000	Lesser Merchants and Traders by Sea	6	48,000
10,000	Persons in the Law	7	70,000
2,000	Eminent Clergy-men	6	12,000
8,000	Lesser Clergy-men	5	40,000
40,000	Freeholders of the better sort	7	280,000
120,000	Freeholders of the lesser sort	$5\frac{1}{2}$	660,000
150,000	Farmers	5	750,000
15,000	Persons in Liberal Arts and Sciences	5	75,000
50,000	Shopkeepers and Tradesmen	$4\frac{1}{2}$	225,000
60,000	Artizans and Handicrafts	4	240,000
5,000	Naval Officers	4	20,000
4,000	Military Officers	4	16,000
500,586		$5\frac{1}{3}$	2,675,520
50,000	Common Seamen	3	150,000
364,000	Labouring People and Out Servants	$3\frac{1}{2}$	1,275,000
400,000	Cottagers and Paupers	$3\frac{1}{4}$	1,300,000
35,000	Common Soldiers	2	70,000
849,000		$3\frac{1}{4}$	2,795,000
	Vagrants; as Gipsies, Thieves, Beggars, &c.		30,000
	So the general Account is		
500,586	Increasing the Wealth of the Kingdom	$5\frac{1}{3}$	2,675,520
849,000	Decreasing the Wealth of the Kingdom	$3\frac{1}{4}$	2,825,000
1,349,586	Neat Totals	$4\frac{1}{13}$	5,500,520

Table 1 Contd.

Yearly income per Family	Yearly income in general	Yearly income per Head	Yearly expense per Head	Yearly increase per Head	Yearly increase in general
£ s	£	£ s d	£ s d	£ s d	£
3,200	512,000	80 0 0	70 0 0	10 0 0	64,000
1,300	33,800	65 0 0	45 0 0	20 0 0	10,400
800	704,000	55 0 0	49 0 0	6 0 0	76,800
650	390,000	50 0 0	45 0 0	5 0 0	39,000
450	1,200,000	45 0 0	41 0 0	4 0 0	120,000
280	2,880,000	35 0 0	32 0 0	3 0 0	288,000
240	1,200,000	30 0 0	26 0 0	4 0 0	160,000
120	600,000	20 0 0	17 0 0	3 0 0	90,000
400	800,000	50 0 0	37 0 0	13 0 0	208,000
198	1,600,000	33 0 0	27 0 0	6 0 0	288,000
154	1,540,000	22 0 0	18 0 0	4 0 0	280,000
72	144,000	12 0 0	10 0 0	2 0 0	24,000
50	400,000	10 0 0	9 0 0	0 16 0	32,000
91	3,640,000	13 0 0	11 15 0	1 5 0	350,000
55	6,600,000	10 0 0	9 10 0	0 10 0	330,000
42 10	6,375,000	8 10 0	8 5 0	0 5 0	187,500
60	900,000	12 0 0	11 0 0	1 0 0	75,000
45	2,250,000	10 0 0	9 0 0	1 0 0	225,000
38	2,280,000	9 10 0	9 0 0	0 10 0	120,000
80	400,000	20 0 0	18 0 0	2 0 0	40,000
60	240,000	15 0 0	14 0 0	1 0 0	16,000
68 18	34,488,800	12 18 0	11 15 4	1 2 8	3,023,700
				Decrease	Decrease
20	1,000,000	7 0 0	7 10 0	0 10 0	75,000
15	5,460,000	4 10 0	4 12 0	0 2 0	127,000
6 10	2,000,000	2 0 0	2 5 0	0 5 0	325,000
14	490,000	7 0 0	7 10 0	0 10 0	35,000
10 10	8,950,000	3 5 0	3 9 0	0 4 0	562,500
	60,000	2 0 0	4 0 0	2 0 0	60,000
68 18	34,488,800	12 18 0	11 15 4	1 2 8	3,023,700
10 10	9,010,000	3 3 0	3 7 6	0 4 6	622,500
32 5	43,491,800	7 18 0	7 9 3	0 8 9	2,401,200

Source: Laslett, **World we have lost – further explored**, pp.32-3.

King acknowledges his debt to Charles Davenant in several places, and information vital to his calculations seems to have been part of what he borrowed.[12] But the counterflow was far, far more important. Davenant embodied a great slab of King's work in his *Essay upon the probable methods of making a people gainers in the ballance of trade*, 1699, so much and of such significance that the little book might otherwise have been forgotten. The most important thing which he reproduced was a very large table of figures under column headings and line headings, the famous *Scheme of the income and expence of the several families of England calculated for the year 1688*, which was actually worked out in 1696.[13] This astonishing array of numbers specified a rank, a size and an income for every household going to make up English society, and then divided up the whole between those 'increasing' and those 'decreasing' 'the wealth of the kingdom'. King had reworked and developed Petty's reckoning of the national income presented in his *Treatise on taxes* in 1662, into a distribution of that income between classes, households and individuals. In this way the whole tradition of looking at societies in their entirety, taking every single member into account, first came into being. The figures King worked out have, as may be imagined, been repeatedly cited since Davenant printed them and have been reproduced on many occasions by modern scholars as we reproduce them here as our Table 1.[14]

It is also true that the brief but brilliant essay for which King's Scheme was composed was printed in full from one of the manuscript versions in 1804 by George Chalmers.[15] Quite apart from the appearance of a few items of them in print, it is not

12 See Holmes, 'Gregory King', pp.46-7 and chapter 8 by Arkell below.

13 Charles Davenant, *An essay upon the probable methods of making a people gainers in the ballance of trade*, London, 1699. This reproduces with minor variation various materials from the manuscript *Natural and Political Observations and Conclusions upon the State and Condition of England, by Gregory King, Esquire, Lancaster Herald of Arms, Ao D 1696*, British Library Harleian MSS. 1898. The variations can be noted by comparing the 1st edition of Laslett, *World we have lost* (pp.32-3) which reproduces the 1696 Scheme with either the 2nd edition (pp.36-7) or 3rd edition (pp.32-3) which reproduce the 1699 Scheme. See also Holmes, 'Gregory King', pp.66-8.

14 See, for example, the list of publications given in footnote 5 of the Introduction above. See also the Addendum to this chapter for a discussion of criticisms and revisions.

15 George Chalmers, *An estimate of the comparative strength of Great Britain ... a new edition ... to which is now annexed Gregory King's celebrated State of England ...*, London, 1804. This was the first full printing of BL Harl. MSS. 1898 and Chalmers' text of it is also reproduced in Laslett, *Earliest Classics*.

Table 2 The household expenses of Gregory King

Expens of my own Family 5 Persons viz.
My self and Wife a Clerk, Serv.t Maid and Boy.

			Self	Wife	Clerk	Maid	Boy
Dyet at 25s p week	65£ p ann.		15.0.0	15.10.0	10.0.0	8.0.0	7.0.0
My own Apparel 10£ p an	10						
My wifes Apparel 10£	10		10.0.0	10.0.0	08.0.0	3.0.0	3.0.0
The Boys Apparel	3						
Fire and Candle	6		2.00.0	2.00.0	01.0.0	0.10.0	0.10.0
Soap and Starch	1		0.5.0	0.5.0	0.4.0	0.3.0	0.3.0
Grocery Spicery Confectionary	3		1.0.0	1.0.0	0.10.0	0.5.0	0.5.0
Mops Brooms etc Brushes Spunges	1		0.5.0	0.5.0	0.4.0	0.3.0	0.3.0
Table Linnen and Sheets etc	2		0.10.0	0.10.0	0.8.0	0.6.0	0.6.0
Utensils Plate China etc	4		1.10.0	1.10.0	0.10.0	0.5.0	0.5.0
Repair of Bedding Hangings etc	4		1.0.0	1.0.0	0.10.0	0.5.0	0.5.0
Coach and Water-ridge	3		1.5.0	1.5.0	0.8.0	0.1.0	0.1.0
Tavern and Aleho. & Coffeeho.	10		4.10.0	2.5.0	3.0.0	0.4.6	0.1.0
Servants wages	15						
Plays, Shews, gifts & Charities	5		3.0.0	1.10.0	0.8.0	0.1.6	0.0.6
Books and Papers	5		4.0.0	0.0.0	1.0.0	0.1.0	0.0.6
Smith, Brickl. Joyner etc Glasier	3		1.10.0	1.0.0	0.5.0	0.3.0	0.2.0
My Share of ye publick charge	4		4.0.0	0.0.0			
	152		49.15.0	37.10.0	26.7.0	13.7.6	12.2.0

Source: **Burns Journal**, p.250 in Laslett, **Earliest Classics**.

impossible that King's investigations of the population, production and income of his country, together with their tendency to grow or to decline over time, made an enduring impression on the actual conduct of government for a century and more after he completed them. There are indications that his tables and calculations, together with the manuscript essay itself, may have served succeeding officials in the Treasury as the basis for estimating the yield of taxation, and for what economic policy they attempted to maintain, during much of the eighteenth century. But the fact remains that King did not see more than a small part of what he had done put at the disposal of all those alive in his own day who were prepared to interest themselves in such matters, and his work as a pioneer was largely wasted.

This is not simply because all his writing other than the passages printed by Davenant stayed in manuscript in his lifetime, but much more because most of his results were never brought together in publishable form. They remained, and still remain, scattered throughout his notebooks, which must originally have made a very considerable series, but only two of which are known to have survived.[16]

In the pages of the *Burns Journal* can be found what seems to be the workings for King's *Natural and Political Observations*. But they also contain notes which appear to be preparatory to a much more ambitious work of economic and of demographic analysis, and other even more specialised treatises. For example, King uses his own family and household to reckon an annual budget of expenditure. The table he drew up for this exercise is reproduced as our Table 2. Where else would you find a record of the amount a household spent annually on fire and candles, or on cleaning materials? And who else but Gregory King would have thought of factoring out the differences of expenditure on every particular between man, wife and servants? This one item is enough to demonstrate that such a writer can provide for the social historian information on everyday life in principled form which can be got in no other way. Incidental references to mops, brooms and sponges, their cost, even their probable life of usefulness, can be expected in letters, diaries, plays and novels. But a calculation over a year is information of an entirely different order: scientific.

Surprisingly enough this fascinating table, a very early attempt by a man to submit himself and his establishment to something like economic analysis, can be checked from outside sources in one very important respect. In the returns made under the Marriage Duty Act of 1695,[17] the assessment for the parish of St Benet Paul's Wharf in the City of London dated 1st May 1696 contains the following entry as one of the households in the Heralds' office:

Gregory King Esq.
Anne his wife
Samuel Stebbing } servants
Margaret Watson }
Charles Jarvaise }

[16] According to Glass, 'Two papers on Gregory King', the bound journal which has acquired the name the *Burns Journal* and which is reprinted in Laslett, *Earliest Classics*, was originally labelled 'G.K. no.51', which implies that it may have been one of a series of similar notebooks. Apparently the only other notebook of this character known to have survived (sometimes called the Kashnor Manuscript from the name of the bookseller who possessed it when Glass worked on it) is now held by the National Library of Australia.

[17] This Act and the records generated as a result of it are discussed in the second part of this volume. The practice of keeping household accounts goes a long way further back than the 1690s; it is its analytic quality which distinguishes King's account of himself and his establishment.

Samuel Stebbing was evidently the name of the Clerk heading the third column in table 2, Margaret Watson the maid and Charles Jarvaise the boy. As for the wife, King was married to Anne, formerly Anne Powell, in 1674. 'A generous way of living to which his own and his wife's inclinations led them' are the words from King's own autobiographical fragment (unfortunately ending with the year 1694) which might be applied to this account of his household expenses. Perhaps more significant for our present purposes is the fact that the table is not quite properly drawn out, as for example in the entries under Apparel. The figures do not add up overall, since the correct total should be £154.1.6., not £152, and these digits are only as close as they are to each other because errors within the first few lines cancel each other out.

In fact it could be said that in this table, as elsewhere, King seems to be satisfied with guesses at the numbers in each cell, rather than recording what had actually been spent in any one year, or as an average over a number of years. He certainly does not here seem to be consulting his own household records for the purposes of making estimates. Informed guesswork of this kind, informed by a man with an excellent head for figures, an astonishing thirst for numerical information and a corresponding capacity for getting access to it, occupying in addition to this an exceptional position in respect of discovering just the materials which he wanted, characterises all of the work which King did. No one else could have produced these figures for his own establishment and, in the years 1695-1700, no one else was in a position to put into his notebooks quite the collection of national estimates which make them so interesting. In this, as Philip Kreager shows, he resembled his predecessor and model, John Graunt.[18]

Not every commentator on Gregory King's estimates takes such a favourable view of their usefulness, or of their reliability for the purposes of scholars in our own day wishing to use them as a source of data, perhaps more often as a standard against which to judge their own results. In the Addendum to this chapter, some of the criticisms and revisions have been set out. King's limitations are obviously of the first importance to those who wish to get at the truth as we define it now, but we must be careful not to think of all of them as defects in quite the same sense which we attach

[18] Kreager, 'New light on Graunt'.

to the errors we make ourselves, in disregard of the standards of accuracy which are now established. Where King can be shown to have overlooked or distorted evidence which we know to have been available to him, then he must indeed be judged as culpable in the same way as we are when we blunder. But where he was setting down only that with which a man of his period and outlook can be expected to have been satisfied, the case is different. His 'errors' of this kind are themselves a proper subject of historical enquiry, as is hinted below.

A necessary consequence of King's failure to get into print has been that less interest has been taken in him as a person than in Graunt, and less has been written in a critical way on his results. Nevertheless, the references made throughout this chapter show that considerably more information is available about his career than might be expected, and that several manuscript remains from his hand have now been identified. David Glass did most to discover the whereabouts of the King treasures.[19] A great deal of further work on him, however, is still both possible and desirable.

Gregory King's purposes and data

A survey of King's papers, and especially a detailed examination of the *Burns Journal*, seems to me to make King's purposes quite plain. He wrote, as others have suggested, with government exigencies in mind. In fact it would seem justifiable to suppose that he was engaged in providing the administration of England during the critical months of an all-out war with France with a realistic account of the taxable resources of the English nation. Sir Richard Stone maintains that the statements King makes in the *Observations* show that he was reckoning how long England could go on fighting the war in which she was engaged in 1696 by calculating the rate at which her resources were being used up. To quote Stone:

> 'When will the war end?' is a question that has been asked throughout the ages. In 1689 the war of the League of Augsburg broke out between France on the one hand and the confederacy led by England and Holland on the other. In 1696 Gregory King in his *Natural and Political Observations and Conclusions upon the State and Condition of England* attempted to answer this question by an application of the new science of Political Arithmetic introduced a generation earlier by Sir William

[19] Glass, 'Two papers on Gregory King'.

> Petty and described by Charles Davenant as 'the art of reasoning by figures upon things relating to Government'.

Stone actually compares King with James Meade and himself, both now Nobel Prize-winning economists, working together in the offices of the British War Cabinet in the summer of 1940. 'Whatever you think of my comparison,' he adds, 'King's analysis is very interesting'.[20]

The actual months when King did his reckonings were very probably those of the winter of 1695-6. Several statements in support of this view can be found in the notebook. In a copy of one letter of explanation dated April 1696, to Stepney, the English ambassador to the Rhineland Princes, King stated that his 'disquisition' was intended 'to form a scheme of the effect which this great and expensive war against France may have upon the power and wealth of England, and thereby to judge of our ability to prosecute and maintain the same.'[21]

It seems unlikely to me that an outsider to government could have collected the information to draw up a document of this kind which King evidently had in mind when making such a claim. This is true even of a member of the Herald's Office, who could look through such official documents as the visitations of the counties for armorial purposes, and one with a fairly comprehensive acquaintanceship inside departments of state. In King's generation it was quite normal for civil servants to communicate official papers of all kinds to their curious and interested friends.

The *Burns Journal* seems to imply that King's mastery of Government administration went further than this. He apparently made careful examination of the official returns from the Window Tax, the House Tax and the Chimney Tax for various dates from 1689 onwards, if not always personally, then through official informants. Though it has been denied that he personally used Poll tax lists and returns, the most valuable series of all from his point of view, King seems to have pored over some of the

20 Stone, 'When will the war end?', p.193. See also King, *Natural and Political Observations*, section 10, pp.61-3. It seems that this was a response to Davenant's *Essays on Ways and Means of Supplying the War*, King agreeing with Davenant that the war could not be sustained beyond 1698. This point is discussed in Holmes, 'Gregory King', p.51.

21 *Burns Journal*, p.171.

assessments for the Marriage Duty Act as they actually arrived at the Treasury during the first months of its operation in the course of 1695. The returning officers themselves, as well as other persons in a position to know, were in correspondence with him.

It is possible to suppose, then, that Gregory King may actually have been invited into the Treasury to report on just the subject which is at issue in his declaration to Stepney, and that some at least of the relevant papers were opened to his inspection over a period of months or even years, perhaps extending from 1695-8. Records of the brief given to him, of the documents he was expected to read, and the payment which he was to receive, perhaps still exist somewhere, though none of these, as far as I know, has so far been discovered.[22]

A state paper?

If all this was so, and considerable further research would be necessary to confirm it, what King composed as a manuscript treatise in 1695-6 can be given a recognisable description. The *Natural and Political Observations* which Davenant saw and quoted and which Chalmers first printed over a century later, can be provisionally classed as a state paper. Now a state paper is not for publication, unless specifically written to that end. But it may well be for quotation by government writers in just the way Davenant in fact did quote figures and tables from King's memorandum. Such circumstances would help to explain why it was that King himself never composed, or had printed, the various works apparently in contemplation when he wrote this manuscript. They seem to have been designed to bear such titles as 'Of the Riches and Poverty of a Nation'; 'An Essay Upon the Numbers of the People in England'; 'An Essay Upon Marriages, Births and Burials'.[23] This would not, of course, be a sufficient explanation by itself of why he did not print any pieces on these subjects under his own name at subsequent dates, when he had ceased to be a government figure so that no issue of permission or

22 Holmes rejects the suggestion that King was working for the government, or had privileged access to government documents, or that he was ever given a brief; Holmes, 'Gregory King'. See the Addendum to this chapter for further discussion. In my comments on Stone's Mattioli lectures I argue that social investigation was advanced significantly during the 1690s due to the involvement of a notable body of intellectuals, of whom King was one, with politicians and administrators. Clearly King's link with government is crucial to this view.

23 *Burns Journal*, pp.161, 106, 160 and 101, respectively.

confidentiality could have arisen. Thus further reasons for his silence as an author will have to be inferred from his biography if ever that can be sufficiently recovered.[24]

If this view of Gregory King's status and activities should be established by future work, or even if some version of it should prove to be correct, that King had limited access rather than the full governmental confidence which has been hypothesised, then his work must be accorded more weight than has hitherto been thought justifiable and the value of his writings raised accordingly. Certain interesting details also fall into place.

It has always been a little mysterious that King's Scheme, though elaborated in 1695 and 1696, should refer to England in 1688. Assertions in the later pages of the *Burns Journal* (especially from p.200 to the end) can be interpreted to show that he was engaged on establishing the history of the population and resources of his country as they developed after the year 1688. This could have been, as Stone suggests, in order to answer the question 'When will the war end?'. But however this may be his concern was evidently the story of what happened to the English population and resources in consequence of the outbreak of hostilities in the following year, 1689, and what might be expected to happen if the war continued. Such might well have been his brief, and he might also have been charged to try to make estimates for France, England's enemy, and for the United Provinces, England's ally, over the same period. Hence the particular attention given in the notebook to these powers over the years.

King's attitude to his predecessors and contemporaries also becomes easier to understand. He used Graunt and Davenant, together with the authors of the books which he cites on France, on the German States, on Japan and so on, for what he could get out of them for his appointed task. It is of the greatest interest that he should have concluded that the population of London and of England had been virtually static between 1689 and 1695, the years of war, and that national resources had been diminishing and would go on doing so until peace was made. In this respect King's manuscript resembles the famous tract published in 1940

[24] King's failure to publish is discussed at length in Laslett, 'English social realism'.

by J M Keynes on *How to Pay for the War*. For Keynes, 1938 was the last year of peace, of normality; for King it was 1688.

We can moreover see, if we wish, in King's obvious determination to take the lowest estimates rather than ever to exaggerate, his sense of responsibility towards the government he was advising. In his manuscript, he reproves Sir William Petty, whose estimates no doubt enjoyed some official standing at the time, for trying to make the population of London and of the kingdom 'greater than they truly were'. He proceeds thus: 'I shall endeavour to give such an account thereof as will bear the touchstone of truth' for the benefit of 'those who sit at the helm to whom a true account of the Kingdom is more necessary than to others'.[25] Petty is cut down to size in various other passages. It may be added, that where we have checked King's estimates from other sources, his desire to be conservative seems to have impelled him to go too low.[26] This is certainly true of mean household size, where he consistently refuses to accept the Graunt and Petty figures of eight or six persons to a household, but goes down to a figure of 4.125-4.17, which is probably too small by a third or a half of a person.[27]

Nevertheless he cannot be expected to have transcended the outlook of his time. A glance at any one of the tediously repetitive estimates he made in various places in his manuscripts of the population of the world at successive periods makes it abundantly clear that he was the prisoner of revelationism. He regarded it as unquestionable that his population figures and his account of population growth had to fit on to the Biblical version of the way these things must happen. With revelationism went also theodicism, the view that God's purpose ensured the imminence of the best of all possible worlds in the world as it was, in respect of population as of everything else. Fantasy is the only word for us to use of the accounts of future growth and change by

25 *Burns Journal*, p.49.

26 See the Addendum to this chapter for details.

27 In *Natural and Political Observations* the mean household size of 4.4 given for 'villages' is actually a misprint for 4.04 (see p.35 of Chalmer's printing). King's proposed mean household size for the whole country was given as 4.17 in *Natural and Political Observations* and 4.125 in the *Burns Journal*, (p.276). For a discussion of mean household sizes in pre-industrial England see Laslett, 'Size and structure of the household'; Wall, 'Mean household size' and Arkell, 'Multiplying factors' and the figures in chapter 12, Table 2, below.

'multiplication'. What else can we think of a man who would carry his forecasts for England and for London to the year 20,000 *Anno Mundi*, and of the globe to the year 500,000 *Anno Mundi*, not even pausing at the year 1695/6 when he was actually writing?[28] More serious perhaps is the impression of arbitrariness given by nearly all his figures. He usually sets them down only to revise them a page or a line or two later, when something else occurs to him.

It does not necessarily follow that because a man is completely confined within a revelationist, a theodicist ideal, that he is for that reason always disposed to make arbitrary judgements on insufficient evidence, and because he is often content with snap estimates that he can never be supposed to present the facts as they were. Occasionally there are signs that he tried to check conclusions done from one body of data with those drawn from another, as for example where he confronts the yield from the Poll taxes by social class against his own earlier estimates of the members in each class.

When, for instance, he takes such pains to calculate the distribution of the English population by age and marital status, allowing as always for differences between London, the great towns and the countryside,[29] King can surely be assumed to be as independent as a man can get of his ideological prepossessions. So it must be when he assembles both the vital statistics of a whole collection of villages in the 1690s, and their populations in 1696, so as to work out rates of fertility and mortality, and of increase or decrease.[30] This collection includes the relevant figures for the now famous parish of Colyton or Culliton, on which E.A. Wrigley carried out the first family reconstitution for an English community.[31] So it must be when he works out the number of persons in England by social group; or the consumption of apparel broken down into incredible detail; of silk and paper; even of medical expenses, beds and bedding, recreation, schooling, tobacco and travel.[32] King actually calculates the value of the people

28 Since in his *Anno Mundi* calculations King assessed that the world began in 3948 B.C., this takes his forecasts for London and England to 16,052 A.D. and to 496,052 A.D. for the world. See *Burns Journal*, p.52.

29 *Burns Journal*, pp.76-7.

30 *Burns Journal*, p.100.

31 See Wrigley, 'Mortality'.

32 *Burns Journal*, pp.200, 203, 205, 206, 210.

themselves, by age and sex, their procreative value as well as their value for 'Business'.[33]

Conclusion: Political Arithmetick and the fundamentals of social and political analysis

Exercises like these make it possible to place the activities of English individuals in the 1690s alongside those of other individuals in other societies and at other times. Hence their value in comparative historical sociology. As illustrations of the wider significance of these natural and political observations on the population of late seventeenth-century England, we may glance at two themes.

One has to do with the overall question of whether the emergence of modern society in England was associated from the very beginning with greater equality between individuals in matters of income and wealth. Was the immensely less affluent order of pre-industrial social and economic relations, with its very obvious inequalities in social status, in education, in personal relations, necessarily a society in which the rich were richer and the poor poorer, in relative terms of course, than is the case in our own wealthy, developed, industrial world? This, it must be acknowledged, is a fundamental theme.

The second theme is not quite so definite, nor so wide-ranging in its implications, but it has also to do with personal relationships of a basic character, those between employer and employed, the possessive, directive, class or classes, and the rest of society. The question asked of the evidence is this. Were all employed persons in the pre-industrial world taken to be personally subordinate to their betters, to their masters, to their employers and directors? Were all but a minority of our ancestors in fact looked upon as servants, in contractual and also in patriarchal subordination?

Very general issues of this character are not likely to be definitely settled, but to stay in permanent debate. Yet the activities of scholars in recent years seem to me to yield surprisingly definite conclusions on the first of them, if not on the second. Two of the foremost authorities on the history of English wealth and its distribution have pronounced that over the era of industrialisation

33 *Burns Journal*, pp.245, 248. Petty had also calculated human capital.

'the classic image of widening class inequality does fit',[34] even though extreme versions of expropriation by the rising bourgeoisie are quite unjustifiable. After decades of industrialising change, they claim along with others, mid-Victorian England seems to mark the climax of inequality in possessions, not only for English history but for the history of all those countries on which we now have information. It was not until after 1900 that the distribution of wealth in Britain returned to the level of inequality characteristic of the society known to Graunt and King, and it was only after that when any marked redistribution became manifest.[35]

This is a result of great significance to all historians and students of social structure. If accepted as conclusive it will make necessary some revision of the standard account, including, for example, that sketched out in the chapter of *The World we have lost*, entitled, 'After the transformation'.[36] From our point of view here, however, the important fact is that no such story could ever have been written without Gregory King's Scheme for 1688 and without his workings. No guide to the society would have existed, and it seems impossible that econometric studies of the past, for all their growing analytic sophistication, could ever have reconstructed such a guide. What is more, as the scholars concerned have made clear, the research itself started in just the way which is pursued by historians of local population, that is by taking local examples, in this case listings of inhabitants, and comparing them with Gregory King's conclusions, correcting, revising, approximating.[37] The same is true of the other great issue in social development.

[34] Lindert and Williamson, 'Revising England's social tables', and their sequential article, 'Reinterpreting Britain's social tables', especially the concluding passage of the second study.

[35] See Lindert and Williamson, 'Revising England's social tables' and 'Reinterpreting Britain's social tables'; compare Williamson, *Britain's capitalism*, p.73.

[36] See Laslett, *The World we have lost – further explored*, chapter 11, where it is assumed that pre-industrial England was always and consistently marked by greater inequality of wealth than industrial England.

[37] Lindert and Williamson, 'Revising England's social tables', lists twenty-six 'local enumerations' which they used to revise the figures in King's classes of status and occupation (see p.387). Quite apart from the conclusions of these two scholars, it is rather disconcerting to have Sir Richard Stone asserting that 'annual real income rose nearly sixfold between the 1690s and the 1940s. ... a solid achievement, but those people who think that we are enormously richer than our ancestors should think again'. 'When will the war end?' p.200.

It was the late Professor Brough Macpherson in his brilliant Marxist essay of 1962, *The Political Theory of Possessive Individualism*, who asserted that all wage-earners in seventeenth-century England were regarded by their contemporaries as servants.[38] He devotes an appendix of that remarkable book to Gregory King's workings so as to show how large a proportion of the population were in receipt of wages or unemployed. Servants, he maintained, could not have political personalities of their own, they could not vote in elections or take any independent political or social action, because they were owned by their masters, subsumed that is to say within the public personalities of their employers. In this sense even the famous Levellers, the only people with persuasive claims to democratic principles in seventeenth-century history, were so much imbued with ruling class, bourgeois values that they were willing to deny the vote to whole masses of the people because they were regarded as servants. Democracy, insofar as it must imply equality of personal status, was out of the question even before economic development got under way.

It has been denied that the Levellers did have this attitude, and to the social historian who has seen how individuals are described in listings of inhabitants or in parish registers, Macpherson's account of servanthood seems quite unconvincing. As students of the micro-social structure as it might be called, we have all got to know who the servants were, life-cycle servants as we have come to call them. Unmarried males and females we observe them to have been, listed in their early adulthood within the households of farmers and craftsmen, but found later in life as married household heads themselves, sometimes employing life-cycle servants in their turn. It seems impossible that such a description could fit Macpherson's theory, and we might expect that Gregory King's guide to the social structure would readily confirm the fact. But it turns out that this is not in fact quite the case. Though King's Scheme and many passages of his writings testify to the status of servanthood as a phase of life, and clearly imply that they were practically universally unmarried, there is a conspicuous inconsistency.

[38] Macpherson, *Political theory*; this book was reviewed by the author of this chapter in the *Historical Journal*, 1964, which began an interchange with Brough Macpherson which continued until his death in 1987.

In the *Natural and Political Observations* King certainly lists servants and children as distinct classes of members of the household, in the way we have become accustomed to. But he also lists no less than 140,000 to 160,000 as 'Children under 16 of servants in husbandry'.[39] The same phrase occurs on several occasions in King's manuscript workings and he sometimes brackets children of 'Day Labourers' with the children of servants.[40] If King is taken as the final authority, Macpherson's view of subordination and servanthood has more to be said in its favour than might be expected from King's other statements and his general account of seventeenth-century English society. In addition, or alternatively, King's account of social structure might have been incoherent, on a point of considerable importance.[41]

Alternatively it could be that the expression 'servant' has two distinct meanings in the social vocabulary of King's day, perhaps several of them, and that he could pass from one to the other without thinking it necessary to give notice to the reader. Such is the view which I myself take. Nevertheless, this puzzle in nomenclature brings home to us that we cannot expect rigorous consistency of usage in the language of our forefathers referring to their own society, even when Gregory King is the writer.

Furthermore it compels us to recognise the fact that no model of a whole society thought up after the event can hope to be complete, and provide against a member of that society suddenly producing a term, an attitude, a classification which is entirely unexpected and could not have been allowed for. This applies to Brough

39 See King, *Natural and Political Observations*, pp.39, 57.

40 *Burns Journal*, pp.70, 73. Since the Poll taxes from 1678 to 1698, inclusive, exempted the children of day labourers and servants in husbandry aged under sixteen, it comes as no surprise that King should wish to estimate their numbers.

41 These points were hinted at in footnote 20 to my 'Introduction' to Laslett, *Earliest classics*. But the possibility that 'servant' could be used to cover married employees with their own families dependent to varying degrees for subsistence on selling their labour seems not to have been recognised at all widely. Kussmaul's authoritative work, for example, assumes that they were always unmarried residents of the households of their employers; see Kussmaul, *Servants in husbandry*. It is known that many servants could be married in parts of Europe (in seventeenth-century Estonia for example, or in Portugal, even in parts of Germany) and isolated examples of married servants do occur in England. But as an accepted social rule, the enforced celibacy of people called servants in England has not been seriously doubted. Thus Gregory King's use of the term 'servants in husbandry' should give us pause.

Macpherson, and it applies just as much to his critics. The general lessons we may learn from considering these *Natural and political observations* may well be as valuable as the astonishing wealth of detailed social information which they offer us.

Addendum

CRITICISMS AND REVISIONS OF GREGORY KING'S WORKINGS AND RESULTS

The way in which King's figures should be used and the caution which should be observed about their reliability for historical purposes have, I hope, been made clear in the text. In what follows, the critical work which has recently been done on his methods and results is briefly surveyed, and references given to the studies in question.

When the listings file of the Cambridge Group for the History of Population and Social Structure was instituted,[42] tables for comparing figures for the characteristics of the household were drawn up to contrast the numerical results of analyzing social structure from these documents with the figures of Gregory King.[43] The outcomes have never been published, but we soon discovered that our figures and his were in fair agreement. There was so little difference that the exercise was dropped for listings analyzed after the text for *Household and family in past time* was completed in 1972.[44] This was striking confirmation of King's accuracy and reliability, though it was true (as is said above) that his results tended to be on the low side, especially in the matter of mean household size. It has also to be admitted that a famous French scholar, Emmanuel Le Roy Ladurie, found his calculations fantastically wrong on the delicate subject of French wines.[45]

42 See the 'General Note' in Laslett, *The World we have lost – further explored*, pp.287-91 and the list of listings published in successive numbers of *Local Population Studies*.

43 Analytic tables making such comparisons for age distribution of Ealing in 1599 and of the status of persons within the households of Clayworth in 1676 appear in Laslett, 'The study of social structure', pp.192-4.

44 Laslett and Wall, *Household and family*.

45 Le Roy Ladurie, 'Les comptes fantastiques'.

The results of demographic comparisons with King's figures and those of Wrigley and Schofield were rather similar to those for social structure.[46] Estimates were pretty close, but King's age structure was too young, and his population total too high, as Glass had already discovered.[47] In 1982 Peter Lindert and Jeffrey Williamson began the series of publications on what they called 'Revising England's social tables', heavily concentrating on Gregory King's Scheme for 1688.[48] They have revised upwards his figures for the numbers of gentry, of lesser clergymen, and especially of shopkeepers and traders (40,000 to 114,000) and inserted some 200,000 families in manufacturing and building trades. King's estimates for the lower social levels are generally accepted,[49] although the incomes of the wealthier English are considerably amended in these new estimates, and the total 'pre-fisc household income' raised accordingly. Those wishing to make use of these fresh results should of course refer to the original publications.

With these exceptions, then, these two acknowledged econometric experts underwrite Gregory King as a source of evidence, praising both his aims and his workmanship. So also does Sir Richard Stone as we have seen and he is a world authority on just the subject King helped to institute, national accounting. His work on the evidence vindicates Gregory King's methods to a remarkable degree, and the volume which is still to come will raise his reputation even further.[50] Stone will be speaking for the most part to the converted, with one partial exception, perhaps, in the last of King's critics we can mention, Professor Geoffrey Holmes, a prominent historian of English politics, administration and intellectual life who is also interested in social structure.

We have already cited an uncomplimentary opinion from the essay which Holmes has published on Gregory King.[51] In spite of the composition of his original audience, Holmes does not conceal

46 For age distribution and population totals see Wrigley and Schofield, *Population history* (2nd edition), pp.210, 579, 218.

47 Glass, 'Two papers on Gregory King'.

48 Lindert and Williamson, 'Revising England's social tables'; 'Reinterpreting Britain's social tables', and further studies.

49 See Arkell, 'Poverty', for a more critical examination of the lower social levels.

50 See Stone, the Mattioli lectures.

51 Holmes, 'Gregory King'.

his slight discomfort with econometrics as applied to the past, and with what is often referred to as the quantitative approach to history.[52] He is generous in his praise for King as an innovator, a creator in the analysis of social structure, but insists that he was deeply affected by his conservative, his Tory, his anti-war convictions, and that this explains his rather unlikely opinion that his country was getting rapidly poorer, indeed was going to the dogs in every way which had to do with production and wealth. King, Holmes claims, grossly and almost culpably underestimated the numbers of the English elite and their riches in his Scheme for 1688. His methods were tortuous and his figures unstable: his debts to Davenant were considerable, and his replies to Robert Harley, who questioned him on some of his conclusions, reveal his weaknesses and his consciousness of them. He was never as close to the centre of power and administration as I have claimed here, and the documents which would have been most revealing about the population and social structure of this country, that is to say the Poll tax lists and returns, were never open to him.

Considerations have been put forward above to moderate these, to me, rather over-emphatic judgements, and Sir Richard Stone's quite contrary conclusions have been extensively cited. There are many points on which further information might have been supplied by Professor Holmes to underwrite his case against King. He gives no demonstration, for example, that the Poll tax documents were closed to him.[53] But the interested reader is left to make up his own mind, or hers, on the points which are raised. It is not often that an eminent historian of what might be called the traditional political cast comes up against an economist of the very highest expertise. Not the least of the benefits of the study which has been recommended in this essay is that it requires that those who pursue it should develop their critical judgements as historians and historical sociologists.

[52] A point on which we are very close; see Laslett, 'Character of familial history'.

[53] For further discussion of this point see the concluding section of chapter 8 below.

Part I

Hearth tax & Compton census

INTRODUCING THE DOCUMENTS

The Hearth tax is the first of the major sources to be discussed in this half of the volume. The many variations in the appearance of the nominal lists derived from its administration can only be understood fully with an appreciation of the context in which they were created. This is described in some detail in the next chapter by Tom Arkell, and as a consequence this introduction to the documents simply surveys in brief some of the main differences in the composition of the better Hearth tax lists.

As a starting point, it is known that somewhere within the Hearth tax assessment list of 1670 for Henley Street Ward in Stratford-on-Avon was the house which is now open to the public as Shakespeare's birthplace (Illustration 1.1). In fact it comprises the inn with six hearths of John Tomes and the first of George Heart's one-hearth dwellings. The houses adjacent to them were pulled down subsequently. Because the names of the exempt householders are interspersed with those of the liable, this list is clearly recorded in some kind of topographical order, rather like the schedules of a nineteenth-century census enumerator. In this instance they start at the bottom of Henley Street nearest to the river and move up the east side before returning down the west side of the street. Here the exempt are identified by a 'C' for 'certified' being placed on the right, as well as the number of their hearths appearing to the left of those possessed by the liable, which ranged in this ward from one to eleven. Three dwellings are clearly indicated as being empty at the time and several others record the inclusion of a forge or an oven within the total of their hearths. Corrections, like the alteration of John to Ann Young, show that this was a working list used for more than one half-yearly collection of the tax. The names were normally those of each householder, but in some instances they belonged to the owner rather than the occupier. In this case no owners were indicated, unlike the sample list of Michaelmas 1664 for Old

Windsor (see Appendix to Chapter 3 below), but it seems probable that at least the names attached to the empty dwellings were those of their owners and it may also explain why some relatively small residences with only two hearths were apparently occupied by gentry or pseudo-gentry with the title of 'Mr'.

The assessment list of Lady Day 1664 for Castle Street Ward, Warwick (Illustration 1.2) begins very obviously with Warwick Castle, where Lord Brooke's vinehouse alone had more hearths than any other house in the ward. (Interestingly, he later reduced his tax bill by apparently removing all but two of his vineyard's hearths). On this occasion some householders were clearly listed according to their social status rather than in topographical order. Those of gentlemen status immediately follow Lord Brooke in descending order and the non-liable appear in their own separate column. This list also omits any reference to forges or ovens, but the inclusion of one exempt householder apparently without any hearths reinforces the warning that little trouble was expended on recording them. Indeed, in other instances a proportion of the poorer exempt may be numbered without being named (Illustration 1.3), which on some occasions may have reflected the amount of space available on the manuscript page, or perhaps just the patience threshold of the clerk. In this instance the liable are all listed before the non-liable and in Hurley the latter are concluded with fourteen unnamed households which are recorded as being on the common and receiving collection or alms. In many lists, however, it is also quite possible that some at least of the poorest householders were omitted altogether. Nevertheless, it should also be stressed that it is the requirement to include the exempt which makes these Hearth tax lists so valuable.

Reliable interpretations of the Hearth tax lists depend primarily on the ability to determine the completeness and accuracy of each one. Because a great diversity of local officials compiled them, there is no such thing as a single best buy or vintage on a national scale. Instead the quality of each list must be examined on a county, hundred and even parish or ward level. Unfortunately, in all but a few exceptional cases, this can only be undertaken by comparing one Hearth tax list with another or resorting to purely internal evidence, so that the fewer lists which survive for a particular area the more difficult it usually is to assess their reliability. Of course when a manuscript is damaged or contains no non-liable householders, it will be unarguably incomplete. But more often uncertainties arise because there is no specific formula for determining when a list achieved a complete enumeration since the proportion of exempt in individual communities ranged from under twenty to over eighty per cent. Eventually the administrators decided that the best means of detecting evasion from the Hearth tax was to list the households in topographical order, as in the case of Illustration 1.1, so that those arranged thus are often, but not always, more reliable than the less topographical ones. Some non-liable householders for example, or even a small hamlet, are more likely to have been omitted from the latter and in this format there is often a tendency for several dwellings to be added together under one name if one landlord was considered to be responsible for them.

In comparison, the records which supply most of our information about the Compton census are very different from those for the Hearth tax. Not only was the census taken within one year, that of 1676, but with very rare exceptions were any names noted. The intention was to record, for each parish, the numbers of men and women over sixteen and, among those, the numbers both of Popish recusants and of Protestant dissenters who absented themselves from church. But, as Anne Whiteman explains in her chapter below, because the first question was so unclearly worded, many incumbents' returns referred to other categories, such as adult males, householders or even all the inhabitants including the children. The so-called Salt manuscript, which tabulated the results for most parishes in the dioceses of the Province of Canterbury, is the main surviving source for the Compton census; manuscripts in the Bodleian Library in Oxford supply figures for some parts of the Province of York. The illustrated example for Clare deanery, Suffolk (Illustration 1.4) shows how beautifully the details were transcribed in the Salt manuscript.[1] But often the 'Conformists' column is deceptive in that it does not record the number of Anglican conformists in a particular parish, but one of the other categories listed above. Moreover, sometimes the figures include a return for a chapelry or chapelries in a parish. Although the actual returns made by the incumbents or churchwardens have come to light for only a few areas to reveal what lies behind the tabulated results, for many they no longer exist. How diverse

[1] For a discussion of the accuracy of its contents based on a comparison with the Hearth tax return of 1674 see pp. 116-8 below.

they were may be seen from the illustrations in the *Critical edition*; compare, for example, those for parishes in Canterbury, Worcester, Exeter, Hereford and York dioceses. Frustratingly, therefore, what appears in the first instance to be a straightforward source to handle is in fact a potential minefield, so that all students of the Compton census will urgently require the expert guidance offered by Whiteman. When an adequate Hearth tax list exists for the same locality, Arkell shows in Chapter 6 how the two sources may be used to help illuminate each other.

Illustration 1.1 Hearth tax – Henley Street Ward, Stratford-on-Avon, 1670.

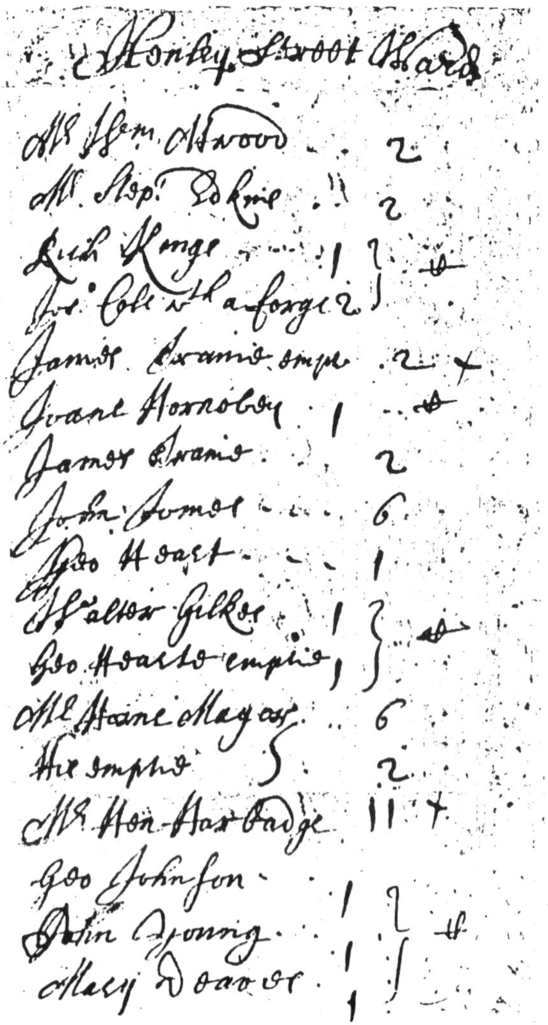
Henley Street Ward
Mr Hen. Atwood 2
Mr Step. Tomkins 2
Rich. Kenge 1
Jo. Cole wth a forge 2
James Evans empty 2
Joane Hornsby 1
James Evans 2
John Jones 6
Geo Heart 1
Walter Gilkes 1
Geo Hearts empty 1
Mr Haine Mayor 6
His empty 2
Mr Hen. Harbadge 11
Geo Johnson 1
John Young 1
Mary Weaver 1

Illustration 1.2 Hearth tax – Castle Street Ward, Warwick, Lady Day 1664.

Kington Hundred in Kenelworth devision

Warwicke

The Castle streete Ward	hearths liable
Robert Lord Brooke in the Castle	47
The Ld Brooke in the Vineyard house	15
John Kerby gent	10
Roger Lodi gent	10
William Land gent	4
Thomas Harrison gent	4
Edward Payne	1
Robert [illegible]	2
Anthony Land	3
Richard Robinson	4
Charles [illegible]	4
William Barttell	6

	Hearths not liable
William Chandler	1
Richard [illegible]	1
Benjamin Smith	1
Elizabeth Moss	1
Mathew Howard	1
Richard [illegible]	1
Thomas Gilstone	1
Robert Wardon	1
Robert Lea	1
Edward [illegible]	1
Johnson Gibbs	1
Widd Walker	1
Mathew Howard	1
Widd Millard	
	14

Illustration 1.3 **Hearth tax – The villages of Hurley and Grendon, Warwickshire, 1670**

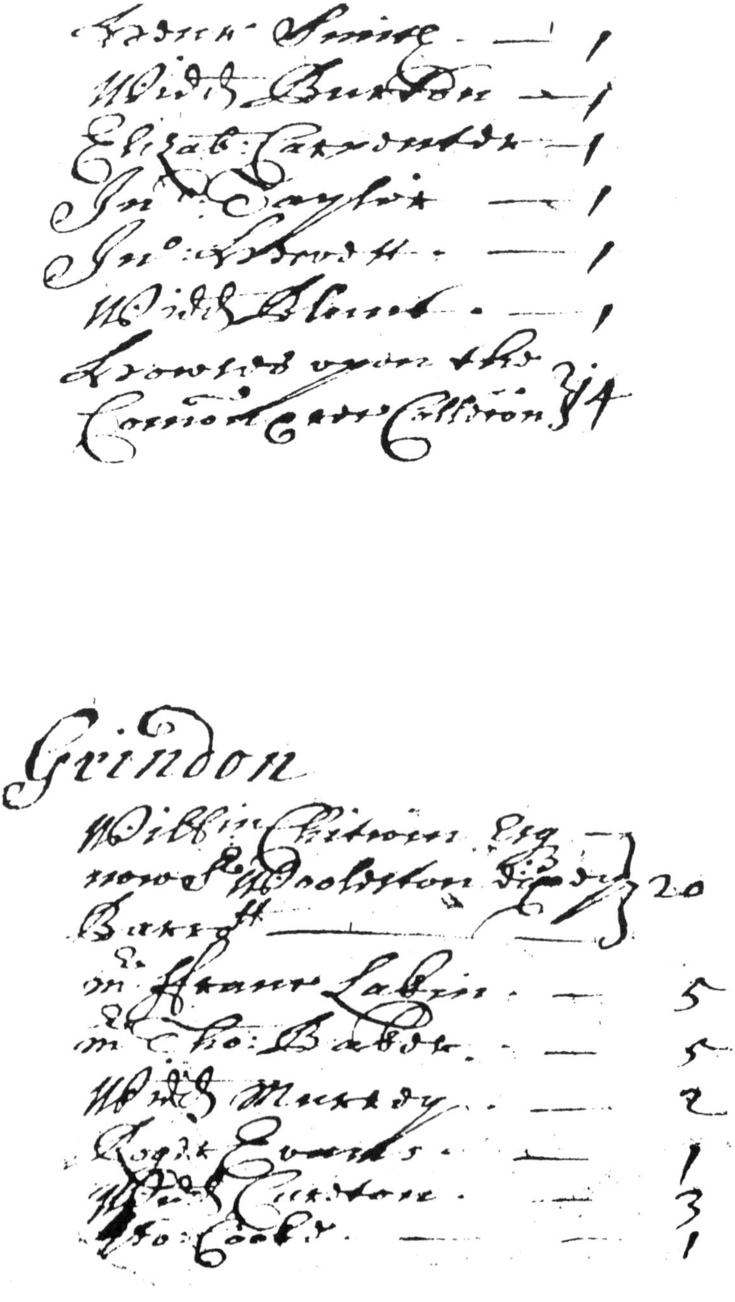

Francis Smithe — 1
Widd: Burdon — 1
Elizab: Carpenter — 1
Jno: Taylor — 1
Jno: Arnold — 1
Widd: Blunt — 1
Erected upon the
Common Cottages 34

Grindon

Willm: Chetwyn Esq —
now Mr Woolaston Esq — 20
Barrtt —
Mr Henry Lakin — 5
Mr Tho: Badder — 5
Widd: Murdy — 2
Roger Evans — 1
Wm Cutlare — 3
Jno: Cooke — 1

Illustration 1.4 **Compton census: Salt manuscript – Fordham and Clare Deaneries, Suffolk, 1676.**

	Conformists	Papists	Nonconformists
Newmarket SStorum	140		
Newmarket Mariæ	340	4	1
Soham	530		21
Snaylewell			
Tudenham	107		2
Worlington	115		
Wicken			
Wooditton	231		6
Wangford	58		
Decanat; Clare			
Barnardiston	81		
Bradly magna	130		1
Bradly parva	39		1
Cowling	140		
Clare	500		50a
Dalham	169		
Denham	57		2

Here the heading 'Conformists' is very misleading because the Salt manuscript's figures for this column included the Papists and Nonconformists in Norwich diocese and several others – see p.85.

3

Printed instructions for administering the Hearth tax

TOM ARKELL

Introduction

The Hearth tax is a frustratingly complicated source to use. At first sight apparently nothing could be simpler than studying a tax which levied one shilling every six months on each hearth in England and Wales in the occupancy of all but the poor for a period of twenty-seven years (1662-89). However, the better acquainted one becomes with the tax, the more the difficulties of interpreting it with certainty become. For example, many lists appear to be either incomplete or not totally accurate, especially in respect of those exempt from it. Some names may not represent the occupiers of separate houses, some of the totals of hearths may disguise evasion and not all the exempt were poor. In part, these difficulties stem from the changing methods of collection used by the different Hearth tax administrations, and from the considerable variations in the practices adopted within the separately administered counties and cities. Others are caused by the fact that the surviving documents come from different stages in the tax's collection – assessments listing those who ought to pay, sometimes retrospectively, returns of those who had paid, forms of combined assessments and returns, collectors' entry-books, working papers, fair copies and so on.[1]

All these issues cannot be clarified in one short chapter, but much needed light can be shed on some of these problems by a critical examination of the two surviving printed instructions made for the collectors in 1664 and 1684.[2] However, a brief survey of the Hearth tax legislation and administration is required first to provide the context for this discussion.

1 Relatively brief general discussions of the Hearth tax can be found in: Meekings, *Hearth tax*; Patten, 'Hearth taxes', pp.14-27; Arkell, 'Student's guide', pp.23-37; Beckett, Barley and Wallwork, 'Introduction', pp.vii-xv.

2 PRO, E179/265/30; *Calendar of Treasury Books*, VII, pp.1362-7.

The Hearth tax legislation

The original Hearth tax bill, which received its first reading in the Commons on 1 March 1662, seems to have been drawn up very hastily and to have enjoyed a relatively rapid passage through Parliament. It was approved finally by the Commons on 12th March and by the Lords on 19th March before receiving the royal assent on 19th May, by when it had already been in force for nearly two months since 25th March.[3] By the terms of the new Act, one shilling was to be levied every six months at Michaelmas (29 September) and Lady Day (25 March) on the hearths or fireplaces of all householders in England and Wales.[4]

The original Hearth tax bill did not distinguish clearly between the liability of owners and occupiers nor did it make any provision for exempting anyone, but a series of amendments added by the House of Commons did both. By one clause, 'the payments and duties hereby charged, shall be charged only on the occupier for the time being of such hearth or stove, dwelling in such house whereto such hearth or stove shall be belonging, his executors or administrators, and not on the landlord, who let or demised the same, his heirs, executors or assigns'. This clause, therefore, made the basic unit of taxation the household or family in the seventeenth-century sense and not the house. However, the working of other parts of the act did create serious doubts about several other issues, such as the liability of payment for empty houses which were technically liable.

Exemption from the Hearth tax was covered by three separate amendments which caused some confusion because their different categories overlapped. By the first clause, 'no person who by reason of his poverty, or the smallness of his estate is exempted from the usual taxes, payments and contributions toward the church and poor, shall be charged or chargeable with any of the duties by this act imposed'. The second clause provided exemption if 'the house wherein any person doth inhabit is not of greater value than of twenty shillings per annum upon the full improved rent; and that neither the person so inhabiting, nor any other using the same messuage, hath, useth or occupieth any lands or tenements of their own or others, of the yearly value of twenty

3 *Journal of House of Commons*, VIII, pp.376-85; *Journal of House of Lords*, XI, pp.408-11, 471-2.

4 14 Car. II c.10.

shillings per annum, nor hath any lands, tenements, goods or chattels, of the value of ten pounds in their own possession, or in the possession of any other in trust for them'. Anyone in this category required an exemption certificate signed by the minister and at least one of the churchwardens or overseers of the poor of their parish and certified by two JPs. Finally, 'this act ... shall not extend to charge any blowing-house, and stamp, furnace, or kiln, or any private oven within any of the houses hereby charged, nor any hearth or stove within the site of any hospital or almshouse for the relief of poor people, whose endowment and revenue doth not exceed in true value the sum of one hundred pounds by the year'. This last clause was badly worded because it did not make it clear that smiths' forges and bakers' ovens remained liable.

Only two subsequent amending Acts were passed by Parliament in the next two years.[5] From 1663 the assessments were required to list the names and hearths of all the non-liable as well as the liable and from 1664 everyone with more than two hearths was made liable even if they were otherwise entitled to exemption. Even though many of the exempt did not need an exemption certificate, this first amendment caused some confusion because it required that all the exempt should be named in the assessment lists. Further confusion was sometimes caused by the fact that the smallest unit of civil government in which the officials were responsible for collecting the tax was often not the parish, which was responsible for issuing exemption certificates, but instead a constabulary, tithing or similar civil unit with boundaries different from its local parish. And so some lists of exempt do not coincide with the areas of the lists of the taxpayers.

This situation has been compounded by the fact that a disturbing number of recent commentators' attempts to elucidate the exemption clauses has suffered from various degrees of inaccuracy. These have included claims, for example, that exemption was given to those with an annual income of not more than ten pounds or with a house worth less than twenty shillings (not per annum) or to those in 'receipt of alms'.[6] The suggestion that 'the Hearth Tax Acts divided the poor into two classes, those exempt by certificate and those, poorer still, who were

5 15 Car. II c.13; 16 Car. II c.3.

6 Patten, 'Hearth taxes', p.18; Russell, 'Introduction', pp.xxii-xxiii; Foster, 'Hearth tax', p.385; Marshall, 'Bedfordshire', p.2; West, *Village records*, p.131.

automatically exempt'[7] is equally erroneous because the hastily-conceived amendments created overlapping rather than logically separate categories of exempt.

Administration

Initially the ordinary machinery of local government was used to administer the Hearth tax.[8] Petty constables, tithingmen etc. were responsible for making assessment lists of the hearths of the taxpayers within their areas and for presenting them to their county's next quarter sessions. There they were to be inspected by the JPs and enrolled by the clerk of the peace who also had to provide the Exchequer with a duplicate. The petty constables then had to collect the tax within six days of Michaelmas or Lady Day, transmit it along with the names of the defaulters to the high constables of the hundreds within twenty days, who then had ten days to pass them on to the county's high sheriff. The sheriff was given a further thirty days in which to make his return to the Exchequer. In cities and towns that were also separate counties, collection was simpler because it was entrusted to the sheriffs and was based on assessments supplied by the constables. The Act of 1662 also provided powers and penalties to help carry out these measures and made provision for recording 'where any increase or decrease of such hearths or stoves shall hereafter happen'.

This machinery proved hopelessly inadequate. In the first year the Exchequer received from the Hearth tax little more than one third of the wildly optimistic estimated yield of £300,000 per annum. Parliament's first revising Act concentrated on alleged deficiencies in assessment and virtually ignored all failings in collection, apart from making the outgoing constables responsible for collecting any outstanding tax at the end of their annual period of office. The sheriffs' administration was finally discredited when the new assessment authorised by this Act of 1663 produced no improvement in the number of hearths taxed.

The first assessment lists under the sheriffs were prepared in the summer of 1662, somewhat later than intended originally because of the delay in granting the royal assent. They contained the names of only the liable, although there are grounds for believing

7 Styles, 'Introduction', p.lxxvii.

8 Much of this section is drawn from the excellent accounts in Chandaman, *English public revenue*, pp.77-109, 316-23 and Meekings, *Hearth tax*.

that sometimes petty constables may have included some householders who should have been exempt. These lists were used for the first three collections of 1662-3. They were followed by a second assessment in the autumn and winter of 1663-4, which listed both chargeable and exempt and was designed for the Lady Day 1664 collection. Sometimes those householders who had pulled down or bricked up some hearths since the previous assessment were recorded among the exempt for their demolished hearths in this assessment (with or without a separate indication) as well as among the liable for their remaining hearths.

In May 1664 Parliament acceded to the king's demands for a major reconstruction of the Hearth tax's administration and agreed that both assessment and collection should be taken over by officers appointed by the king. From Michaelmas 1664 to Michaelmas 1665 the tax was administered by receivers with staffs of sub-collectors, who were soon known as chimney men, and at the same time most county boroughs were brought under the same administration as their adjacent counties. Petty constables or their equivalent were still needed to accompany the chimney men when they exercised their rights to enter and search a house once a year to check the accuracy of its assessment and also to distrain and sell the householders' goods if the hearth money remained unpaid within one hour of their demanding it. This transfer of most of the responsibility for the Hearth tax from local government officers and the stricter administration, which included the production of a printed manual of instructions discussed below, increased the unpopularity of the tax. The anticipated improvement from administration by royal officers therefore did not materialise. This situation was further exacerbated by the effects of the plague and war against the Dutch, so that a government desperate for money agreed to privatise or farm out the tax to three London merchants in March 1666 for seven years.

The receivers were appointed so hastily in 1664 to replace the sheriffs that most could not make their first assessment until the autumn or winter of 1664-5, i.e. after their first Michaelmas collection was due. Because it was made retrospectively it often took the form of a combined assessment and return and further potential deficiencies arose from the fact that many were revisions of the original assessment of 1662 and not of the more recent one for Lady Day 1664 as intended. In many counties this list for Michaelmas 1664 was also used for the two collections in 1665, although some made new assessments for one or even both of them.

The collection for Lady Day 1666 was also seriously disrupted because the farmers replaced the receivers in the spring of 1666 with very little warning. In a few counties, therefore, the receivers collected all or part of it, but in most the sub-farmers took it over retrospectively and acted as receivers for this one collection. Their books, which were made in the summer of 1666 and eventually submitted for audit to the Exchequer, were again in the form of combined assessment and return, but often omitted many of the exempt.

However, the farming of the Hearth tax proved to be a total failure and was made worse by the fire of London, which even destroyed the newly-established Hearth Office. Popular hatred of the tax reached its peak in 1666-7 and often concentrated on opposing payment for smiths' forges. The farmers surrendered their farm at their earliest possible opportunity (after three years) at Lady Day 1669. From Michaelmas 1669 to Lady Day 1674 the Hearth tax was again administered by receivers with staffs of sub-collectors and help from petty constables under the general supervision of a small central office called the Agents for the Hearth tax. Under their tight control there was a striking increase in the efficiency of collection (although not of assessed value), helped by a higher rate of payment for the receivers, printed certificates for exemption and a comprehensive manual to guide the sub-collectors.

Because the receivers were not appointed until the summer of 1670, they had the difficult task of making three collections simultaneously at Michaelmas 1670. Not surprisingly, therefore, this first assessment, which was made in the summer and autumn of 1670, was again combined with their return. Three further assessments were normally made between Lady Day 1671 and Lady Day 1674, mainly in the same form of combined assessment and return, with copies enrolled by the clerks of the peace in addition to those submitted to the Exchequer. The form of these assessments, however, was far from consistent, with some listing only the changes since the last assessment, while others ranged from lists of taxpayers alone to those which named all or many of the exempt and perhaps numbered those who were claimed to be paupers receiving alms or 'collection'.

The administration of the Hearth tax settled down at last into a regular pattern of different administrations every five years in the 1670s and 1680s. The second receivers were succeeded from Michaelmas 1674 by two farms, each of five years. Finally, from Michaelmas 1684 the government returned to collecting the Hearth tax directly through a special Commission set up to manage both the Excise and the Hearth tax. Under the last the average yield from the Hearth tax shot up to £216,000 per annum from about £150,000 per annum under the three previous administrations. But this success was shortlived. In 1689 William and Mary agreed to abolish the Hearth tax in England and Wales to help win support for their new regime, but the Irish and Scots were not so fortunate. The Hearth tax continued to be levied in Ireland for another hundred years and was first introduced into Scotland in 1691.

Almost all the surviving detailed English Hearth tax lists come from the two rather disjointed periods of 1662-66 and 1669-74, when the machinery of local government was involved in its collection and detailed accounts were sent for auditing to the Exchequer. In general eight assessments were produced in most counties in these nine years, but there is great diversity in the quantity and condition of the material which is now available for each one.[9] The accounts of the farmers and of the commissioners were also audited in the Exchequer, but the supporting vouchers which they had to produce did not include detailed lists of taxpayers and exempt from the local areas so that comparable detailed lists from the more settled and possibly more efficient last fifteen years of the Hearth tax's administration are not available in the Public Record Office.

The manual of 1664

The first of the two surviving copies of the manuals of instructions for collecting the Hearth tax dates from 1664 and was designed for the three collections from Michaelmas 1664 to Michaelmas 1665 of the first receivers' administration. It contained sixteen numbered paragraphs and was accompanied by

9 For the best summary of those which have survived see Gibson, *Hearth tax*.

a specimen form for Old Windsor that was intended to illustrate with even greater clarity how the instructions should be implemented.[10] They were part of the government's larger initiative to improve the collection and increase the yield of the Hearth tax. Both documents were reprinted by Meekings in his volume on the *Dorset Hearth Tax Assessments 1662-1664*, but their existence does not seem to be known widely nor the unwitting confusion which they created over the recording of the Hearth tax data appreciated.[11]

Sir Edmund Sawyer, the senior exchequer auditor who had helped to draft the original Hearth tax bill in 1662, prepared the manual to inform the receivers in each county on how the previous returns for Lady Day 1664 should be revised. His instructions were designed to ensure that the collectors did not make new lists for Michaelmas 1664, but simply revised and checked the old ones, confirming when they were correct, inserting all omissions and recording all changes and the reasons for them. The details demanded included the landlord's name if the occupier was only a tenant, the names of the executors if the occupant had died and the date when he or she had left if the house stood empty. They were also instructed, by the two following paragraphs, to record accurately all those who were legally exempted from paying the tax:

> '8. If you find any party dwell in a house not worth xx*s*. by the year, and are qualified according to the first Act, or the Tenants by reason of their poverty be not Rated to Church and Poor, yet if the Houses contain above two Hearths, they are not to be exempted from payment; but for such of the natures aforesaid as exceed not two Hearths, you are to note them in the Margent of your Book against such party, that they are such ...'
>
> '11. And if you find any persons that dwell in Houses not worth xx*s*. per Annum, or Cottages Erected by poor people upon Commons or Waste Grounds, or such persons as receive Alms of the Parish, which are omitted out of the first Roll, then you are to enter the same in your Book, at the end of the Parish, in which they are, expressing them to be such'.[12]

10 See Appendix to this chapter below.

11 Meekings, *Dorset*, pp.110-3; Patten, 'Hearth taxes', p.17; Chandaman, *English public revenue*, p.90.

12 PRO, E179/265/30.

The collectors were also instructed once a year, 'to examine all Increases and Decreases, and other things according to the aforesaid Instructions, and to certifie the same to the Clerk of the Peace' and 'to observe the same method in writing the names of Hundreds, Parishes, Places and Persons, with the numbers of the Hearths that was in the Rolls now sent unto you, with the variations; to the end that His Majesties Auditors may the more readily and certainly compare and reexamine them'. In addition, the collectors were instructed to return the books they had been given with their comments and additions to the Clerk of the Peace for their county, who would have them approved by the justices and then have a copy engrossed in parchment for returns to the Exchequer.

The specimen form was divided into four columns (see Appendix). The first listed in shillings the money received as arrears for the half year due at Michaelmas 1664 (and so should have corresponded with the number of hearths that were liable).[13] The second and third columns copied the names of the householders and their number of hearths from the earlier roll. The last column recorded the collectors' remarks as directed by the instructions: *Ex.* (for *examinatur*) if the former entry was correct, but when the householder was merely a tenant the name of the owner was to be inserted and so were all changes from, and mistakes in, the previous list. A separate section for those 'Hearths not mentioned in the former Return' came at the end.

Lost instructions

A brief entry in the *Calendar of Treasury Books* for 12th March, 1672 concerning the Excise proves that a manual for the guidance of the collectors of the Hearth tax was in use at that time. The relevant passage reads somewhat cryptically: 'The Attorney General called in, says there is a manual for the Customs and a manual for the Hearth money and moves to have an able person to make such another manual for the laws of Excise with an index.'[14] This Hearth tax manual was produced by the Hearthmoney Office which had been established in 1670 to organise the direct collection of the Hearth tax by royal officers

[13] The money was received in arrears because the receivers' administration was set up in great haste in the middle of its first half year. Meekings, *Hearth tax*, 3rd page; Meekings, *Dorset*, p.x; Styles, 'Introduction', pp.xxxviii-xlii.

[14] *Calendar of Treasury Books*, III, p.1049.

under the second receivers' administration of 1669-74.[15] Unfortunately no copy of the manual appears to have survived to show how closely these instructions from the early 1670s followed those of 1664, or if they had been substantially modified by then.

Instructions of 1684

The only other surviving printed instructions date from 1684. They were made at the start of the English Hearth tax's final phase, when it was collected with the Excise until 1689 by a specially established joint commission.[16] These instructions differ substantially from those of 1664. They can be found in the *Calendar of Treasury Books* for 16th October, 1684 when it was agreed that they should be printed and published in two parts.[17]

The first part of the instructions was for the Commissioners, officers and deputies involved in the collection of the Hearth tax and contained fifteen paragraphs. Most summarised clearly the relevant clauses of the three Hearth Tax Acts of 1662-4 or provided a helpful interpretation of how they should be carried out. For example, blowing houses and stamp furnaces which were exempt, unlike smiths' forges, were defined as 'houses wherein the mineral ore is smelted down into metal'. Private ovens which were also exempted (but not public ones) were described as those, 'wherein provisions for the family only and not for gain, are baked and dressed' (para 3). The next paragraph covered exempt households as follows:

> 'If the churchwardens and overseers of the poor of the parish and the minister thereof or any two of them (the minister being one) shall in writing certify that any house is not of greater value than 20s. per an. upon the full and improved rent and that no person inhabiting or using the said house has or uses any lands or tenements of their own or others of the value of 20s. per an. nor has any lands, tenements, goods or chattels of the value of 10*l*. in their own possession or in trust for them, then such certificate on being allowed by the two next justices of the peace shall discharge the person and house so certified from the duty for the year only in which such certificate is made. Certificates departing from any of the above detailed points are illegal and void and cannot hinder the levying of the duty'.

15 Chandaman, *English public revenue*, pp.95-8.

16 Chandaman, *English public revenue*, pp.104-6.

17 *Calendar of Treasury Books*, VII, pp.1362-7.

Paragraph 7 dealt with those who moved house in the middle of a half year, No 8 empty houses and Nos 9 and 10 hearths that were covered, stopped up, etc. Paragraph 11 urged the deputies to make sure that they recorded all parishes, places, houses, etc. that might have been omitted from previous views (surveys), as well as all recently erected chimneys. Nos 12 and 15 provided guidance in the distraint of goods and the alternative measures to be taken against those who refused or failed to pay, No 13 on the giving of receipts to those who had paid and No 14 on the procedures to be adopted by officers who were injured or opposed in the performance of their duties.[18]

The second part of these instructions, which applied to the Commissioners and chief officers, is in ten paragraphs and is somewhat more illuminating on how the tax was collected. In every town, parish and place, except cities and market towns, the inhabitants were to be warned in advance, either in church or by the constable, of the time when the duty would be collected so that 'persons may not be surprised by your sudden coming but may have some reasonable time to provide the duty or in their absence to leave out the same'. The text continued along similar lines, 'In taking the names of the inhabitants in each parish, town or place (with the number of hearths in each house) you and your deputies are to enter them as they lie most contiguous, whereby the duty may be more easily collected; inscribing all empty houses and their number of hearths in their due places with the names of the persons who by the law are chargeable with the duty for the same'. In addition, the officers 'are so to demean yourselves that you may avoid all just occasion of offence that so this affair may be better advanced and carried on'.[19]

Comparison between the instructions of 1664 and 1684

Taken together, these instructions demonstrate the meticulous care with which the collection of the Hearth tax was to be undertaken, but a comparison also reveals some striking differences between the two. Chiefly these are as follows:

[18] *Calendar of Treasury Books*, VII, pp.1363-5.

[19] *Calendar of Treasury Books*, VII, pp.1365-7, paras 4, 5 and 8.

Topographical order

The instructions for 1684 stated categorically that the names of the inhabitants must be listed in strict topographical order, including the empty houses, and by implication, the non-chargeable ones. Sawyer's instructions, on the other hand, demanded that the collectors should follow the same order as in the previous lists and insert omissions at the end. Almost certainly this major difference reflects the fact that by the 1680s experience had shown that strict recording in topographical order was the best method of preventing omissions and evasions.

Exemption

Although the laws affecting exemption remained unaltered after 1664, the two manuals of instructions did not reflect this continuity.[20] Somewhat surprisingly, those of 1684 made no mention of the first exemption clause passed in 1662 involving exemption from paying rates, but they did paraphrase very accurately the second one concerning the valuation of houses as well as the third referring to blowing houses.[21] On the other hand, although the earlier instructions referred to all three exemption clauses, overall their treatment was bedevilled by errors, omissions and confusion.

For a start, both paragraphs 8 and 11 were wrong to state that houses not worth 20s. per annum were exempt; it should have been those worth not *more than* 20 shillings.[22] This manual of 1664 also made no reference to the exemption of blowing houses, stamps, furnaces, kilns and private ovens. In addition, paragraph 11 failed to mention those who were not rated to church and poor, and so implied rather dubiously that no one in this category could have been omitted from previous assessments by mistake. More importantly because persons that dwell in houses worth not more than 20 shillings per annum covered all the rest of the exempt, the instruction in paragraph 11 to record cottages upon commons or wastes and those who received alms of their parish is potentially a quite superfluous and misleading innovation, whatever Sawyer's motives for their inclusion may have been.

20 Arkell, 'Student's guide', p.25.

21 14 Car. II c.10, ss.16, 17, 19.

22 If it seems pedantic to present this discrepancy as an error, it should be recalled that rents of £1 per annum were common but not those between 19s. 6d. and £1.

These flawed instructions were certainly the main source for many of the errors made by recent commentators mentioned above, but the explanations for them can only be surmised. The error in the manual of 1664 over the value of exempt houses, together with the confusion in paragraph 11, suggests that the document was drafted in considerable haste, without adequate checking. The reference to poor people living on commons or wastes and receiving alms can probably be explained best by the fact that Sawyer wanted all property, however poor, to be included in the revised lists and these two categories were both easy to detect and the most likely to have been omitted. By the 1680s, however, exemptions appear to have been granted only to those with legal certificates which were based on the value of their houses, so that the alternative qualifications of those who were potentially exempt through not paying rates were ignored, because experience had probably shown that all were normally subsumed within the former category.[23]

Poverty

The later manual made no reference to poverty as a cause of exemption, but the earlier one clearly did. Paragraph 9 from the manual of 1664 offers a partial explanation: 'And in case where the Landlords pay the Rates to Church and Poor for all their Tenants' Lands, and the Tenant is not left out of the said Rates by reason of his Poverty, but by reason his Landlord payeth the same..., such houses... are to be Rated as others are'.[24] Thus the houses of those who did not pay rates because their landlords paid them were not exempted from the Hearth tax, but only the houses of those who did not pay rates by reason of their poverty or the smallness of their estate (to use the words of the Act of 1662).[25] Omission of this latter phrase may seriously alter the meaning of this exemption clause if it leads to 'by reason of their poverty' being interpreted in a modern sociological sense and not exclusively in the context of exemption from rates.[26]

23 Arkell, 'Poverty', pp.29-36.

24 PRO, E179/265/30, paragraph 9.

25 14 Car. II c.1, s.16.

26 Various aspects of the question of poverty raised here are discussed at some length in Arkell, 'Poverty', pp.38-47.

Format of the returns

Despite, and probably even because of, Sawyer's attempts to encourage uniformity nationwide in the Hearth tax assessments there was great diversity in the format of the returns made in 1664-5. Some of those which have been reprinted appear to have ignored them completely, including the returns for Norfolk, Oxfordshire and the Isle of Wight. In other counties, such as Dorset, Surrey and Worcestershire, the general plan was followed but not the precise details, although the surviving documents from elsewhere do indicate that in many other counties the prescribed form was followed very closely.[27]

The main reason for this failure to impose a uniform format on all the receivers' returns stemmed from Sawyer's original intention to base this revision on the lists for Lady Day 1664. Unfortunately it must have been realised too late that these returns would not reach the Exchequer in time for them to be copied and then dispatched to the receivers for the Michaelmas 1664 collection. The receivers were therefore supplied with copies of the assessments for 1662, and a preamble seems to have been added to their instructions urging them, if possible, to acquire and use a local copy of the Lady Day 1664 assessment as the basis for their new returns. Many receivers failed to do this and then apparently found themselves in the frustrating situation of trying to follow inappropriately worded instructions which referred specifically to the 'Roll for our Lady day 1664' in both of its first two paragraphs.[28]

[27] Meekings, *Dorset*, pp.xvi-xvii; Frankel and Seaman, 'Norfolk'; Weinstock, 'Oxfordshire'; Russell, 'Hearth tax returns'; Stoate, *Cornwall*; Dwelly, 'Somerset'. See also Meekings, *Dorset*, p.xv for a brief note on the limitations of the Somerset volume and Stoate, p.x for an indication of how the Cornish returns departed from Sawyer's manual.

[28] This conclusion is based on a close reading of the text and does not follow the interpretations in Meekings, *Dorset*, p.xvi; Styles 'Introduction', p.xlii or Stoate, *Cornwall*, p.x. Meekings argued that, although Sawyer would rather have provided the receivers with copies for the Lady Day 1664 assess ment, the Exchequer's printed manual of instructions was designed for revising the 1662 assessment. Styles echoed this interpretation, stating that it was assumed in Sawyer's instructions that all receivers would be furnished at the outset with the books containing copies of the 1662 assessment and adding that 'Sawyer would have preferred – surprisingly enough – to take the second assessment as a basis'. Stoate, on the other hand, deduced that the instructions intended that non-liable hearths were to be included in the 'hearths not formerly returned' section and concluded that Sawyer was not

Sawyer's failure to tailor his instructions precisely for a revision of the 1662 lists proved particularly confusing over recording the exempt. The assessment for Lady Day 1664 had been the first to follow the instructions in the first revising Act of 1663 to record the non-liable in 'a booke or roll fairely written wherein shall be two columnes, the one containing the names of the persons and number of hearthes and stoves in their respective possessions that are chargeable by the said act, and the other the names of the persons and number of hearthes and stoves in their respective possessions which are not chargeable by the said act'.[29] Sawyer's manual for Michaelmas 1664 appears to have assumed initially that all the collectors were working from an assessment that listed the two separately, and so ordered them to record at the end of each parish both the liable and non-liable houses that had been omitted from the former lists. But because the specimen form for Old Windsor contained no separate list of exempt, it seems to have been one from 1662 and so further confused the collectors. Many must have assumed that they were no longer required to follow the pattern established at Lady Day 1664 by the Act of 1663 so that in some counties the non-liable were omitted entirely, while in others they were all grouped together not at the end of each parish, but at the end of the entire assessment. Even more individuality was displayed in the returns for Cornwall where the non-chargeable were listed after the chargeable who had not been mentioned previously in the parishes for only two of its nine hundreds.[30]

really concerned about their inclusion. One other potential misunderstanding concerning the instructions of 1664 is an erroneous statement in Meekings, *Dorset*, p.xvii that the manual instructed the collectors to record an exempt person as a 'pauper'. Even though this was a common practice in the Dorset returns for Michaelmas 1664, the word 'pauper' was nowhere mentioned in Sawyer's manual.

29 15 Car. II c.13, s.1. Initially the government had hoped that the collection at Michaelmas 1663 would be based upon it; see Introduction by Meekings in Edwards, *Derbyshire*, p.xxiv.

30 Meekings, *Dorset*, p.xvi; Styles, 'Introduction', pp.xlii-xlviii; Stoate, *Cornwall*, pp.40-51, 135-45; Frankel and Seaman, 'Norfolk' pp.viii, 115-27. It is also possible that some returns may have included separate lists of non-chargeable which have been lost subsequently. One peculiarity of the Cornish returns which may be worth noting is that all the householders of 1662 who were listed as exempt in 1664 were reported as being poor and not rated to church and poor, but not as having houses worth 20 shillings per annum or less.

This diversity of practice in recording the non-chargeable continued in 1669-74 under the second receivers' administration. Then, for instance, all the recorded exempt were named and listed separately from the liable at the end of each parish in Devon, Exeter and the Isle of Wight.[31] However, in Bedfordshire and Essex some unnamed paupers who received 'collection for their support' were mentioned after the lists of those who were discharged by legal certificate.[32] Both practices occurred in Warwickshire as well as lists in which the non-liable were interspersed topographically with the liable, mainly in the first assessment lists of 1670 that were based upon those for Lady Day 1666.[33] Finally, among the surviving returns for Derbyshire there are very few certified paupers and those who were recorded were listed with the liable.[34]

These great variations among the surviving Hearth tax documents for the early 1670s make it impossible to guess what instructions were contained in the manual for the second receivers' administration. As yet no coherent pattern can be discerned among such apparent random diversity so that it is impossible to say how much they were affected by, for example, the introduction of printed exemption certificates in 1670, or how much influence the individual receivers or their deputies had upon their final format.

Because very few Hearth tax lists survive from the 1680s, the instructions of 1684 are unlikely to generate much interest unless it can be shown that they were modelled closely on those for some previous administrations. The available evidence is limited but suggestive. In 1678 the collectors or sub-farmers for the city of Worcester set out the names of all householders, including the non-liable, so topographically that it is still 'possible to trace the route which the collectors took through the city' and they did their job so thoroughly that their book is 'virtually a gazetteer of all the households in the city in 1678'.[35] The format of their book

31 Stoate, *Devon*; Hoskins, 'Exeter', p.65-86; Russell, 'Hearth tax returns', pp.137-99.

32 Marshall, 'Bedfordshire', pp.65-159; Patten, 'Hearth taxes', p.18. A similar format was used in York in 1671 and 1672, see Hibberd, 'Data-linkage', p.60.

33 Styles, 'Introduction', pp.lxxiii-lxxv and plates iv-vi.

34 Edwards, 'Derbyshire', pp.34-111, 136-98.

35 Meekings, Porter and Roy, 'Hearth tax', pp.18, 32.

and the comments which their successors made as they collected the tax in the next two years clearly indicate strong connections between their instructions and those of 1664, even though these must have been modified somewhat. Because *'Ex'* was not used for unchanged entries, most in this Worcester list had no collectors' comment, but a range of other remarks similar to those of 1664-5 were appended to a substantial minority. These included the names of new owners and landlords, empty houses, changes in the number of hearths and of those who were certified exempt, the discovery of concealed hearths, distraint, disputes over payment and so on.[36]

Surviving documentation from the later 1670s and 1680s is so meagre that it is impossible to tell if the Worcester example of keeping collectors' books was normal or exceptional in the later stages of the Hearth tax. Nevertheless, it does seem plausible to suggest that by then, and probably some years earlier, the normal practice may have been to apply the detailed instructions for recording the collection of the Hearth tax consistently to the collectors' books and that this included setting out the households in strict topographical order long before the manual of 1684 was drawn up.

Conclusion

Despite their inconsistencies over recording the exempt, the very detailed instructions of 1664 have created a good opportunity in several counties for a careful study of the many changes that occurred to both the occupants and their hearths in the first two years of the tax's collection. So far this has not been undertaken, although preliminary analyses of the material have been made for Cornwall and Warwickshire.[37]

However, the conclusion that emerges most strongly from this comparative study of the surviving Hearth tax instructions is that Sawyer's well-meant but muddled manual must bear much responsibility for the inconsistent state of the extant Hearth tax lists from Michaelmas 1664 onwards. Without any doubt the ambiguities created by his instructions and their accompanying form exacerbated the confusions over exemption contained within

36 Meekings, Porter and Roy, 'Hearth tax', pp.12-16, 40-116.

37 Stoate, *Cornwall*, pp.xi-xiii; Styles, 'Introduction', pp.xliii-xlv.

the Acts of 1662 and 1663 and also made it impossible for the receivers and their collectors to reconcile all Sawyer's directions with the innovations that had just been established at Lady Day 1664. This perverse outcome was clearly the reverse of his intentions.

Appendix

INSTRUCTIONS FOR COLLECTING THE HEARTH TAX – MICHAELMAS 1664

What follows is a reproduction of the complete text of the instructions issued for collecting the Hearth tax at Michaelmas 1664. The original copy of this document is held in the Public Record Office[38] and we are grateful for permission to reproduce this unique document in this volume. The instructions are set out in sixteen numbered paragraphs and are followed by a worked example relating to Old Windsor, Berkshire. It should also be noted that pages 7 and 8 were left blank.

[38] PRO, E179/265/30.

(1)

Inſtructions

To the Officers appointed for receiving the Duty and Revenue ariſing and belonging to His Majeſty by Fire-Hearths and Stoves, &c.

Nprimis, Having received from His Majeſties Auditors, Books of the former Certificates, and Returns of the ſaid Duty and Revenue, which are Ordered to be delivered unto you, you ſhall endeavour to procure from the Conſtables or Tythingmen, *&c.* Copies of the Taxations of the ſaid Duty for the half year ended the 25th of *March* 1664. And in caſe you can readily have them, you are by comparing them with the ſaid Books, to make the beſt uſe of them you may for His Majeſties Service; But if they cannot readily be had, you are nevertheleſs to proceed, and in your proceeding to obſerve theſe Rules following.

1. IF the party in the former Roll be an Owner of the Houſe, and continue ſtill in Poſſeſsion, and you find his Hearths by your view the ſame number

A tha

(2)

that were certified in the former Roll for our *Lady-day* 1664. That then you write againſt the name of ſuch party in the Book ſent you, *Ex*. And if any of the Chriſtian Names be wanting, to add them.

2. If the Owner of the Houſe be changed, then againſt the name of ſuch party, write the name of the preſent Owner; and if there be any Increaſe, either by the Roll for our *Lady-day* 1664. or by your own view, then to expreſs the ſame accordingly; and whether the ſame were by omiſsion in the former Certificate, or by New Buildings: And if there be any decreaſe, then likewiſe to expreſs the reaſon; whether it were by miſtake in the former Certificates, or by Fire, or any other caſualty, or by wilful ſtopping up; and to note the ſame, with the time when the ſame was done.

3. If the party be a Tenant, and continue the ſame, and no alteration in the Hearths, then to write againſt it, *Ex*. and the name of the Owner.

4. If the Tenant be changed, write againſt his name, the name of the new Tenant, and the name of the Owner: And if there be any alteration in the number of Hearths, expreſs the reaſon as before.

5. If you find any parties named in the Roll dead, and the Duty due from ſuch party not anſwered, then expreſs who is the Executor or Adminiſtrator: and if there be any new Tenant, expreſs his name; and if there be none, then the name of the Owner. And if there be any alteration, then expreſs the reaſon as before.

6. If

(3)

6. If you find the party named in your Book gone, expreſs the time when; and if there be a new Tenant, expreſs his name, and alſo the name of the Owner; and if there be no new Tenant, then the name of the Owner: and if there be any alteration in the number of Hearths, then expreſs the ſame as before.

7. If you find any houſe empty, expreſs the Owner, and the name of the laſt Tenant; and if there be any alteration, expreſs the ſame as before.

8. If you find any party dwell in a houſe not worth xx *s.* by the year, and are qualified according to the firſt Act, or the Tenants by reaſon of their poverty be not Rated to Church and Poor, yet if the Houſes contain above two Hearths, they are not to be exempted from payment; but for ſuch of the natures aforeſaid as exceed not two Hearths, you are to note them in the Margent of your Book againſt ſuch party, that they are ſuch. And in all caſes of Diviſion of Houſes, or Letting the Houſes from the Land, you are to obſerve the particular Directions in the Act.

9. And in caſe where the Landlords pay the Rates to Church and Poor for all their Tenants Lands, and the Tenant is not left out of the ſaid Rates by reaſon of his Poverty, but by reaſon his Landlord payeth the ſame, or for ſome other cauſe other then his Poverty, ſuch Houſes, if they exceed the yearly value of xx *s.* the year, then their Hearths are to be Rated as others are, according to the number of their Hearths.

10. And

10. And if you find any Charge in the former Roll for Hospitals, or Alms-houses, not Chargeable by the Act, then to note against them in your Book, that they are such; and if you find any such omitted in the former Roll, to enter them at the end of the Parish in which they are, expressing them to be such.

11. And if you find any persons that dwell in Houses not worth xx*s. per Annum*, or Cottages Erected by poor people upon Commons or Waste Grounds, or such persons as receive Alms of the Parish, which are omitted out of the first Roll, then you are to enter the same in your Book, at the end of the Parish in which they are, expressing them to be such.

12. And if you find any Hundreds omitted out of the former Certificates, you are to enter them particularly at the end of your Book: And if you find any Parishes omitted, you are to enter them at the end of those Hundreds of which they are parcel. And if you find any Houses omitted in any Parish, That then you enter them at the end of every such Parish: And for the names of the persons, and number of Hearths so omitted, you shall find them in the Roll, in the hands of the Constables which Collected the said Duty there in the former years; and after you have Entred them in your Book, to note in the Margent against such party, according to your former Instructions for such as were Entred in your Book.

12. In all which Examinations you are to require the

(5)

the Aſſiſtance of the Conſtable, Tythingman, or other Officer of the place, who are to joyn with you in making a Certificate to the Clerk of the Peace, of all Increaſes and Decreaſes of Hearths, which you ſhall find upon your ſaid Survey and Examination, to the Clerk of the Peace, to be by him certified according to the Tenor of the ſaid Act. And further, That at the end of the Rolls of every Pariſh, both you, and ſuch Officers as aſsiſt you, ſubſcribe your names.

14. You are once a year, during the time of your Employment, to examine all Increaſes and Decreaſes, and other things according to the aforeſaid Inſtructions, and to certifie the ſame to the Clerk of the Peace, as by the ſaid Act you are required.

15. You are to obſerve the ſame method in writing the names of Hundreds, Pariſhes, Places and Perſons, with the numbers of the Hearths that was in the Rolls now ſent unto you, with the variations; to the end that His Majeſties Auditors may the more readily and certainly compare and reexamine them.

16. You are to return the Books delivered unto you, with your Quotations upon the ſame, and your Additions thereunto, under your Hands, and the Hands of your Deputies who acted in the ſame, for the places they reſpectively acted, and the Hands of the Conſtables and Tythingmen that aſsiſted them, to the Clerk of the Peace, to be approved by the Juſtices, and to be by him Engroſſed in Parchment, and returned into the Office of His Majeſties Remembrancer in the Exchequer, as by the ſaid Act is directed.

B And

(6)

And laſtly, You and your Deputies are to execute and perform all other the Powers and things compriſed in the ſeveral Acts, for the viewing of the ſaid Hearths, and for the Collecting and Levying of the ſaid Revenue according to the Tenor and Directions of the ſaid Acts concerning the ſame, and to give us a true accompt of your doings and proceedings therein from time to time, that thereupon we may give you ſuch further Orders and Directions as ſhall be meet,

(9)

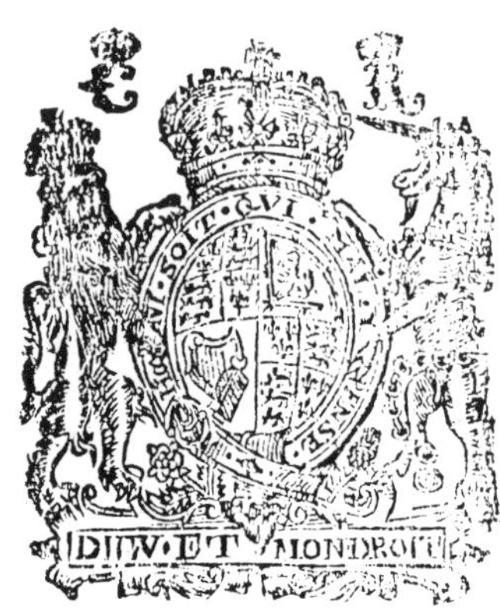

A FORM

TO BE

Obſerved by the Officers appointed for receiving the Duty and Revenue ariſing and belonging to His Majeſty by Fire-Hearths and Stoves, in their Books to be made and Returned upon the View and Survey of the ſame.

Com. Berks. } *Hund. de Ripleſmeere.*

{ *The Money for the half year.* }

Shillings. **Hearths.**

xxv. The Mannor-Houſe——xxv. *Examinatur*. Now Sir *Edw. Nicholas* Tenant to His Majeſty.
v. Thomas Smyth————v. Ex.
iij. William Slan————iij. Ex.
vj. Ralph Baldwyn————v. Now *John Baldwyn*, returned one too little.
iiij: John Berry, *Eſq*;————v. Returned one too many by miſtake.
v. Southwood————v. Ex.
viij. William Powel————viij. Ex.

Shillings.

(10)

Shillings. **Hearths.**

ix. Robert Stiles *for tile-place*-vii. Encreafed two by new building.
o Mary Platt, *widow*, ——ij. The houfe pulled down, or burnt, as the cafe requireth.
ij. William Ruffell-——ij. Ex. Dead, and *A. B.* his Executor.
ij. Henry Trotter——ij. Ex. Gone after the Duty grew due, & now liveth at *Eafham*.
ij. Peter Fowler——ij. Ex. Gone before *Michaelmas*, *A. B.* Owner.
o Ralph Woods——j. Not worth xx s. *per annum*.
iij. Chriftopher Todd——iij. Tenant to *John Pearfe*.
ij. Thomas Tiggnalls——ij. Now *John Tiggnall*.
vj. William Carpenter——vj. Ex.
iiij. Edmund Saunders-——iiij. Ex.
iiij. Henry Lynne——iiij. Now empty, *John Spratt* Owner.
vj. James Sedgley——vj. Ex.
v. Michael Jenkins-——v. Now *John Jenkins*.
ij. John Saunders——ij. Ex. Tenant to *Thomas Johnfon*.
ij. Thomas Croffe—— *A houfe void*—— } ij. Now *Thomas Joanes*.
o Robert Pefmore——ij. Not Rated to Church or Poor, by reafon of his poverty.
o Thomas Gaffon-——iij. The houfe burnt down.
iiij. Thomas Skeldin——ij. He hath two more then were Returned.
ix. VVill. Smyth, *Gent*.——x. He ftopped up two fince the return.
ix. John Powney, *Gent*.——ix. Ex.
Humphrey Michell——xiij. Ex. Now *John Michell*.
John Lever——viij. Ex. Tenant to *John Michell*.
Thomas Newman——iiij. Ex.
VVilliam Michell-——ij. Ex. Tenant to *James Pearfe*.
VVilliam Streatenig——vj. Ex.
o VVilliam VVhitle-—— *A houfe void* } ij. *A. B.* the Owner.
James Smyth, *Gent*.——ix. Ex.
James Sedgeley——iij. Ex. Dead, the houfe empty, *John Spratt* Owner.
VVilliam Streatenig——ij. Tenant to *John Spratt*.
viij. VVilliam Carpenter, *A houfe of Dr. Gylls.* } ix. Returned one too many by miftake.
Ralph Bennett——iiij. Ex.
VVilliam VVhitle, *for a houfe he dwells in* } ij. Ex.
vj. Samuel VVoods——iij. Returned three fhort.
Edward Lane——vj. Ex.
Henry Danford——iij. Tenant to *John Robinfon*.
VVilliam Harding——iij. Now widow *Harding* Tenant to *John Robinfon*.
Richard Danford——iij. Now *John Danford*.
o Anne Atlee-——ij. Not Rated to Church nor Poor by reafon of her poverty.
John Lane-——ij. Ex.

Number of Hearths in *Old Windfor*—— } CCXIX.

Hearths

(11)

Hearths not mentioned in the former Return.

John Dawſon————iiij.
Peter Smyth————.—ij.
John Thomſon————j. Not worth xx s. *per annum*.
John Simpſon————ij. Not Rated to Church nor Poor by reaſon of his poverty.
An Almes-houſe———v.
The Hoſpital of———

4

Hearths, wealth and occupations: an exploration of the Hearth tax in the later seventeenth century

CHRIS HUSBANDS

Introduction

The population of later seventeenth-century England was neither evenly distributed nor socially homogeneous.[1] Whilst the demographic characteristics of local communities have been elucidated through aggregative and nominative reconstitutions, the detailed social structures which underlay these remain inaccessible. One way in which historians have attempted to reconstruct these local social structures, however, is to analyse community listings made between 1662 and 1689 for the Hearth tax.[2] These listings, in principle socially comprehensive, provide data on the number of hearths possessed by each head of household. Under the Chimney Money Act of 1662, a shilling was due for each hearth 'within every dwelling, House and other Edifice' that was not exempt at Lady Day and Michaelmas each year.[3] Since the number of hearths was generally likely to have been proportional to size of house, and since size of house was likely to have been a reflection of personal wealth, Hearth tax listings have been used by commentators since the 1680s as a guide to the distribution of wealth. But the extent to which hearth totals are a reliable indicator of personal wealth is somewhat questionable. It will be examined below, together with the occupational labels of some householders, in an attempt to establish how much the Hearth tax can be expected to elucidate contemporary social structure.

1 Much of the subject matter in this chapter has been discussed at greater length in Husbands, 'Hearth tax'.

2 See for example, Hoskins, *Industry*, and Skipp, *Crisis and development*.

3 On Hearth tax administration see Arkell's chapter 'Printed instructions'.

The Hearth tax returns as an indication of wealth

Sir William Petty, writing in 1662, had provided a justification for the introduction of the Hearth tax as a permanent feature of the royal revenue:

> 'Of all the Accumulative Excizes, that of Harth Money or Smoak Money seems the best, and that onely because the easiest and clearest and fittest to ground a revenue upon: it being easie to tell the number of *Harths*, which remove not as *Heads* or *Polls* do... Moreover (it accords with) the Naturall Justice that everie man shal pay according to what he actually enjoyeth'.[4]

As early as the last decade of the seventeenth century, the Hearth tax material was being plundered by political arithmeticians for information on wealth distribution. Both King and Davenant argued from Hearth tax data about the proportions of national wealth located in the south and the north.[5] For contemporaries, there was a clear relationship between hearths and wealth.

Until recently, historians followed these political arithmeticians and made a straightforward connection between hearth totals and an abstract concept of 'wealth'. In the nineteenth century, Thorold Rogers drew on Gregory King's work on the mis-dated '1690' Hearth tax for his survey of wealth distribution over six centuries.[6] Equally, according to Styles, the Hearth tax was a 'fair and effective means of tapping national wealth'.[7] More recently, Hoskins and Patten have both worked from Meekings's analysis of Hearth tax accounts in their discussions of the relative wealth of urban centres in the sixteenth and seventeenth centuries.[8] Similarly, in their survey of English towns, Clark and Slack have made direct connections between hearth occupancy or ownership

4 Hull, *Economic writings*, vol.I, p.94.

5 See Thirsk and Cooper, *Seventeenth century*, pp.798-9, 808-10; Whitworth, *Charles D'Avenant*, vol.1, pp.26-9, 34-6, 38-9, and Laslett's chapter above.

6 Thorold Rogers, *History of agriculture*, vol.6, pp.117-8. It has proved impossible to trace the original data, but the incorrect transcription also appears in Davenant; see Whitworth, vol.1, p.38.

7 Styles, 'Social structure', pp.96-117, especially p.115.

8 Hoskins, *Local history*, p.104 and App.2; Patten, *English towns*, pp.109-11, 115-17. The source is Meekings, *Dorset Hearth tax*, App.2. Patten also draws together secondary research on population size between 1660 and 1680, but combines estimates making different, contradictory, assumptions about the nature of the material.

and wealth.[9] Clearly, it has been widely supposed that the total number of hearths assigned to individuals within a community provides a rough index of their relative wealth.[10]

Whilst making the same fundamental assumption, local historians have deployed Hearth tax materials somewhat differently. In a variety of studies extant local assessments have been used to construct wealth schedules through which the social structure of local communities in the 1660s and the 1670s is described and compared.[11] In one of the most influential of such studies, Skipp suggests that changes in the economy of three north Warwickshire parishes were directly reflected in the pattern of hearth distribution.[12] From his work on Wigston Magna, Hoskins argued for a strong relationship between inventoried wealth and hearth totals, whilst a similarly strong positive correlation between assessed personal wealth in probate inventories and hearth totals has been suggested for Cambridgeshire by Spufford.[13] Styles examined the relationship between Hearth tax assessments and other contemporary sources, such as the 1661 Free and Voluntary Gift or Present in Kineton hundred, Warwickshire.[14] Such work has given apparently strong empirical support to the assumption that the Hearth tax provides valuable evidence on local social structure in the seventeenth century.

However, the abundant empirical research into local hearth distribution patterns has been conducted in many cases without resolving the central question of how closely hearth totals correspond to levels of wealth or without any precise definition of the concept of wealth which is being adopted. Obviously,

9 Clark and Slack, *English towns*, p.113. Of those listed in the various Hearth tax documents some were non-resident owners of the properties concerned, but most were either tenants or owner-occupiers. Usually it is impossible to distinguish these different categories except perhaps in the case of vacant dwellings. In this chapter the term 'accountability' is used to cover all three possibilities.

10 Although the assumption is near universal, Rogers sounds a warning note when he observes that 'it is a long path from the number of rooms or hearths to one's place in local society.....Size of house does not necessarily equal wealth any more than wealth necessarily equals influence or prestige'; see his *Approaches*, p.224.

11 In addition to the studies cited below, see Tennant, 'Brailes', and Wales, 'Poverty and parish relief'.

12 Skipp, *Crisis and development*, pp.78-9.

13 Hoskins, *Midland peasant*, pp.299-301; Spufford, 'Significance', pp.53-64.

14 Styles, 'Social structure', pp.96, 98, 100-2.

individuals accountable for houses of forty taxable hearths would have been wealthier than those accountable for dwellings with only one or two hearths, but such contrasts were extreme, and differences in wealth between individuals inhabiting two-hearth houses and those inhabiting three- or four-hearth houses might be less easy to describe and could sometimes have been non-existent. 'Wealth' itself is an ill-defined concept; it may be held in a variety of forms for a variety of purposes.[15] Such problems need to be addressed before it can be determined whether it is legitimate to use hearth totals and patterns of hearth accountability as a means of comparing the social and spatial distribution of wealth within different communities. If, for example, crude hearth totals varied as a result of elements other than wealth, such as architectural style, then further doubt may be cast on the value of hearth tax-based analyses of wealth.

Variations in housing

Architectural historians are agreed that the sixteenth and seventeenth centuries constituted a crucial stage in the evolution of English vernacular architecture, although there are differing accounts of the pace and timing of change.[16] The 'Great Rebuilding', stretching over a period from about 1570 to about 1710, was simply the most important element in this development, and it involved the introduction of new styles and larger houses. The 'Rebuilding' affected different areas and social strata at different times. It has been described by Barley and Clifton-Taylor as the diffusion of distinctively Renaissance styles originating in East Anglia and the south-east, and moving gradually westward and northward during the course of the seventeenth century, at the same time as diffusing down the social scale.[17] In north-east Oxfordshire, an area for which perhaps the best survey of traditional domestic architecture exists, the transformation of the physical structure of houses was at full flood between 1645 and 1675; precisely the period of the

15 Wealth is conventionally described as a *stock* whilst income is defined as a *flow*. See Atkinson, *Economics*, pp.7, 120-21; *Royal Commission on the Distribution of Income*.

16 The debate is traced in Hoskins, 'Rebuilding', pp.131-49; Machin, 'Great rebuilding'; Borsay, 'English urban renaissance', pp.581-604.

17 Barley, 'Rural housing', pp.722-4,736-7, 766-7; Clifton-Taylor, *Patterns*; Brunskill, *Traditional farm buildings*, pp.2, 34; Portman, 'Vernacular building', pp.135-66.

Hearth tax.[18] In general, despite the pervasive influence of new, extra-local styles, it is usually suggested that the rebuilding did not fundamentally disrupt regional architectural styles, and this was certainly true in north Oxfordshire.[19] Wood-Jones concludes that the different hearth numbers might in some cases represent different types of house, so that in general the Hearth tax returns 'enable the composition of the seventeenth century village to be determined with some accuracy'.[20]

Unlike Clapham, who argued that one-hearth houses were normally occupied by cottars, Wood-Jones concluded that in north-east Oxfordshire single hearth houses were often too elaborate for cottagers, 'but were the houses of smaller husbandmen, tradesmen and craftsmen... and fine workmanship does not depend on size of house'.[21] In their classic study of Monmouthshire, Fox and Raglan noted two features which also counter the conflation of one-hearth houses with cottar dwellings: the appearance ot 'two-unit' houses around a central hearth and the development in the later seventeenth century of service rooms without hearths.[22] Brunskill has shown that in the Highland Zone, the traditional longhouse form could become an elaborate dwelling without any increase in hearth numbers,[23] and two-unit houses around a central hearth were common in Sussex and Kent in the later seventeenth century.[24] Although the Royal Commission on Historical Monuments formally abandoned its plan to produce descriptive analyses of historic buildings by county in 1980, its already published volumes depict a picture of local complexity and variety which precludes the formulation of early generalisations about the relationship between architectural style and hearth numbers.[25]

18 Wood-Jones, *Traditional*, pp.107-9.

19 Innocent, *Development*, pp.312-5; Wood-Jones, *Traditional*, pp.141, 163-6, 286.

20 Wood-Jones, *Traditional*, p.286. However, Wood-Jones's study, which was based on surviving buildings, fails to take account of buildings which were destroyed for rebuilding in the years following the Hearth tax but which, therefore, would have been assessed for Hearth tax.

21 Wood-Jones, *Traditional*., pp.163-4.

22 Fox and Raglan, *Monmouthshire houses*, pp.131-6; Sheppard, 'Vernacular buildings', p.33, 35; Dyer, 'Urban housing', p.211.

23 Brunskill, *Traditional farm buildings*, pp.45, 50, 52.

24 Sheppard, Vernacular buildings', p.39; Chalklin, *Seventeenth century*, pp.248-57; Brandon, *Sussex*, pp.167-9.

25 Fowler, 'Royal Commission', pp.106-14.

Testing the validity of the Hearth tax returns

In searching for a source against which to check the Hearth tax, historians have typically turned to probate inventories. In many ways, probate inventories and Hearth tax returns may be seen as complementary, and together they might provide a powerful tool for the analysis of the social hierarchy. Students of inventories have often made the point that they present an image only of movable wealth, excluding capital invested in domestic improvements, additional land or new techniques, and that the wealth of certain inventoried groups is therefore under-represented.[26] Furthermore, inventories were a socially selective source, since those too poor to require probate papers were excluded; this latter group possibly made up between sixty and eighty per cent of the entire population.[27] Conversely, the Hearth tax returns constitute a guide to fixed capital wealth, as represented through the size of houses.[28] They were also, in principle, socially comprehensive in listing all heads of households. But comparisons are fraught with difficulty. Since each was addressed to different types of wealth, one should not expect a complete or perfect 'fit', but it is by no means clear what precise relationship between inventoried-wealth and hearth-wealth would be predicted.[29]

A strong relationship is suggested by Spufford on the basis of a comparison between the Cambridgeshire Hearth tax and Cambridgeshire probate inventories. However the precise statistical relationship between the figures Spufford derived from the Hearth tax and inventories is less than her impressionistic conclusions would suggest.[30] Clearly, direct comparison between Hearth tax households and probate inventories is complicated and normally yields only very low sample sizes, especially when it is restricted to those who died within a few years of their assessment for the Hearth tax. Spufford, for example, used very strict standards for nominal linkage and so was unable to identify positively more than 101 Hearth tax householders from the 340

26 Emmison, 'Jacobean household'; Havinden, *Household*, and Overton, 'Estimating crop yields'.

27 Barley, 'Farmhouses', p.112.

28 See Howell, *Hearth tax*.

29 The wealth-income relationship is explored in Atkinson, *Economics*, pp.120-3.

30 See Spufford, 'Significance', p.64 for the data, with n=325 a correlation coefficient r-0.5712 is produced between the two variables.

inventories that survive for Cambridgeshire in the 1660s. This group represents less than one per cent of all the households in the county.[31] Similarly, for a sample of 1,213 households listed in the Michaelmas 1664 Hearth tax roll for part of north Warwickshire, the present writer managed to trace only thirty-four inventories - a success rate of 2.8 per cent.[32] Several factors contribute to an explanation for such apparent failure: the inventories covered mainly the middle ranks of society and excluded most labourers,[33] there were high mobility rates, especially in urban areas,[34] and a gap of up to forty years could occur between assessment for the Hearth tax and appraisal of goods at death. In addition, for many areas a paucity of inventories survive for the years immediately following the Restoration before the administration of the ecclesiastical probate courts settled down after the Interregnum.[35] On their own, therefore, probate inventories are an inadequate source of evidence against which to place Hearth tax wealth data.

Comparison between the sums paid in the various taxes levied after the Restoration provides an alternative way of 'testing' the Hearth tax.[36] In 1661 the Crown raised a Free and Voluntary Gift or Present, and the returns from this, although highly socially selective, have been used together with Hearth tax assessments in a number of studies.[37] However, an examination of the returns from the Gift and the 1665 Hearth tax from the exceptionally well-documented and well-researched market town of Banbury suggests that there was a fair correlation between them.[38] Nevertheless, and this is demonstrated by the various groups in Table 1, such research findings based on nominal record linkage

31 Spufford, 'Significance', p.53.

32 PRO, E179/259/10,ms. 50-55; inventories: Lichfield Joint Record Office. See also Alldridge, 'Restoration Chester', p.40.

33 Weatherill, *Consumer behaviour*, pp.3, 176.

34 See Souden, 'Pre-industrial'. This is traceable through closely-related Hearth tax assessments. Wolverhampton, Staffs., is particularly well sourced and reveals an annual mobility rate of 12 per cent between 1666-1673. See Husbands, 'Hearth tax', pp.368-71, and Hibberd, 'Data-linkage', pp.59-79.

35 This probably explains why Arkell, 'Poverty', p.33, managed to trace nearly 8 per cent of the inventories for 5,016 Warwickshire households in the period 1663-75.

36 On Restoration taxes, see Chandaman, *English public revenue*.

37 Styles 'Social structure'; Hoskins, *Exeter*.

38 See, for example, Everitt, 'Banburys', pp.28-39.

Table 1 Hearths per chargeable dwelling and contribution to the 'Gift' of 1661

		Chargeable hearths				
Value of gift		1-2 %	3 %	4-5 %	6+ %	Total %
1s - 2s 11d		57	38	30	0	35
3s - 6s 11d		30	41	24	25	31
10s +		13	21	46	75	34
Total	%	22	32	35	11	100
	n	23	34	37	12	106

Source: PRO, E179/255/5, E179/164/514.

between the Hearth tax and other contemporary material must be treated with caution before any firm conclusions are drawn.

The Hearth tax as a guide to occupational structure

Occasionally the problems involved in relating the Hearth tax to occupational information can be circumvented, either because the Hearth tax listings themselves provide additional socio-economic data on householders, or because such information can be obtained from alternative sources. Such examples are rare, but significant for the light they throw on the problems of Hearth tax interpretation. Normally the Hearth tax assessments recorded only status labels for individuals and not occupational descriptions.[39] Rolls providing full occupational information are particularly rare: those for some London wards for Lady Day 1666 have been analysed in great detail and with much perception by Michael Power.[40] In addition, the much smaller Michaelmas 1664 roll for a number of Sussex tithings records full occupational designations for those with chargeable hearths.[41] As Table 2 suggests, the relationship between occupation and hearth accountability was not straightforward. Each occupation was characterised by a range of hearths, but the width of the range and its location varied systematically. Only gentlemen and yeomen occupied houses of more than five hearths, whilst the percentage of individuals in the 'middle' range of two to four hearths was highest for craftsmen. More labourers inhabited one-

39 On status labels, see Cressey, 'Describing the social order', pp.29-45.

40 Power, 'Restoration London'.

41 PRO, E179/258/16.

Table 2 Occupational titles and hearths per chargeable dwelling in four Sussex tithings, 1664

		Chargeable hearths					
Occupation	mean	1 n	2 n	3 n	4 n	5-8 n	Total n
Gentleman	3.7	1	1	1	1	2	6
Yeoman	3.5	5	7	5	5	8	30
Husbandman	1.8	12	6	4	-	1	23
Tailor	1.6	3	1	1	-	-	5
Labourer	1.5	15	5	2	1	-	23
Mercer	4.0	-	-	-	2	-	2
Butcher	3.0	-	1	1	1	-	3
Clerk	3.0	-	1	-	1	-	2
Smith	3.0	-	1	-	1	-	2
Shoemaker	2.0	-	2	-	-	-	2
Carpenter	1.6	-	1	2	-	-	3
Miller	1.0	2	-	-	-	-	2
Others	2.7	1	1	3	1	-	6
Total	2.5	39	27	19	13	11	109

Notes: The four tithings are as follows: Dallington, Ewhurst, Iden, Pleaden.
Source: PRO, E179/258/16.

hearth dwellings than did any other group, but the extent of the difference between them and the husbandmen may have been masked by the absence of the non-chargeable. Overall, though, knowledge of occupation is a poor predictor of hearth accountability in individual cases, and vice versa. In part this reflects the fact that none of these occupation groups was homogeneous so far as wealth was concerned and also suggests that society was not so rigidly hierarchical as is often assumed.[42]

For Leicester, the Hearth tax material, organised by ward, may be compared with the Freemen's Roll to provide information on freemen admitted between 1630 and the end of the century. This comparison is set out in Table 3.[43] Once again, broad distinctions emerge from the comparison; hearth occupancy was highest among metalworking trades and lowest among weaving

42 For an illuminating discussion see Wrightson, 'Social order', pp.177-202.

43 PRO, E179/240/279, ms. 1-3; Hartopp, *Roll of the freemen*, Hartopp, *Roll of the Mayors*, pp.91-156.

Table 3 Number of hearths per dwelling and occupational groups in Leicester, 1670

Occupational group	Mean	Exempt	Hearth numbers 1	2	3	4	5-8	9+	Total
Construction	2.23	7	7	9	3	-	2	1	29
Woodworking	2.39	2	6	7	3	2	-	1	21
Leatherworking	1.96	12	22	16	14	5	1	-	70
Metalworking	3.20	5	7	8	4	6	3	-	24
Textiles	2.12	6	13	4	2	5	1	1	32
Dealing	2.55	9	21	8	14	9	11	-	72
Service	2.75	4	18	10	10	6	7	2	57
Agricultural	3.08	-	1	2	5	3	1	-	12
Miscellaneous	3.75	3	7	5	3	8	11	2	39
Total	2.55	45	101	89	58	45	34	8	366

Notes: The occupational categories in the above table are composed as follows: **Construction** = Slater, Joiner, Roughlayer, Mason, Bricklayer; **Woodworking** = Carpenter, Cooper, Basketmaker, Wheelwright, Turner; **Leatherworking** = Cordwainer, Fellmonger, Tanner, Sadler, Shoemaker, Currier; **Metalworking** = Blacksmith, Ironmonger, Cutler, Brasier, Locksmith, Gunsmith, Tinplateworker; **Textiles** = Weaver, Jerseycomber, Draper, Silkweaver, Hosier, Dyer, Laceworker; **Dealing** = Butcher, Baker, Tallowchandler, Haberdasher, Brewer, Fishmonger; **Service** = Tailor, Victualler, Vintner, Barber, Apothecary, Glazier, Painter, Cook, Roper, Pipemaker, Gardener; **Agricultural** = Maltster, Shearsman, Grazier; **Miscellaneous** = Mercer, Gentleman, Clerk, Labourer.

Source: See text.

and leatherworking trades, with mercers, drapers and blacksmiths standing out as the best endowed individual occupations.[44] Historians have generally argued that mercers and smiths were amongst the wealthiest sections of the urban community, but the ranking of other occupations in Leicester provides new insights into the less wealthy sections. However, the general picture is a complicated one. The Hearth tax roll for 1670 includes individuals admitted to the freedom up to thirty or forty years before, or only a year or two before, as well as identifying a few tradesmen who were admitted in 1671 or 1672. Therefore it is essential to consider the roll as constituting a slice through a society with individuals at various stages of the life-cycle: the

[44] A note of caution is needed here. Because trade and business hearths were often taxed along with the household ones, the mean number of hearths for metal workers with forges might be raised significantly. See Alldridge, 'Restoration Chester', p.44.

twenty-four mercers included some extremely prosperous ex-mayors,[45] some possibly retired individuals and others who would achieve influence, and possibly wealth, only in the 1690s.[46] In general, highest levels of hearth accountability were located among those who were admitted to the freedom between 1645 and 1655.[47] In this case, just as Alldridge discovered in Chester, the Hearth tax distribution is found to have been complicated by social and economic elements excluded from it.[48]

Regional comparison

Clearly, social status and wealth cannot be read off directly from Hearth tax totals, even though contemporaries did believe that the Hearth tax was an effective means of tapping personal wealth. As far as individuals' wealth was concerned, they were over-confident. The Hearth tax returns present a broad continuum, with the rich at the top of the scale, the poor at the bottom, and much overlap of groups in between. They present, too, a static image of a fluid society. Nevertheless, the information portrayed in Tables 1-3 has revealed a degree of correlation between hearth totals, personal wealth and occupational status, although it often breaks down in individual cases.

The weakness of the Hearth tax in understanding the wealth and status of individuals is less apparent at an aggregate level. By taking communities as a whole, broad comparisons between the relative wealth and prosperity of different communities can be advanced. In this respect, the Hearth tax returns offer a common criterion on which to compare local communities. This is not to assume, of course, that hearths were a measure of wealth, however defined or measured, but simply to adopt the assumption of those responsible for devising and managing the Hearth tax, that hearth accountability was an observable and real, if crude, social and economic discriminator. Differences between communities and regions were reflected in the Hearth tax returns. Broad distinctions between locations of similarly sized houses and

[45] For example, William Franke, seven hearths, mayor in 1658; Edward Craddock, eight hearths, mayor in 1646 and 1657.

[46] For example, John Goodall, four hearths, mayor in 1680, 1690; William Bently, three hearths, mayor in 1688.

[47] Amongst twenty-three individuals traced in the Hearth tax and known to have been admitted between these years, hearth accountability averaged 4.21. In the city as a whole, it was 2.86.

[48] Alldridge, 'Restoration Chester', pp.48-50.

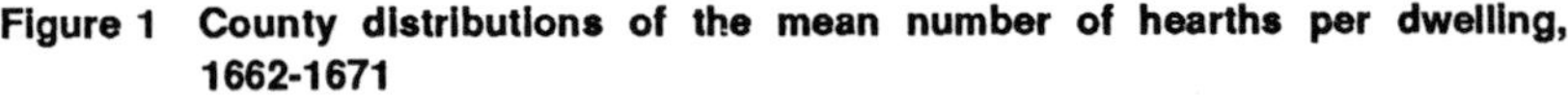
Figure 1 County distributions of the mean number of hearths per dwelling, 1662-1671

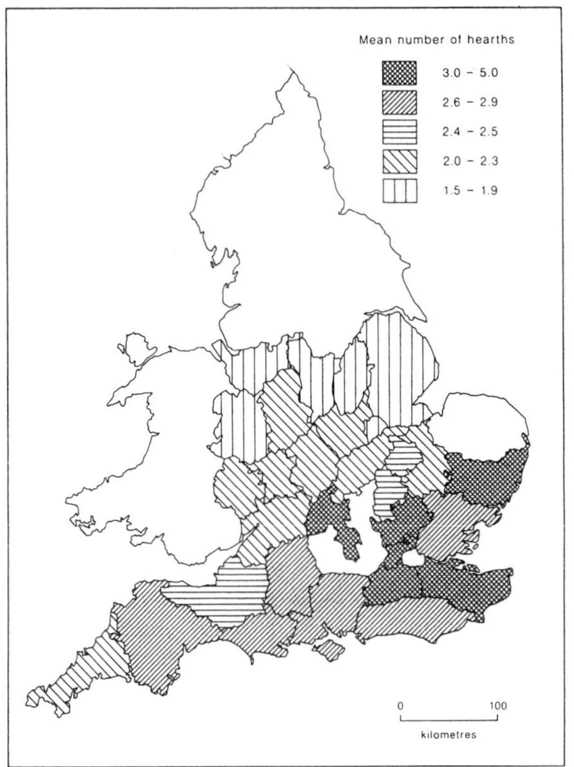

those where there were marked differences in the distribution of hearth accountability can be distinguished, and general tentative conclusions on the social geography of the later seventeenth century can thereby be reached.

It is for such reasons that I have argued elsewhere that 'alone amongst mid and late seventeenth-century taxes, the Hearth tax allows historians to draw general, comparative conclusions about local economies' and that, in contrast to the other available sources, it makes a study of comparative per capita wealth possible with relative ease.[49] Thus, it is possible to outline a composite analysis of the distribution of chargeable hearth occupancy at county level based on an analysis of 859 randomly

[49] Husbands, 'Regional change', pp.348-9.

sampled communities in English counties south of the Humber over the period 1662-1671.[50] Although using rather crude data, the results of this exercise, displayed in Figure 1, conform to general expectations, with generally high levels of hearth accountability in the south and east, particularly in metropolitan areas, and lower levels in the north and midlands.[51] Counties recording the highest number of mean hearths per dwelling did not form a compact group; although predominantly south-eastern, the ten counties recording the highest numbers of mean hearths per dwelling included east Anglian counties such as Essex and Suffolk as well as Oxfordshire and Devon.[52] Conversely, those counties recording the lowest numbers of mean hearths per dwelling were more compact. Of the ten counties at the bottom of the list, all but two – Worcestershire and Cambridgeshire – lay in a contiguous unit across north central England.

Conclusion

The Hearth tax returns, analysed as a whole, present significant variations in hearth accountability across southern and central England, variations which can be explained in terms of a number of existing models. Because hearth numbers as a wealth surrogate pose numerous methodological difficulties and, within individual communities, may often be rather weak tools for analysing the social hierarchy, historians need to approach the Hearth tax with considerable caution. However, relatively rich rewards can be garnered from a sensitive handling of the data. But, as yet, much of the potential of the Hearth tax to provide a general framework for the socio-economic history of the later seventeenth century still remains to be exploited at both local and national levels.

50 For more details see Husbands, 'Regional change', p.350. Buckinghamshire has been omitted from this analysis because it was represented by only one community. In addition the counties of London, Berkshire and Norfolk were excluded from this study.

51 See Langton, 'Industry', pp.173-98, and Clarkson, *Pre-industrial economy*, pp.215, 223.

52 Compare Everitt, *Change*, pp.54-5, with Husbands, 'Hearth tax', pp.162-3, 193.

5

The Compton census of 1676

ANNE WHITEMAN

The Critical edition

It has long been recognised that demographic, ecclesiastical and local historians would all benefit from the publication in full of the so-called 'Compton Census'. It is therefore hoped that *The Compton Census of 1676: a critical edition*[1] will fill the gap. This work edits key texts both for the Province of Canterbury and the Province of York.[2] Where possible these are supplemented by the use of incumbents' returns and tabulations of the census results made at archidiaconal and diocesan level, and comparative material is supplied to help in the interpretation of the figures.

This chapter sets out to summarise some of the findings about the census, and to explain briefly some aspects of the book which may need elucidating.[3] Originally I conceived my task primarily as

1 Whiteman, *Critical edition*. For reasons of space it is impossible here to give a full list of all the libraries and record offices, and their archivists, to whom I owe so much, or to the many colleagues who have so generously helped me over the years; in the edition of the census my debt to them is fully recorded. It would not be right, however, to omit a special word of thanks to Mary Clapinson, who has shared so much of the work with me, and also to other friends in the Bodleian Library, including Molly Barratt and David Vaisey. I am deeply grateful for help from the Cambridge Group for the History of Population and Social Structure, and especially to Peter Laslett, Tony Wrigley, Roger Schofield and Richard Wall. Among the many others who have assisted me at various stages of the work I should like to mention particularly Richard Clark, Tom Arkell, Stephen Green, Vivien Russell, Michael Greenslade, the late Frank Emery and Dorothy Owen.

2 The texts respectively are MS. Salt 33, held in the William Salt Library, Stafford and MSS. Tanner 144 and 150, held in the Bodleian Library of Oxford University. I owe special thanks to Margaret Midgeley and the late Marguerite Gollancz for making possible my use of MS. Salt 33 in the early stages, to the Trustees of the William Salt Library at Stafford, and to the Curators of the Bodleian Library for permission to print the manuscripts of the census in their custody, and to the British Academy for undertaking the book's publication.

3 I have not provided full notes for this chapter, since documentation for what I have said below is in the edition of the census, set out at length both in the General Introduction and the appendices to it, and in the introduction to each diocese.

trying to establish how accurately such incumbents' returns as I could find had been reproduced in the Salt manuscript at Stafford, which is our only source for most of the census figures for dioceses in the Province of Canterbury. It soon became apparent, however, with what inconsistency the returns had been made at local level, and how crucial were the editing processes which had transmuted them into the smooth uniformity of the Salt manuscript. What could be found about the census for every diocese had to be separately scrutinised and assessed, as had likewise what survives of it for the Province of York, mostly now in the Bodleian Library. The question to be asked became increasingly not just that of the accuracy of the transmission of the figures, but what the figures in any particular parish actually represented. This led inevitably to an attempt to test the 1676 returns against other sources which might help to throw light on them.

For reasons stated in the General Introduction to the *Critical edition*, comparative tables are difficult to prepare for returns of papists and nonconformists. But if the census is to be tested as a guide to population, several sources may be used: the Hearth tax returns, the Protestation returns of 1641-2, the 1603 returns of communicants, papists and non-communicants, and various other seventeenth-century surveys from which population estimates can be worked out. All these present their own difficulties of interpretation, and for various reasons it did not prove possible to use them as consistently as might in retrospect seem desirable; but perhaps a certain eclecticism does no harm in pointing to the variety of comparative material available for future exploitation. I have, of course, come to certain conclusions about the census and its value which I have attempted to sum up below, but I should like to emphasise that I regard my work on it mainly as opening it up as a source, the first step in making full use of it. A macro-study of this kind will have much wrong with it which can only be cleared up at local level in a series of micro-studies using, for example, parish registers, and based on a much more critical examination of the returns in their particular environment.

The work on the census was begun some years ago – before, in fact, efficient pocket calculators, word processors and easy access to computing facilities were available. The use of computers may of course discover much about the returns which have escaped my scrutiny, but at any rate some of the snags of taking the returns at their face value will have been disclosed before highly sophisticated methods are used to extract the fullest possible information from them.

The taking of the census

Posing the questions

What we call the 'Compton Census' was known to contemporaries as 'the Bishops' Book'; when it got its modern name I have not been able to discover. Henry Compton, Bishop of London, was not its originator, but merely served in his capacity as Dean of the Province of Canterbury to circulate to the bishops in the southern province Archbishop Sheldon's letter with the questions to be answered appended, and to assemble the results of the enquiry. The Archbishop of York, and those responsible for parishes in peculiar jurisdiction, were told of the enquiry by letters from Sheldon. But Sheldon was not the moving spirit behind the launching of the enterprise either: that was the Lord Treasurer, Danby, anxious to persuade Charles II that a policy in support of the Church of England was safe since Anglicans made up the bulk of the population.[4]

Much confusion has been caused because, by bad luck, in assembling material for his *Concilia Magnae Britanniae et Hiberniae* (1727), David Wilkins chose the draft of Sheldon's letter and the draft of the questions[5] for printing in his collection of documents, and these were copied by Edward Cardwell, in the *Documentary Annals of the Church of England* (1839). The actual letter, as sent out, consisted of only one part of the text Wilkins printed; the tendentious, latter part, with which Thomas Richards (the influential critic of the census) made much play, was never circulated.[6] Likewise, the wording of the first question asking, in the draft, 'what number of persons or at least Famely's' inhabited in each parish, was circulated in a version which dropped any reference to families. The questions ran as follows:

4 On Danby's initiative, see Browning, *Thomas Osborne* (Vol.1, p.146. seq.); H.M.C., *Eleventh Report*, Appendix, Part VII (MSS. of the Duke of Leeds), pp.14-15; British Library, Harleian (hereafter BL Harl.), MS. 7377, f.62v; MS. Tanner 42, f.219; Pett, *State of England*.

5 Now in Bodleian MS. Tanner 282.

6 Whiteman, *Critical edition*, pp.xxiii-xxix which includes a further discussion of T. Richards, *Religious census* (1927).

> 1. What number of persons are there by common accompt and estimation inhabitting within each parish subject unto your jurisdiction.
> 2. What number of Popish Recusants or persons suspected for such Recusancy are there resident amongst the Inhabitants aforesaid.
> 3. What number of other Dissenters are there in each parish (of what Sect soever) which either obstinately refuse or wholly absent themselves from the Communion of the Church of England at such times as by Law they are required.

Compton's covering letter was a short and simple one. It did not indicate in any way the kind of answers that the authorities wanted.[7]

Unfortunately the questions were too short and simple, and two bishops at least (there may have been others) asked for elucidation, for the circulated version said nothing about the age and sex of those to be counted as inhabitants. It transpired in correspondence that the authorities expected a return of men and women of age to communicate (translated in practice into those over sixteen),[8] but not everyone responsible for playing his part in the taking of the census understood this. Had the wording of the first question been properly thought out, the results would of course have been much more uniform, and it must be a matter of regret that Sheldon's draughtsman was less precise in setting out the 'population' question than Whitgift's had been in 1603.[9] The fortunate survival of some papers concerned with the census at local level enables us to see that the first question was asked in various different ways in different dioceses, but for some no such information is forthcoming. It is likely that in a number of dioceses, the interpretation of the question was left entirely to the incumbents; in others there may have been verbal guidance.

In his covering note enclosing Sheldon's letter and the questions, Compton suggested that the answers should be collected at the Easter visitation of the archdeacons, and this was done in a

7 Guildhall Library, MS. 9531/17, f.9v (Henry Compton's Register).

8 MS. Tanner 42, f.219; Harl. MS. 7377, f.62v (Edward Reynolds, Bishop of Norwich to Henry Compton, Bishop of London, 28 Jan. 1675/6, and draft reply from Sheldon, to whom the question had been referred, in Sheldon's Letter-Book); Leicestershire Record Office, 1 D 41/43/162-5 (correspondence about taking the census in the archdeaconry of Leicester, Lincoln diocese).

9 Whiteman, *Critical edition*, p.lx.

number of dioceses. In Hereford diocese and perhaps that of Llandaff, however, the officials were quick off the mark, because the returns seem to have been made in February. Elsewhere things went more slowly, and it was probably August before the returns for the Province of Canterbury were collected in London. In that month at any rate Danby knew how many papists had been reported in the twenty-two dioceses. York was far behind; the Archbishop of York had obviously put Sheldon's letter into his pending-tray, and woke up to the fact that time was getting short only in March, with the result that in his province returns were still being assembled as late as October.

Collecting the answers

The fortunate survival of the incumbents' returns for parishes in some dioceses enables us to see in some detail how the procedure for collecting the answers worked. The questions, sometimes reworded at diocesan or even archidiaconal level, were probably distributed by the apparitors,[10] sometimes with a covering letter; an 'official form' might be sent out, incorporating the questions, with a certain amount of explanation, and gaps left for the answers to be inserted. In some cases, about two to three weeks elapsed between the despatch of the questions and the visitation itself; this interval may have varied. Of course it is only in a comparatively few cases that we have any information about how the incumbent (or curate or churchwardens) set about preparing the answers to be returned; but there is enough evidence to show that in a number of parishes the request for information was taken very seriously. William Sampson, of Clayworth in Nottinghamshire, was not the only incumbent who made a list of all those who lived in his parish:[11] so, for example, did Francis Nicholson, curate of Goodnestone-next-Wingham, in Kent,[12] and the incumbents of four other parishes in that county, whose zeal to be accurate is undetectable from the final results of the census. On the other hand, some undoubtedly took very little trouble, or seem to have done so. It is, however, worth noting that the Easter Book kept by some incumbents would provide a reasonably sound

10 Apparitors were the messengers who carried citations (i.e. summonses) from the ecclesiastical courts to persons required to attend at court; they were extensively used to convey other papers emanating from the courts or the bishop's or archdeacon's registry round the diocese or archdeaconry.

11 Gill and Guilford, *The Rector's Book*, pp.14-18.

12 Whiteman, *Critical edition*, pp.635-44.

estimate of those who had to pay Easter dues, since part of their income depended on this record.[13] It would be going far beyond the evidence, nevertheless, to claim that all returns were conscientiously made.

Conscientiousness, however, did not solve the problem of what categories in the population ought to be counted if the form of the first question as received was uninformative. Consequently incumbents in some dioceses made their answers in varying terms: men and women over sixteen, men only, households (or families), or the whole population irrespective of age. In Canterbury diocese registry officials made an attempt to sort things out in some of the parishes; but it is often the case that the user of the census cannot tell what the figure for the parish in which he is interested represents – more will be said on this point later. A few surviving incumbents' returns, however, provide some clues. For example, it could be detected that in parts of Worcester diocese men over sixteen only were commonly reported before any comparative material was consulted. The way in which the first question was framed is therefore of the greatest importance, but unfortunately in a number of dioceses it has so far not been possible to establish it. And so, if there is no indication to the contrary, it seems safest to assume that the question was worded in the way in which it was sent out from Lambeth or York.

A crucial stage in the transmission of the returns to London or York was that at which the figures given in answer to the three questions were arranged in three columns. Editing of this kind inevitably entails firm decisions; much detail has to be discarded, ambiguities resolved, arbitrary choices made. Where the editing can be checked against the incumbents' returns, it has been found to be reliable and honest; those concerned did their best to distil correct answers to the three questions from the often inconsistent or unclear returns which they were handling, but they could not in the three-column framework indicate which figures related to which categories of population, or pass on any qualifications the incumbent had included. In some dioceses this initial process of editing was carried out at archidiaconal level, in others, at the diocesan one; the problems were the same at both. Only in one diocese, Peterborough, does an 'editor', in this case Archdeacon John Palmer, seem to have imposed his own pattern of what he

13 See Wright 'Easter books'; Wright, 'Guide'.

thought the returns ought to represent on the actual figures sent in to him. He was convinced that the whole population in each parish should have been counted and applied his own rules to try to ensure that the returns conformed to this.[14] There is not enough evidence to make it possible to state categorically that other editors did not do something similar; but it seems unlikely. All other indications are that the actual figures given in by the incumbents were faithfully reproduced in the version of the returns sent to London or York. It has not, perhaps, been recognised hitherto how important was this editing phase in the transmission of the census figures. Only when original returns from the incumbents were traced and some of the local tabulations into three columns came to light could the problems of the initial editing become clear. How many times the figures were copied and recopied in various later stages of editing cannot be established; but it must be remembered that at each stage transcription slips may have occurred and further editing been undertaken. One version of the returns for Canterbury and Salisbury dioceses[15] almost certainly represents a re-copying of the figures actually sent up to London.

The Salt manuscript

The great majority of the returns for dioceses in the Province of Canterbury survive only in the Salt manuscript.[16] This is a superbly written document, in a formal bookhand, perhaps prepared for the eyes of Charles II, almost certainly commissioned by Bishop Henry Compton of London. The figures for each parish are set out under uniform headings throughout the book: Conformists; Papists; Nonconformists. In the case of some dioceses – in fact probably the majority – the figures under the heading *Conformists* are not figures for conformists at all, but of

[14] Whiteman, *Critical edition*, pp.375-81.

[15] MS. Lambeth 639.

[16] For some areas no returns appear to have survived (e.g. Dorset archdeaconry in Bristol diocese), but new evidence about the census continues to come to light. For example, a return for Worlingham parish, in the archdeaconry of Suffolk, has now been identified by Tim Wales, of the Institute of Historical Research, University of London, in a Parish Book 1653-1729. Dated 15 March 1675[/6], it lists seventy-nine inhabitants over sixteen, no papists, and eight nonconformists (Suffolk Record Office, Lowestoft, 167/A2/1). The presumption that returns were made for at least some parishes in the archdeaconry is thereby established (Whiteman, *Critical edition*, pp.190, 192). I am indebted to Mr T. Wales for telling me about the list and to Miss Amanda J. Arrowsmith and Miss R.A. Rowse of the Suffolk Record Office for locating it for me.

inhabitants including papists and nonconformists, or whatever category or categories of population were reported by the incumbents in answer to the first question. The volume begins with the returns for Canterbury and London; here the heading is at any rate not misleading, since any papists and/or nonconformists reported have been subtracted from the returns for inhabitants (or whatever category was counted) to produce figures for conformists. The same has been done in the case of the returns for Salisbury and Chichester. But the returns for Winchester, sandwiched in the volume between those for London and Salisbury, are for 'inhabitants', as are those for Ely, Worcester and Norwich, which follow Chichester; also for Exeter and Peterborough, and almost certainly for most of the rest of the dioceses, though direct evidence is not equally strong for all of them. In Lincoln diocese a return of conformists was asked for, and so the figures given in the Salt manuscript are correctly described as conformists, as are most of the returns for Hereford diocese and those for the archdeaconry of Derby, although figures for the rest of Lichfield diocese are probably for inhabitants or their equivalent. Presumably a decision was made at the beginning of the compilation of the Salt manuscript to arrange the returns so that figures for conformists were prepared from inhabitants' figures by the subtraction of any papists and/or nonconformists reported, but this policy lapsed as the writing of the volume progressed, though there are of course some anomalies.[17]

The few extant returns for the Province of York do not present the same problems.[18] We have them only in tabulated form except for those for Nottingham archdeaconry, and it is unlikely that they were ever set out formally as were those for the Province of Canterbury. But using the Salt manuscript version of the Canterbury returns is not as easy as it might seem. The beautiful uniform dress cloaks much that is not uniform; consequently the figures for each diocese, or even sometimes for each archdeaconry, must be considered on their own. Fewer generalisations about the census would have been put forward had all the returns looked like those for the dioceses of York and Carlisle, and its composite nature would always have been more obvious.

17 For example, the returns for Gloucester diocese are particularly puzzling.

18 MSS. Tanner 150 and 144.

Demographic interpretations

What has been said so far about the Compton census might suggest that the returns are of little value. This is not the case, particularly so far as demographic studies are concerned, but it must always be remembered that it was very different from more modern censuses. Since the mid-nineteenth century the taking of the census has been a relatively standardised procedure, the questions are uniform throughout the country, answers are made on the same day, enumerators and census clerks sort out ambiguous replies, editing is done on the same principles and the results are presented in a uniform way. In comparison, for the census of 1676 the form of the questions varied from diocese to diocese (sometimes from archdeaconry to archdeaconry), returns were made, according to the area concerned, from February throughout the summer and perhaps into the early autumn, the amount of elucidation of unclear answers was variable and probably in some dioceses non-existent, principles of editing were left to individuals, and inconsistency dogs the form in which most of the returns have come down to us. Generalisations about the 1676 census are, therefore, bound to be misleading. My aim in the *Critical edition* was to take it apart, as it were, and to examine the returns for each diocese separately. In doing this sometimes there is a great deal to be said about the consistency and reliability of the figures, and sometimes very little, for the relevant evidence varies considerably in quantity and quality. It should, however, now be possible for anyone wanting to use the returns for demographic purposes for any particular area to find out at the outset something about their characteristics, and how confidently they may be relied on.

If the incumbents' returns survive for only a very few parishes in a diocese, they may yet tell us a good deal about how the enquiry was conducted, and what category or categories of population were counted. For a number of dioceses, however, nothing has come to light, and it is only by comparing the 1676 figures with estimates of population extracted from other evidence that it is possible to discover, or to make a reasonable conjecture about, what part of the population was included. The Hearth tax returns are an obvious comparative source, and if a good run survives from 1670 to 1674 it can be most illuminating, as it is for example for Peterborough and Worcester dioceses.[19] Hearth tax returns for earlier years may also prove helpful. But the quality of some Hearth tax returns is mediocre or poor and can afford little assistance. If those exempt from paying the tax are not recorded, the returns are virtually useless as a check on the 1676 figures.

Totals of households drawn from the Hearth tax returns can be used in two ways: either a multiplier can be applied to produce an estimate of the total population (and normally a range of multipliers is better than a single one) or Arkell's method of dividing the 1676 figures by the total number of households to indicate what categories of population were counted.[20] Both methods tend to give the same results; however, a number of returns, inevitably, remain obscure whichever method is applied. In certain cases a comparison between Hearth tax returns and the Compton census returns may be bedevilled by the doubt whether they relate to the same area; parish boundaries and boundaries observed by Hearth tax officials did not always coincide, especially in some parts of the country. On the whole, however, the Hearth tax returns prove very helpful in identifying the category of population reported in 1676. Poll tax returns may also turn out to be useful, but their patchy survival made it difficult to use them for comparison in preparing the *Critical edition*; moreover, the omission of the names of those exempt from paying the tax greatly reduces their value.[21]

For the *Critical edition*, however, use was made of other sources of information about population which, though they date from other parts of the seventeenth century, have also contributed a great deal to an understanding of the 1676 figures. They include the 1603 enquiry into communicants, papists and non-communicants, the results of which are available for a number of dioceses, including the large one of Lincoln.[22] These often indicate

19 Whiteman, *Critical edition*, p.lxxi.

20 See the following chapter by Arkell for a discussion of the most appropriate multipliers and of these methods. Ratios between 2.1 and 3.7 generally point to a count of men and women over sixteen, over 3.7 to a count of men, women and children, 1.1 to 1.9 to one of men over sixteen only, and 1.0 or 1.1, of households.

21 See the chapter by Cooper which discusses the poll books for King's Lynn.

22 These dioceses are Gloucester, Lincoln, Norwich, Winchester, Bangor (part), Chichester (Lewes archdeaconry) and York (Nottingham archdeaconry). See forthcoming edition of the returns for 1603 by D.M. Palliser.

that the same part of the population must have been counted both in 1603 and 1676, and point to that part being men and women over sixteen, who were often simply called 'communicants'. The Protestation returns of 1641-2 are also helpful, and have been widely used. Because they listed males over eighteen years of age the multiplier is a relatively simple one, since a count of men has only to be doubled to give a rough estimate of both men and women in a parish (though of course there were some parishes with an unusual ratio of men to women).[23] For a few areas a local source of information is available, for example the *notitiae* for parishes in the north Welsh diocese of St Asaph which date from the 1680s, and Denton's count of households in Cumberland, in Carlisle diocese.[24]

In compiling the tables in the *Critical edition* use has been made throughout of the 1811 census and, since this includes population figures for the whole country, it has proved invaluable in suggesting the categories reported in 1676. As Wrigley has pointed out, the population of England and Wales roughly doubled between 1676 and 1811, so that if we assume that two-thirds of the population consisted of men and women over sixteen, we should expect the ratio of the 1811 to the 1676 figure to be 3 to 1, if men and women over sixteen had been counted in 1676; 6 to 1 if only men over sixteen had been counted; and 8 to 1 if households were the category counted. Of course in practice the ratios do not conform as neatly as this, especially in urban parishes. In general (though regional differences must always be kept in mind), ratios up to 2:1 indicate a count of men, women and children; from 2.1:1 to 3.5:1, one of men and women over sixteen; from 3.6:1 to 5.1:1, one of men over sixteen only; from 5.2:1 to 6.5:1, one of either men or households; and over 6.6:1, one of households. There are occasions when contemporary evidence goes against such an interpretation and a decision needs to be made on a balance of probabilities. Overall, however, the use of the 1811 census figures is both easy and profitable, though regard must be paid to the degree of industrialisation arrived at by 1811 in any particular area.[25]

23 Whiteman, *Critical edition*, p.lxi, indicates their survival and discusses their reliability.

24 Whiteman, *Critical edition*, pp.492-504, 618-21.

25 See Wrigley and Schofield, *Population history*, pp.33-7, for another example of the use of the Compton census and 1811 census data for estimating population totals in their 404 parishes.

An analysis of the various tables included in the *Critical edition* of the 1676 census in which at least two comparative figures are available for each parish (including the 1811 census figure) throws light on the categories of population reported in 1676. Over 1,200 parishes in seventeen dioceses in the Province of Canterbury and two in the Province of York are included, although the samples for each diocese vary in size; returns for parishes in a few dioceses which are known to be atypical (e.g. Peterborough) are omitted.[26] The percentage of returns which may be conjectured to represent counts of men and women over sixteen varies from diocese to diocese, from eleven per cent in parts of Lichfield and Worcester dioceses to eighty-eight per cent in Lincoln diocese; it may also vary considerably from archdeaconry to archdeaconry. The percentage for the whole sample works out at sixty-five per cent. There is, therefore, a good chance that in a considerable number of dioceses a figure given for inhabitants will represent adults of both sexes; in some areas, a very high chance indeed. The percentage conjectured to represent men, women and children works out from the same sample as about eleven per cent; that to represent men only, or households, as about sixteen per cent; the interpretation in about eight per cent is uncertain. It must again be stressed that the returns for each diocese must be interpreted in their own terms and that the percentages given above are merely findings from a sample which is in no way weighted, and which, on further investigation of the 1676 census, may turn out to be in some ways unrepresentative. It is only further research that can correct the picture, both locally and overall.

The inconsistency with which the returns are presented in the Salt manuscript constitutes another problem in using the figures. As pointed out above, the uniform heading 'Conformists' is certainly misleading in a number of dioceses, and probably so in most. In handling the returns for Canterbury, London, Salisbury, Chichester, part of Hereford and part of Lichfield dioceses, and in the case of Lincoln diocese, it is necessary to add any figures for papists and nonconformists to the 'Conformists' figure to produce a total for 'inhabitants' (in some instances, of course, other categories of population may have been reported). This is almost certainly the case for some of the returns for Gloucester diocese, which seem to be inconsistently reproduced in the Salt

26 Whiteman, *Critical edition*, pp.lxii-lxxi.

manuscript. We still know too little about the way in which the questions were asked in some other dioceses to be certain that we can assume that the figure given in the Salt manuscript under the heading 'Conformists' is a report of persons inhabiting in the parish (whether adults of both sexes, men over sixteen or the whole population irrespective of age), and therefore papists and nonconformists need not be added to reconstitute an inhabitants' total. Yet the evidence suggests that the great majority of the figures are in the same form in which the incumbents reported them, and the probability is that most of them answered a form of the questions which asked for a count of inhabitants, which the organisers intended should be a count of men and women over sixteen.

Overall assessment

Doubt has often been cast on the accuracy – and therefore the value – of the Compton census returns. Correlation with population figures derived from such sources as the Hearth tax is for certain areas variable and sometimes downright poor. It does not follow, of course, that when there is a marked difference in estimated totals for a parish (and most estimates involve multipliers which are in themselves contentious) it is the Compton census figure which is 'wrong'. It may simply be that the area over which the count was made was not the same. Difficulties may arise about boundaries as was mentioned above. Part and not the whole of a parish may also have been omitted (or the record of it lost) in either count, or it may be a question of the inclusion or exclusion of a chapelry. Some enumerators were more careful and accurate than others. We know, moreover, that there was a good deal of migration in the later part of the seventeenth century. Equally the size of a community might be affected by the incidence of plague; the destruction by fire of a number of houses might reduce habitable dwellings in a parish; the 'big house' might be occupied or the family might be in residence elsewhere. It is perhaps unreasonable, for these specimen and other reasons, to assume that the population of a parish did not vary, and sometimes considerably, even within a few years. It is moreover possible that a count of persons, which in most cases the Compton census is, will tend to be an underestimate; it is obviously easier to count well-established families than to take cognisance of all individuals. Vagrants and migrants, Gregory King's 'transitory' sort of people, may easily have escaped enumeration. In general terms, however, it is the agreement between population estimates arrived at from sources like the Hearth tax and the Protestation returns which is more striking than the differences. There is from many dioceses a good chance, as we have seen, that the Compton census figure will represent men and women over sixteen; if instead, men over sixteen only, households or the whole population irrespective of age were reported in 1676, useful comparisons can also be made.

Doubt has often been cast on the credibility of the 1676 returns by pointing to the considerable number of figures which end in a round number: 0, 00, or 000. It is tempting to identify accurate returns with a low percentage of round numbers and to mistrust those with a high one. The matter does not appear to be so simple; the figures for Peterborough diocese, with 67 per cent of the returns for 'Conformists' ending in 0 or 00, obviously came under suspicion early on in the compilation of the *Critical edition*, and (as it turned out) rightly so; however, the percentage of returns ending in round numbers is high in some other dioceses, the figures for which correlate well or reasonably well with estimated population totals based on other sources. It is essential to recall that (as many of the incumbents' returns testify) the usual unit for counting at the time was the score; it would have seemed sensible in many cases to level a count up (or perhaps down) to the nearest score, if there were some doubt about the absolute correctness of an enumeration. In reckoning up the population of a small parish, such a practice might produce a sizeable distortion; in a larger one, the difference between 140 and 160 communicants – seven score or eight score – might not have seemed to some incumbents or churchwardens of much significance. It all depends on how accurate to a man, woman or perhaps a child, we can expect our ancestors to have been in making their returns. It is not helpful to be too pernickety, since none of our sources for seventeenth-century demography is beyond criticism.

The census as a religious record

The questions

The treatment by the Compton census of the figures for papists and nonconformists requires a separate discussion. In general incumbents do not seem to have found it difficult to decide what number of papists they should report; this is not of course to say that the number they gave always carries conviction when compared with other sources of information, and fear and favour may have interposed to affect their answers. But the form of the second question, asking for recusants or those suspected for recusancy, had no hidden snags. However, this was far from the case when it came to answering the third question, which asked, in the form sent out from Lambeth, what in each parish was the number of dissenters, who 'either obstinately refuse or wholly absent themselves from the Communion of the Church of England at such times as by law they are required'. Was this asking for a return of the number who never came to church at all or of those who only sometimes or very seldom came to church, or possibly of those who did not receive Holy Communion at the seasons when they were enjoined to do so? What did 'the Communion of the Church of England' mean? Did 'Communion' in this context mean 'fellowship' or did it refer to 'the Lord's Supper'? Incumbents were understandably puzzled and some set out their doubts at length. Very few indeed seem to have thought that the number of their parishioners who did not receive Holy communion was the proper answer to the question; some did in fact report this, but almost always had something also to say about those who did not come to other services in the church. Most, perhaps all, were clear that they should report total separatists (generally Quakers or Baptists), but were worried whether they should also include partial conformists (generally Presbyterians and Independents) who attended their parish church in the morning but might yet go to a conventicle in the afternoon. Others were anxious that careless neglecters should not be confused with wilful absentees.

For these reasons a total count of nonconformists was impossible at the time and consequently the census figures, contributed by perplexed incumbents, can only give a very patchy and inconsistent body of evidence about the strength of Dissent in 1676. The incumbents in the Province of York might be thought to have experienced less difficulty in knowing whom to report in answer to their third question, which asked for refusers or absentees from the Communion of the Church of England 'at such times as by law they are required *to communicate*' [my italics]. But the extant answers for parishes in the province seem to suggest that incumbents there also found it difficult to know how to reply. Whether in the 'Lambeth' or the 'York' form, the question had been poorly drafted.

Partial Conformity

Although the Compton census is supplemented by many other contemporary sources of information about Protestant dissenters, several other reasons conspire to make it even more difficult to identify their numbers accurately in any particular locality.[27]

Religious allegiances are sometimes represented as clear-cut and virtually immutable: a man or woman was either 'Church' or 'Chapel'. There is abundant evidence to show that this was far from true in the second half of the seventeenth century, as indeed careful study of answers to the 1851 census has shown it to be equally untrue even in the nineteenth century.[28] The adherents of certain religious groups, particularly the Quakers and in general the Baptists, had no truck with the established Church at all.[29] But this was by no means the case with many Presbyterians and some Congregationalists, whose disagreement with the restored Church of England was primarily over the form of church government. Presbyterians in particular favoured a national church; it was their sadness that the settlement of 1662 made it so difficult for them to remain wholly within it. But there was a strong sentiment that total separation from the Church of England even as reestablished was wrong; this persuaded many Presbyterians and others that a link should be kept with it wherever and whenever possible. Yet it was common for many of them also to feel that the emphasis on preaching the Word, a central part of their concept of worship, was seldom adequately provided for by the Church; hence the enthusiasm to attend a conventicle where a preacher of the right kind might be heard. In consequence what may conveniently be called partial conformity was widespread:[30] attendance at the parish church in the morning, and perhaps also in the afternoon, and at a conventicle either in a private house, a larger building like a barn, or even in the open air later in the day. For many this pattern of worship became the normal practice.[31]

27 For discussion of these sources in the archdeaconry of Exeter see the chapter by Jackson below.

28 See Ambler, *Lincolnshire Returns* and Tiller, *Church and Chapel*, especially p.xx.

29 Watts, *The Dissenters*, pp.224-8.

30 This term is to be preferred to 'occasional conformity', which later became a term to describe, in particular, reception of Holy Communion according to the Anglican rite as a qualification for political office.

31 Watts, *The Dissenters*, pp.228-9; Clapinson, *Bishop Fell*, pp.xviii-xx.

Evidence of partial conformity from the Compton census is abundant, and well illustrates the complex nature of post-Restoration dissent. The rector of Frittenden in Kent disclosed that besides two or three obstinate Presbyterians, thirty-one Anabaptists or suspected to be such, two Quakers and two Brownists, his parish included between thirty and forty 'Newtralists between Presbiterians and Conformists', eleven or twelve 'Licentious or such as profess no kind of Religion', and between thirty and forty 'other infrequent Resorters to their Parish Church'. The curate of Maidstone, another parish in Kent, reported that he had in his parish of 3,000 inhabitants a total of 316 dissenters. Of these, ten were Anabaptists and Quakers; the rest being 'Presbyterians, who doe usually come to Church, and to divine service, one part of the day, and goe to a Conventicle the other, haveing a Non-Conformist Teacher in the Towne, whom they maintaine to Exercise to them'.[32] According to Archdeacon Parker of Canterbury, such Presbyterians were not returned as 'wholly dissenters' in the diocese in 1676 but there was probably much inconsistency in this throughout the various dioceses.[33]

The presence of an ejected minister in or near a parish obviously made such arrangements easier.[34] Some ejected ministers made a point of attending the parish church before and sometimes also after holding a service and preaching either in their own house, a neighbouring property, or perhaps out of doors. Calamy's biographies of ejected ministers provide some examples of such partial conformity. Joshua Barnett, ejected from Wrockwardine in Shropshire, went to church twice each Sunday; 'when he preach'd at home at Noon, [he] would carry his whole Auditory to Church with him afterwards'. Edward Bury, who had been rector of Great Bolas in the same county, 'attended with his Family on the Publick Ministry in the Morning, and preach'd to his Family and Neighbours in the Afternoon'.[35] The activities of such men does much to explain why the Five Mile Act of 1665 was passed since their influence was likely to be even greater if they were still living in the midst of their former parishioners.

32 Whiteman, *Critical edition*, p.xxxix.

33 Whiteman, *Critical edition*, p.7.

34 Clapinson, *Bishop Fell*, pp.xv-xviii.

35 Matthews, *Calamy revised*, pp.29-30, 91. There were of course some Presbyterians and Congregationalists who strongly objected to attendance at the parish church: for example, William Alleine and Francis Holcroft (pp.8, 271-2).

It cannot have been easy for those responsible for presenting the names of dissenters to decide which, if any, of such partial conformists should be reported. The eye of charity might see them primarily as churchmen, though given to unfortunate lapses from orthodox behaviour about which it was kind or prudent to keep silent. But others who were either personally committed to enforcing strict conformity or were persuaded to do so by directions from the bishop or from Whitehall would have had no doubt that nonconformity in any form should be reported and duly punished.

Fluctuations in central politics meant that whereas sometimes messages were received from Whitehall, through the judges on circuit, proclamations or other means, that the laws against nonconformity should be put into strict execution, at other times the pressure for presentment and prosecution was relaxed or even discouraged; Charles II's Declaration of Indulgence in 1672-3 temporarily suspended the operation of the laws against dissent. During the 1660s the so-called Clarendon Code, backed by a fear that conventicles might provide a cover for dangerous plotters,[36] probably tended to ensure that in most districts prosecution of those presented was kept at a high level. The 1664 Conventicle Act and the more stringent provisions of its 1670 successor made attendance at religious assemblies outside the church hazardous and sometimes highly dangerous; but by no means all justices and other officials were zealous to implement them. It was probably only with the Stuart Reaction after the Popish and Rye House Plots that anything like systematic presentment of dissenters took place, and a real attempt made to silence nonconformist preachers. This of course collapsed soon after the accession of James II, as the king tried to make dissenters his allies in his campaign for toleration. There is some evidence to suggest that throughout the period many people were unhappy with a policy of persecution of men and women who did not seem to pose any danger to Church or State, and that a growing fear of Roman Catholicism began to supersede the suspicion of dissent.[37]

The problem of deciding who was a dissenter was therefore difficult and widespread; accurate figures for them were unlikely to emerge from such a background. What can be achieved varies a

36 Greaves, *Deliver us*.

37 See Watts, *The Dissenters*, pp.221-62, for the background. On the Conventicle Acts see Fletcher, 'The enforcement'.

great deal from area to area and whether the parish or parishes under review are urban or rural ones. The names of the leading dissenters, and sometimes the size of their following, may often be recovered for rural parishes, especially if they were nuclear rather than large and dispersed. So far as urban dissent is concerned the size and number of the parishes in the city or town is probably of crucial importance. Great Yarmouth, a stronghold of dissent, consisted of one large parish; ecclesiastical discipline within it must have been virtually impossible and the identity of committed dissenters, as opposed to hangers-on, very hard to establish. In a city like Exeter or Norwich, on the other hand, a number of relatively small parishes meant that the incumbent and the parish officials could know a good deal about their parishioners and their religious persuasions, if they were so minded.[38]

There are, therefore, several reasons why a comparison between the numbers reported as nonconformists in the 1676 Compton census and of those named in visitations or brought to court, in the same parish and about the same time, do not always confirm each other. In addition, all over sixteen may have been included in the count of 1676, whereas householders alone were more often presented either in an ecclesiastical visitation or to the quarter sessions or assizes. This generalisation needs more testing. Peter Jackson's chapter in this volume of essays is a valuable piece of pioneering research, which could with advantage be undertaken for other areas and which might reveal a wider discrepancy than that found by Jackson.[39]

Conclusion

When I began my work on the Compton census, I had little idea what the returns represented, and often wondered whether it was worth editing. I now feel confident that it is a source of major importance for assessing population in the later seventeenth century, and in a different way, valuable for the history of recusancy and dissent. But it does not give up its secrets easily, and there are many more to be discovered.

38 Watts, *The Dissenters*, pp.245-6; Exeter is generally accounted to have had twenty parishes and Norwich thirty-six.

39 See chapter by Jackson.

6

A method for estimating population totals from the Compton census returns

TOM ARKELL

Students of later seventeenth-century social and demographic history owe a large debt of gratitude to Anne Whiteman and her assistants for their herculean labours on the Compton census returns.[1] Her *Critical edition* contains a definitive version of the Compton census and the scholarly introduction to the volume provides essential information on many problems encountered in its interpretation.[2] In this chapter I will attempt to repay a small portion of this debt by trying to elucidate further aspects of three important and related issues. These are the multipliers that should be used to convert the Compton figures for each parish into a population estimate; the possible alternatives that the figures given in the Compton records represent; and the potential reliability of these figures. Selected Hearth tax returns will be employed for the last two of these tasks, in which it will also be suggested that sometimes the Compton figures may be used in a reciprocal exercise to vet the quality of some Hearth tax lists.

Multipliers

Any attempt to calculate population estimates from the Compton census returns must tackle first the question of what multipliers should be applied to three of the four different categories recorded by the various incumbents. Clearly, different multipliers will need to be applied if the census takers enumerated households, adults or male adults only. Alternately, if incumbents counted the total number of inhabitants in their jurisdiction then, of course, no further adjustment is required.

1 Since the first draft of this chapter was written several years ago I have received much valuable help and encouragement from Anne Whiteman.

2 An outline summary of her findings is given in her chapter above.

Households

I have argued elsewhere that the mean household size in both rural and urban areas outside London was normally about 4.3, yet at the same time warning against the use of a single multiplier to obtain population totals for separate communities, suggesting a range of at least plus or minus 10 per cent, and possibly 15 per cent, around the central multiplier. Even this measure of flexibility will not allow for the full range of local variations, since a few communities had an even smaller or larger mean household size.[3] In particular, the mean household size figure may have been highly variable in very small parishes, in which a few large households could have had a marked effect on the overall mean. Consequently, a multiplying range of perhaps 3.7 to 5.2 should be applied to the Compton figures that record households. This range will cover the mean household size of the great majority of places, although possibly not all of them.

Adults

Whiteman has now resolved all doubts about the nature of those who were returned as 'communicants' or 'of the age to communicate'. The former should be regarded as being synonymous with the latter and at this period it was accepted consistently as being aged sixteen and above. It is perhaps clearest to refer to them as adults and to those below the age of sixteen as children.[4]

Children

Determining what proportion of the population was normally aged under sixteen, and should therefore be added to the Compton totals of adults or communicants, is much more problematical. According to two different estimates by Wrigley and Schofield, little more than 30 per cent was under sixteen at the time of the Compton census. Their first 'rough and ready procedure' using model life tables yielded a proportion of 30.6 per cent, while 'back projection suggests that 31.2 per cent of the population was under sixteen in 1676'.[5] Although undertaken with scrupulous scholarship, neither calculation was based directly upon

[3] Arkell, 'Multiplying factors', p.55.

[4] Whiteman, *Critical edition*, pp.xxxiii-xxxvi. See also the perceptive discussion on confirmation and first communion in Wright, 'Catechisms', pp.212-7.

[5] Wrigley and Schofield, *Population history*, pp.35, 570.

contemporary sources, so that further evidence is needed to resolve this issue.

Archdeacon Palmer of Peterborough diocese recalculated the Compton returns of those parishes which he thought had omitted everyone under sixteen by adding one for every two people listed. This simple arithmetic calculation also suggests that he assumed that 'children' formed one third of the population.[6] In addition, Whiteman has made a detailed study of the *notitiae* for 136 parishes in the diocese of St Asaph for the 1680s which recorded children aged under eighteen. She found that the mean percentage under eighteen for this group of parishes was 34.3, yet since she also was well aware that all were not equally reliable, she settled eventually on 33 per cent as being an acceptable proportion of those aged under sixteen.[7] This proportion matches the assumption of one third made by Hoskins for Wigston Magna and comes close to the 29 per cent quoted by Styles for Wellesbourne in Warwickshire in 1676. However, it is clearly at variance with the proportion of 40 per cent that has been accepted by Marshall, Chalklin, Patten, Skipp and others.[8]

Gregory King was the first and most persuasive advocate of the case for a significantly higher proportion of children in the population. Using a detailed enumeration of his native city of Lichfield, together with other comparable sources, King estimated that in England 42 per cent of males and 40 per cent of females were aged under sixteen and that this proportion was lower in London and higher in the countryside. The Lichfield data is difficult to interpret accurately because it recorded no one with an age under one so that either an allowance must be made for the omission of infants, as well as for any other under-enumeration, or else it must be assumed that those recorded as more than sixteen, for example, were fifteen and in their sixteenth year. Altogether some 37 per cent of the Lichfield enumeration was aged either under fifteen or one-to-fifteen so that an allowance for the missing year band suggests that a minimum of 40 per cent was aged under sixteen in Lichfield in 1695. Although, this question was not tackled directly by Glass in his discussion of

6 Whiteman, *Critical edition*, pp.375-6.

7 Whiteman, *Critical edition*, pp.lxvii, 492-504.

8 Hoskins, *Provincial England*, pp.187-8, Styles, *Studies*, p.280, fn.17; Marshall, 'Rural population', p.11; Chalklin, 'Compton census', p.157; Patten, 'Population distribution', p.59; Skipp, *Crisis and development*, p.117.

King's calculations of the age composition of the population, he did consider that in general terms they were unlikely to be 'far from the truth'.[9]

Most other attempts to calculate proportions of children under sixteen from ordinary Marriage Duty assessments are doomed to frustration because both bachelors aged under twenty-five and all spinsters living at home with their parents were not normally differentiated from children of fifteen and under.[10] Other contemporary census-type lists, such as the well-known ones for Clayworth and Goodnestone-next-Wingham, are similarly incapable of sustaining such analyses because they do not indicate the children's ages. However, the lists for three other large parishes with populations ranging from 779 to 1,626 do include sufficient information. Forty-one per cent of the inhabitants of Chilvers Coton in north Warwickshire were aged under sixteen in 1684 and an identical proportion of children was recorded in 1701 in Stoke-on-Trent, which was then still rural. Some doubts surround the ages of those recorded as '00' in the less reliable list for Buckfastleigh (Devon) of 1698, but under most interpretations its proportion of children aged under sixteen was approximately 35 per cent.[11]

Additional support for a higher proportion than that derived from the theoretical calculations of Wrigley and Schofield is supplied by further working of the St Asaph *notitiae*. Anne Whiteman's doubts about the accuracy with which many were compiled have already been mentioned; consequently a sample study has been undertaken of twelve parishes which provide some of the most detailed returns. The information from these select parishes shown in Table 1 suggests that altogether 35.5 per cent of the population in this part of north Wales was aged under sixteen, but ranged from 31 to 46 per cent in the individual parishes. However, all of these figures should not be taken at face value because, even in this sample, the detail is not always equally reliable. For example, the ages of the children were not given in two of these parishes and in only two others was anyone listed

9 Glass, 'Two papers on Gregory King', pp.204-16.

10 Styles, *Studies*, pp.96-7. Chalklin, 'Compton census', p.157 was apparently unaware of this discrepancy in the definition of 'children'.

11 Warwick County Record Office, *Newdigate of Arbury papers*, CR 136 V 12, pp.64-73; Staffordshire Record Office, D(W) 1742/55; British Library, Harleian MSS. 6832 and written communication from Miss E.M. Knowling.

Table 1 Proportion of the population aged under 16: Diocese of St Asaph,* 1685-90.

Parish	H'holds	Pop.	MHS	Aged <16		Aged '0'
	n	n		n	%	%
Llanddulas	19	67	3.5	21	31	n.k.
Llandegla	45	208	4.6	89	43	4.3
Llanelian-yn-Rhus	84	339	4.0	109	32	0
Llanerfyl	94	433	4.6	143	33	0
Llanfair Caereinion	286	1289	4.5	449	35	0
Llanfaethln*	50	242	4.8	91	38	n.k.
Llanferris	58	263	4.5	83	32	0
Llanfihangel Glyn Myfyr	68	297	4.4	115	39	2.4
Llangadwaladr	40	155	3.9	72	46	0
Llangwtenin	70	265	3.8	87	33	0
Llansantffraid Glan Conwy	98	449	4.6	165	37	0
St George	43	196	4.6	66	34	0
Total	955	4203	4.4	1490	35.5	

Notes: * The parish of Llanfaethln is in the diocese of Bangor.

with an age of '0'. Since these parishes also had two of the highest proportions of under sixteen year-olds (39 per cent and 43 per cent), considerable doubt must arise over how many infants under one were included in the other returns. In these parishes the proportions of children may therefore need to be increased by as much as three per cent to account for the under-registration of infants.[12]

Unfortunately, no undisputed mean figure for the percentage of children under sixteen in the later seventeenth century has emerged from this discussion. Nonetheless, although the weight of recent scholarship has tipped the scales towards 33 per cent or less, some of the best empirical evidence which has been considered here suggests that it may often have come very close to the more traditional 40 per cent. Therefore some doubt must now be cast on the confident assertion by Wrigley and Schofield that the national age structure of the later seventeenth century was markedly different from that of the early nineteenth

12 The National Library of Wales, Aberystwyth SA/Misc/1372-1428; Carreg Lwyd 1476. I am very grateful to Richard Wall for first drawing my attention to the potential of these documents. Those who were recorded as being aged sixteen and seventeen have been omitted from these calculations.

century.[13] In the meanwhile, a fairly broad range of 29 to 41 per cent will be proposed to cover the likely proportion of children in most individual communities.

Adult males

If the proportion of adults normally ranged from 59 to 71 per cent, it is tempting to conclude that one half of them were males (29 to 36 per cent). However, Gregory King estimated that there was a ratio of 93.8 adult males per hundred adult females nationwide, and Souden's recent work on the Marriage Duty assessments of 1695-1705 has revealed considerable variations in the total sex ratios, due primarily to differential migration rates, though not specifically those for adults.[14] He concluded that the cities and more important towns 'tended to have female-dominated populations, and smaller, especially rural agricultural, settlements...tended to be balanced or to be male-dominated.'[15] The overall sex ratios for the sample areas which he studied ranged from 83 males for 100 females for the large towns to 90 for the small towns and 100.5 for the villages, with the small town of Lyme Regis registering the greatest female domination (ratio 70), and with no others falling below 80.

As yet there is insufficient evidence to show if the adult sex ratios were significantly different, but since there was a tendency then, as now, for the surplus of females to increase among the older population, the numbers of adult females may well have been somewhat higher than males. Among five communities for which we have reasonably reliable data, the adult sex ratio of males per 100 females ranged from 99 in Buckfastleigh and 94 in Llanfaethln (Bangor) through 86 in Stoke-on-Trent and 85.5 in Chilvers Coton, to as low as 72 in Lichfield. This last figure may be slightly suspect because the list contains a very small proportion of men in their early twenties. Overall the proportion of adult males in each population rose from 26.25 per cent in Lichfield to 27 per cent in both Chilvers Coton and Stoke, for which we have the best two lists, and 32 per cent in Buckfastleigh. Taking into account the possibility that this small sample may be skewed in favour of communities with large proportions of children, it appears reasonable to suggest that the

13 Wrigley and Schofield, *Population history*, pp.217-8.

14 Glass, 'Two papers on Gregory King', p.211; Souden, 'Migrants', pp.150-8.

15 Souden, 'Migrants', pp.157-8.

normal range for the proportion of adult males in most communities was from about 27 to 36 per cent.

Compton/Hearth tax ratios

Once established the relevant range of multipliers still cannot be applied to the Compton figures for individual parishes until it is established what the returns actually represent. When virtually complete Hearth tax returns exist for exactly the same area that is covered by the Compton census, they can be used to help determine the nature of the Compton figures.[16] This method entails dividing the Compton total by the Hearth tax total. When, for example, it yields a ratio of approximately one, it implies that the incumbent returned the number of households in his parish. Similarly ratios of around 4.3 will indicate total inhabitants and intermediate ones of around three indicate total adults and 1.5 adult males.

The main problems posed by this method entail determining reliable outer limits for each category. The exercise requires as much judgement as mechanical application since it is attempting to establish for each parish only their *probable* mean household size combined with *plausible* proportions of adults or adult males. In addition, some allowances must be made for possible imperfections in either list. It has been suggested above that a viable range for mean household size in this period was about 3.7 to 5.2 and that in most communities the proportion of adults normally ranged from 59 to 71 per cent and of adult males from about 27 to 36 per cent. Clearly smaller communities were most prone to stray beyond these limits, but if for the moment one can accept the plausibility of these ranges, then they can be used as the basis for interpreting the Compton/Hearth tax ratios.

Table 2, which is based directly on these proposed ranges, suggests that a ratio of 3.7 could reflect either total inhabitants or all adults, and a ratio of 1.0 either adult males or households. However, apart from these extremes one should have little difficulty in interpreting the ratios.[17] Yet these calculations assume, unrealistically, that the available Hearth tax returns are both contemporaneous and entirely accurate, which many are not.

16 For guidance on the problems of interpreting the Hearth tax returns see my chapter on 'Printed instructions' above.

17 Unless they contained either 2.0 or 2.1, which according to these calculations they should not.

Table 2 Compton/Hearth tax ratios

Compton category	Possible ranges		ratio
Inhabitants	upper limit -	(100 per cent of 5.2)	5.2
	lower limit -	(100 per cent of 3.7)	3.7
Adults	upper limit -	(71 per cent of 5.2)	3.7
	lower limit -	(59 per cent of 3.7)	2.2
Adult males	upper limit -	(36 per cent of 5.2)	1.9
	lower limit -	(27 per cent of 3.7)	1.0
Households			1.0

Some adjustments should therefore be made to cater for the possibility of even apparently complete Hearth tax returns being slightly defective. A suggestion of how this might be done is given in Table 3, in which the upper limits of some categories of Table 2 are increased slightly to allow for small omissions from the Hearth tax totals. In addition, when Hearth tax lists from the 1660s are used, further adjustments may be required to allow for possible population changes in the intervening period.

Interpreting the Compton returns

According to Chalklin, Archdeacon Parker claimed that all inhabitants over sixteen had been included in the Compton returns for the diocese of Canterbury. This assertion can of course be tested by applying the method detailed above to a sample of ten parishes contained in Chalklin's study of the Compton census in Kent. Even though the Hearth tax details were drawn from the 1664 assessment, Table 4 indicates that, whereas all the returns for a similar-sized sample from the diocese of Rochester were for adults, the incumbents in only half the sample Canterbury parishes appear to have returned all adults. One of the others returned all the inhabitants and four adult males alone.[18]

More recently Edwards has used the Compton/Hearth tax ratios as advocated here to make a meticulously detailed comparison for

[18] Chalklin, 'Compton census' p.155. See also Whiteman, *Critical edition*, pp.7, 15-16, where it is also demonstrated from the evidence of some incumbents' returns for Canterbury diocese that Parker was clearly misinformed. In making these calculations I have been advised by Anne Whiteman that for the Canterbury diocese figures as given in the Salt manuscript the number of papists and nonconformists should be added to the conformists to give the Compton census total for each parish, but not in Rochester diocese where the 'conformist' column probably included the papists and nonconformists.

Table 3 Compton/Hearth tax ratios

Compton category	Possible ranges	ratio
Inhabitants	upper limit	5.5
	lower limit	3.9
Inhabitants/Adults	upper limit	3.8
	lower limit	3.7
Adults	upper limit	3.6
	lower limit	2.2
Adults/Adult males	upper limit	2.1
	lower limit	2.0
Adult males	upper limit	1.9
	lower limit	1.2
Adult Males/Households		1.1
Households	upper limit	1.0
	lower limit	0.9

much of Derbyshire between the Compton census and Hearth tax assessments, mostly for 1664.[19] The Derbyshire figures given in Table 4 are taken from his work, but omit sixteen groups of combined parishes or places from Edwards's list because of doubts over their geographical composition.[20] In some other counties Hearth tax assessments from the early 1670s can be used to reduce the chronological gap between them and the Compton returns to only a few years and so eliminate the possibility that significant population changes might have occurred between them. For example, in Bedfordshire Compton returns exist for all but four of the 121 complete parishes which were covered by the Hearth tax of 1669-70.[21]

19 Edwards, 'Population in Derbyshire', pp.106-17. As he acknowledged very handsomely, Edwards used an earlier unpublished version of this paper as the basis of his calculations, which will partly explain why the limits for some of his categories do not coincide exactly with those advocated here.

20 These omissions are: Ashbourne, Ashover, Bakewell, Brailsford, Chesterfield, Derby, Dronfield, Eckington, Eyam, Glossop, Gresley, Longford, Mugginton, Stapenhill, Tideswell and Youlgrave.

21 The Bedfordshire Hearth tax returns for 1669-70, which are in the PRO, were published in *Bedfordshire Historical Record Society*, XVI, 1934, pp.65-159, where they were headed very misleadingly '1671', even though they were described as being for the year and a half to Michaelmas 1670 on p.159.

Table 4 Compton/Hearth tax ratios

	Samples from four counties					
	Kent					
Ratio	Canterbury diocese	Rochester diocese	Derbyshire	Bedfordshire	Warwickshire	Total
	1664		c1664	1670	1673-4	
0.5					1	1
0.7					1	1
0.9					1	1
1.0					15	15
1.1					15	15
1.2			1		10	11
1.3					18	18
1.4					16	16
1.5				1	6	7
1.6				1	11	12
1.7	1		1		10	12
1.8	1			3	2	6
1.9	1			4	1	6
2.0	1(**M**)		2(**A**)			3
2.1			1(**A**)	4(2**A**,2**M**)	3(2**A**,1**M**)	8
2.2				4	1	5
2.3			2	6		8
2.4		1	2	10	7	20
2.5		1	3	12	6	22
2.6	2	1	7	5	3	18
2.7	2		4	5	5	16
2.8	1	1	2	10	4	18
2.9		1	5	8	4	18
3.0		1	6	11		18
3.1			5	3	4	12
3.2			3	3	1	7
3.3			4	4	3	11
3.4		2	2	6	3	13
3.5			6	3	2	11
3.6		2	3		1	6
3.7			1(**I**)	5(4**A**,1**I**)	2(**A**)	8
3.8			1(**A**)	2(**A**)		3
3.9			7			7
4.0			4	1		5
4.1			3	1		4
4.2			1	1		2
4.3			4			4
4.4						0
4.5			1	1		2
4.6			2			2
4.7				1	1	2

Table 4 cont.

Ratio	Kent: Canterbury diocese 1664	Kent: Rochester diocese 1664	Derbyshire c1664	Bedfordshire 1670	Warwickshire 1673-4	Total
4.8			1		1	2
4.9			2			2
5.0	1					1
5.1			3			3
5.2						0
5.3			4			4
5.4						0
5.5					1	1
5.6						0
5.7				1		1
5.8						0
5.9			1			1
6.0				1		1
6.1			1			1
6.2			1			1
6.6			1			1
7.4			1			1
9.6			1			1
13.3			1			1
Totals	10	10	100	117	159	396

Samples from four counties

Notes: Suggested interpretations: **A** = Adult communicants; **I** = Inhabitants; **M** = Adult Males

The county with the best set of Hearth tax returns is Warwickshire, where six virtually complete assessments survive for the whole county, as well as very substantial parts of two more.[22] A comparative study shows that those from the 1670s were generally the most complete, and the Compton/Hearth tax ratios have been created mainly from the returns for 1673-4, supplemented by those for 1672-3 when appropriate.[23] In the 1670s Warwickshire contained some 200 whole parishes, but for

[22] Arkell, 'Assessing the reliability', pp.183-97.

[23] Calculating precise Hearth tax households is never easy. Sometimes the largest totals may not be the most reliable because they may include a few empty or demolished houses as well as some from adjacent areas. In addition, for example, the Warwickshire returns for 1672-3 appear to contain as many as twenty duplicates in the parish of Ansley.

various reasons reliable Compton/Hearth tax ratios can be established for only about four-fifths of these. Compton returns do not exist for twenty parishes, of which eleven were peculiars, four were so small that they had virtually ceased to operate as separate organisations[24] and in the other five the state of their parish registers in the early months of 1676 suggests that their incumbents were either dead, absent or too ill to make a Compton return. In addition, ten very small extra-parochial places, with a total of thirty-one Hearth tax households, did not appear in the Compton census, and in one instance the figures for two little parishes were joined together. A further twenty parishes for which there are Compton returns have been omitted from Table 4 because of doubts over their Hearth tax assessments. In eleven instances where there were several scattered settlements within one parish or the parish had detached portions, it has not been possible to establish with certainty the precise number of their households, in particular those not liable for payment.[25] The other nine parishes were in Coventry where the most recent surviving Hearth tax return dates from 1666.

The figures given in Table 4 show that in Warwickshire, unlike Bedfordshire and Derbyshire, most Compton returns were for adult males.[26] However, precise proportions cannot be established for the different categories until doubts concerning some anomalies and uncertainties have been resolved. In Warwickshire there were three anomalous ratios below 1.0. Since the parish with 0.9, Ladbroke, had a Compton return of 50 compared with 55 Hearth tax households, it suggests that its Compton figure may have been rounded down and its real ratio should have been 1.0. The other two parishes, with ratios of 0.7 and 0.5, equally had Compton returns that were either defective or covered smaller areas than the Hearth tax.[27]

24 These included tiny Compton Wynyates with five households where Henry Compton himself was born.

25 Seven of these parishes were in the Arden Forest to the east of Solihull and four in the Avon valley west of Stratford.

26 The Warwickshire calculations in this table are greatly indebted to the invaluable advice of Anne Whiteman, whose own researches had already revealed the prevalence of adult males and households in the Compton returns for Warwickshire. Her assurance that the papists and nonconformists were already included in the 'conformists' column in the Warwickshire Compton returns enabled me to unravel the significance of my own findings from what had previously been some rather confused statistics.

27 The parishes are Stretton-on-the-Fosse (0.7) and Haselor (0.5).

The two potentially incompatible parishes in Bedfordshire both had ratios above 5.5. However, both were so small, with four and thirteen Hearth tax households which were also much larger than the norm, that their high ratios of 5.7 and 6.0 probably reflect their mean household sizes rather than incomplete Hearth tax assessments.[28] In Derbyshire, with its longer intervening gap of twelve years, seven places had ratios of between 5.9 and 13.3. An examination of the evidence seems to suggest that the two with the lowest ratios probably returned all their inhabitants. Boylestone, the parish with the 5.9 ratio had, rather curiously, a higher total of households listed in the 1662 Hearth tax return when the exempt were omitted than in 1664 when they were included. This would imply that its total of 29 households was not complete. Equally the other Derbyshire parish with a ratio of 6.1, Hognaston, had just 33 households in 1664 compared with 200 inhabitants returned for the Compton census. However, if the former were increased slightly and the latter assumed to have been rounded up, it would produce a more plausible ratio. Inadequacies in the Hearth tax data seem to account for the other five high ratios which are not susceptible to putative revisions like these. And so in this sample a ratio of 6.1 is interpreted as being the probable maximum for denoting Compton census returns of all inhabitants in a particular parish.[29]

Another principal cause of uncertainty in interpreting the ratios given in Table 4 stems from the potential overlap of credible ratios for adult males and households, as well as those for inhabitants and adults, plus the small gap in ratios between those for adults and adult males. In theory ratios of 2.0 and 2.1 should not exist unless some places had the unlikely combinations of a mean household size under 3.7 with over 41 per cent children, or a mean household size over 5.2 with over 36 per cent adult males, but in practice such ratios may be the product of defective documents. Clearly further research is needed on what factors tended to generate these extreme values, but in the meanwhile a somewhat arbitrary decision has been taken in an attempt to resolve the uncertainties, assuming that those places which had many small households and/or exempt from the Hearth tax were

28 The four households in Higham Gobion (5.7) had 7, 6, 5, and 2 hearths respectively and only three of the thirteen in Hatley Cockayne (6.0) had one hearth each.

29 The five parishes are South Wingfield, Clowne, Trusely, Newton Solney and Stretton en le Field. See Edwards, *Derbyshire*, pp.lix-lxvi.

more likely to have lower mean household sizes with fewer servants and more children than the norm.[30] This was the basis on which it was decided putatively that the Compton returns for four of the eleven parishes with ratios of 2.0 or 2.1 were for adult males, while the other seven were for both men and women. (See Table 4 for additional details.)

On the current evidence it is no easier to unravel the adults and inhabitants from the overlapping group of those with ratios of 3.7 and 3.8. The two Warwickshire parishes with a ratio of 3.7 for example, were so small (13 and 20 households) that they conceivably had higher than normal mean household sizes and returned both adult men and women. For similar reasons it appears that no more than two of the other nine parishes in this overlapping category are likely to have had Compton returns for all their inhabitants. It has already been pointed out in reference to Table 2 that the ratio for the lower range of adult males overlaps with that for households. On reflection this is not surprising since about one sixth of households were headed by females, and it is possible that in some places no more than one sixth had additional males aged sixteen and over. Nevertheless, a ratio of 1.0 is so much less likely to have denoted adult males than households that this possibility has been discounted and the ratio of 1.0 has been assumed invariably to represent households. The real problem therefore concerns a ratio of 1.1, which appears in Table 4 only among the Warwickshire parishes. On current evidence one cannot resolve whether those with a ratio of 1.1 were returned as households or adult males without guesswork. So that on balance I am inclined to assume that all the 1.1 ratios relate to adult males and not household returns.

If the interpretations of the uncertain Compton ratios discussed in this section are acceptable, it would make the median ratios for adult males 1.4, for all adults 2.8 and for inhabitants 4.3.

Analysing the Compton ratios

The suggested interpretations for these ratios are summarised in Table 5 which shows that little more than half the parishes in this sample returned adult men and women in the Compton

30 Laslett, *World we have lost – further explored*, pp.64-5; Laslett, 'Mean household size', p.155.

Table 5 Analysis of sample Compton/Hearth tax ratios

	Inter-ratio range	Kent		Derbyshire		Bedfordshire		Warwickshire		Total	
		n	%	n	%	n	%	n	%	n	%
Inhabitants	6.1-3.7	1	5	35	37	8	7	3	2	47	12
Adults	3.8-2.0	15	75	58	61	98	84	48	31	219	56
Adult Males	2.1-1.1	4	20	2	2	11	9	90	57	107	28
Households	1.0-0.9	-	-	-	-	-	-	16	10	16	4
Totals		20	100	95	100	117	100	157	100	389	100

Notes: In the Warwickshire sample two parishes were omitted in the inter-ratio range of 0.7-0.5, and five in Derbyshire in the range of 13.3-6.2.

census. It must be stressed, however, that this proportion should in no way be taken as representative for the country as a whole.[31] Instead the main validity of this analysis lies in the differences which it reveals between the counties. Adult returns clearly predominated in Bedfordshire, even more than in Derbyshire, where a significant minority also registered all the inhabitants. In Warwickshire the norm was adult males and a few even returned households. More insight can be gained into the vagaries of these Warwickshire Compton returns by reconsidering them separately in their deaneries. Table 6 discloses that in two deaneries most Compton returns were of all adults and in the other four the proportion that returned adult males only was even greater than for the county as a whole.

This technique can also be used as a check on the validity of those few surviving original Compton census returns in which the incumbents indicated what category was being enumerated. The form in which the first question was posed in the archdeaconry of Sudbury in Suffolk was: 'What number of persons male and female by common account are inhabiting in your parish of age to receive the holy Communion'. In Clare deanery most incumbents replied that their figures represented people of age to receive Holy

31 In the much larger sample of over 1,200 parishes in nineteen dioceses studied by Anne Whiteman (see her chapter above p.89), nearly two-thirds returned adults. It should perhaps be stressed as well that the work of scholars such as Smith and Unwin who have assumed that all the Compton figures for their areas referred solely to adults must inevitably be suspect. See, for example, Smith 'Population' pp.142-3 and Unwin, *Seventeenth century taxation*, p.31.

Table 6 Warwickshire Compton/Hearth tax ratios

	Category and inter-ratio range									
	Inhabitants 5.5 - 4.7		Adults 3.7 - 2.1		Adult males 2.1 - 1.1		Households 1.0 - 0.9		Totals	
Deanery	n	%	n	%	n	%	n	%	n	%
Coventry and Lichfield Diocese										
Arden			16	55	13	45			29	100
Coventry			3	21	9	64	2	14	14	100
Marton			2	8	23	88	1	4	26	100
Stoneleigh			2	8	16	67	6	25	24	100
Worcester Diocese										
Kineton	1	3	5	15	24	76	2	6	33	100
Warwick	2	6	20	65	4	13	5	16	31	100
Total	3	2	48	31	90	57	16	10	157	100

Communion, while a few others reported that they were communicants or over sixteen. In addition, one curate claimed to have returned the 'whole number of our parishioners', while one lone incumbent gave no indication to the identity of his figures.[32]

The information in Table 7 shows that the Compton/Hearth tax ratios based on the apparently reliable Hearth tax returns of 1674 confirm all but a handful of these claims.[33] Three parishes with ratios of between 4.3 and 4.7 must have returned all their inhabitants, not just their adults, while the one which claimed to have returned all its parishioners appears to have counted only its adult males. Some doubts must also arise over the accuracy of the figures for Kentford, but the ratios of 2.3 to 3.6 for all the other 23 parishes indicate how reliable most of these Compton returns were. It must be stressed, however, that the few rogue returns could not have been detected without a doublecheck from an alternative source, such as the Hearth tax. And the relatively high proportion of parishes with ratios above the previous median of 2.8 for those returning all adults over sixteen suggests that some of these Hearth tax returns had omitted about five to ten per cent of their households, which probably received alms.

32 Whiteman, *Critical edition*, pp.189, 232-4.

33 The Hearth tax returns for Risbridge hundred coincide with Clare deanery. Those for 1674 are in PRO, E179/257/14 and have been published in Hervey, *Suffolk*.

Table 7 Compton census and Hearth tax comparisons: Clare Deanery, Suffolk

Parish	Hearth tax 1674 exempt %	Hearth tax 1674 total n	Compton census total n	Compton census Incumbent's return	Compton/ Hearth tax ratio
Great Wratting	49	39 (1)	184	HC	4.72
Gazeley	34	29 (1)	175	HC	4.38
Hawkedon	34	29	125	HC	4.31
Great Thurlow	41	39	141	HC	3.62
Little Thurlow	36	39	137	C	3.51
Great Bradley	39	38	130	C	3.42
Chedburgh	0	16	52	HC	3.25
Haverhill*	64	173	610	HC	3.19
Denham St Mary	44	18	57	HC	3.17
Ousden	42	38	120	o16	3.16
Withersfield	56	63	199	o16	3.16
Stansfield	33	45	141	C	3.13
Lidgate	54	72 (4)	223	HC	3.10
Stoke by Clare	36	96 (1)	295	HC	3.07
Depden	29	28	c.84	HC	3.00
Dalham	40	57	169	C	2.96
Denston	50	36	104	HC	2.89
Wickhambrook	47	157	c.445	HC	2.83
Little Bradley	43	14	39	HC	2.79
Clare	56	199	540+	HC	2.71
Stradishall	56	90 (1)	236	HC	2.62
Little Wratting	46	13 (2)	34	HC	2.62
Hundon	49	137	356	HC	2.60
Poslingford	45	40 (1)	103	HC	2.57
Kedington*	53	88	206	HC	2.34
Barnardiston	44	36	81	-	2.25
Kentford (chapelry)	59	22	44	HC	2.00
Cowlinge	42	76 (3)	140	P	1.84

Notes: * = The part of the parish in Essex has been included.
Figures in Hearth tax total column in brackets represent dwellings recorded as empty. These have been included in their respective totals as well as the Compton/Hearth tax ratios.

The key to the incumbent's return column for the Compton census is as follows: **C** = Communicants; **HC** = of age to receive Holy Communion; **o16** = over 16; **P** = whole number of our parishioners.

Estimating population totals

If the data are sufficiently reliable to establish the nature of a parish's Compton return, they can then be used as a basis for estimating, very approximately, its population total. When the

Compton/Hearth tax ratio shows that it recorded inhabitants, for example, the Compton figure can naturally be treated as a surrogate population total, but obviously the other three categories of ratio need to be multiplied by one or more credible multiplying factors.

For those parishes which returned households, a multiplying range similar to that advocated previously for Hearth tax households should be appropriate.[34] This will entail a range of about 3.8 to 4.8, although one might extend the upper limit somewhat to 5 or even 5.2. Alternatively, a simpler but much less reliable method would be to apply a single multiplier of 4.3, which coincides with the median for those places in Table 5 that had 'inhabitant' Compton ratios.

If one accepts 29 to 41 per cent as the reasonable limits for proportions of under sixteen year-olds and 3.8 to 4.8 for the mean household size, then a multiplying range of 1.4 to 1.7 should be applied to the Compton totals which represented adults to indicate the probable outside limits of their population totals. Again a simpler approach which accepts the median ratio of 2.8 as the norm and makes no allowance for variations between the different parishes would suggest a single multiplier of about 1.55. A more sophisticated approach would take account of the precise ratios of each place and apply different multiplying ranges to their Compton totals depending on their ratios. Thus a parish with a low ratio, say 2.4, should have a higher multiplying range than one with 2.8 because if it were multiplied by 1.4 it would give a mean household size of only 3.4. Therefore the Compton totals of those with a ratio of 2.4 should in theory be multiplied by 1.6 to 2.0 in order to yield mean household sizes of between 3.8 and 4.8, while those with a ratio of 3.2 should similarly be multiplied by a figure of 1.2 to 1.5. However, the data are almost certainly too unreliable to bear such sophisticated interpretations so that for safety one might limit the multiplying range of a ratio of 2.4 to, say, 1.5 to 1.7 and of 3.2 to 1.4 to 1.6.

For the category recording adult males, a multiplying range of 2.7 to 3.5 would allow for some imbalance between the sexes, but like all such exercises is rather arbitrary. In this instance a single multiplier of around 3.1 would reflect the median ratio of 1.4 and the assumption of a mean household size of 4.3. Again one might

[34] Arkell, 'Multiplying factors', p.55.

Table 8 Population estimates from the Compton census and Hearth tax: selected parishes from Warwick Deanery

Parish	Compton/ Hearth tax ratio	Compton census total	Compton census multipliers	Hearth tax 1670-4 total	Hearth tax 1670-4 multipliers	Population estimates
Inhabitants					**x3.8-4.8**	
Arrow	4.8	302		63	239-302	302
Adults			**x1.4-1.6**			
Warwick: St Nicholas	3.5	596	834-954	168 (1)	638-806	810-830
Coughton	3.4	331	463-530	97 (1)	369-466	460-470
			x1.4-1.7			
Great Alne	2.9	153	214-260	53 (2)	201-254	220-250
Budbrooke	2.7	163	228-277	61 (2)	232-293	240-270
Claverdon	2.7	244	342-415	89 (1)	338-427	360-410
Warwick: St Mary	2.7	1264	1770-2149	473 (8)	1797-2270	1800-2150
			x1.5-1.7			
Hatton	2.5	273	410-464	110	418-528	420-460
Barford	2.4	178	267-303	73 (1)	277-350	280-300
Ullenhall (chapelry)	2.3	130	195-221	56 (1)	213-269	210-220
Adult males			**x2.7-3.5**			
Tanworth-in-Arden	1.4	400	1080-1400	292 (2)	1110-1402	1110-1400
Rowington	1.3	171	462-599	135 (3)	513-648	520-600
Households			**x3.8-4.8**			
Alcester	1.0	280	1064-1344	275 (2)	1045-1320	1100-1300
Aston Cantlow	1.0	112	426-538	108	410-518	430-500
Henley-in-Arden (chapelry)	1.0	139	528-667	137 (2)	521-658	530-650
Lapworth	1.0	91	346-437	93	353-446	356-430
Wootton Wawen	1.0	62	236-298	65	247-312	250-300

Notes: The figures in brackets after the Hearth tax totals represent dwellings recorded as empty. These have been included in their respective totals and Compton/Hearth tax ratios because empty dwellings were not always recorded as such, especially if their tax had been paid.

consider applying different multiplying ranges to the totals of those with higher and lower ratios, perhaps 3.1 to 3.5 to a ratio of 1.2 and 2.7 to 3.1 for a ratio of 1.6, but such an approach cannot be sustained when there are doubts about the accuracy of the relevant Hearth tax or Compton census data.

A safer method of creating more precise population estimates for individual parishes is to use the Hearth tax returns as an additional contemporary source on their own. A comparison between the spans of different estimates deriving from the Compton census and the Hearth tax totals will often reduce substantially the gap between the estimated outer limits because the less they overlap, the smaller will be the range of the final estimate. The application of this method to a block of relatively large parishes that stretched westward from Warwick across the Arden forest is demonstrated in Table 8. In this exercise the Compton totals for each parish have been multiplied first by a range of multipliers appropriate to their Compton/Hearth tax ratios. Then the largest Hearth tax total from one of the three surviving assessments from 1670 to 1674 has been multiplied by the mean household size range of 3.8 to 4.8. Finally, the probable population estimates for each parish have been derived from a comparison of these two alternative ranges. This span is naturally much greater for some than for others and in one instance there is even no overlap at all, but despite such inconsistencies this approach does help target the probable population totals as closely as the somewhat unreliable nature of the data will allow. In addition, this approach underlines the fact that these totals are estimates rather than enumerations, which the rigid application of a single multiplier often tempts one to assume.[35]

Conclusion

This method of unravelling the secrets of the Compton census is clearly dependent upon the reliability of the Compton returns and Hearth tax lists that are used, as well as upon the ability to match the boundaries of the Compton census places with the areas assessed for the Hearth tax. It will therefore not be applicable to all parts of the country.[36] However, where it can be used it should prove extremely helpful in interpreting the Compton returns, especially when one remembers that the nearer any Compton/Hearth tax ratio comes to the centre of one of the ranges for adult males, adults or inhabitants, the more likely it will be that the suggested interpretation of this particular Compton census figure is correct.

35 See, Edwards, 'Population in Derbyshire', pp.112-5, for another example of the application of this method.

36 Yet this method is applicable to much of Nottinghamshire for example. Whiteman, *Critical edition*, pp.582-8 made some use of it in a way which helps to demonstrate that it could have improved the validity of some of Unwin's rather dubious conclusions that were based on the assumption that the Compton census consistently recorded adults above the age of sixteen. See Unwin, *Nottinghamshire*, pp.31-9; Webster, *Nottinghamshire Hearth tax*.

7

Nonconformity and the Compton census in late seventeenth-century Devon

PETER JACKSON

Introduction

Analysts of the Compton census tend to fall into two camps according to their assessment of the accuracy of the figures for nonconformists: namely those who conclude that for political reasons the returns underestimate the number,[1] and those who claim that, treated with caution, they provide a reasonably reliable record of persistent nonconformity.[2]

The difficulties with interpreting the returns arise partly from the ambiguous wording of the third question asking about nonconformists, as circulated on Archbishop Sheldon's behalf.[3] They arise also because local perceptions of who should be included in the count must have differed widely, even if local instructions supplemented the written instructions when the returns were handed in.[4] Whiteman has investigated the possibility that the results of the enquiry were distorted at the higher levels of ecclesiastical administration in order to keep the ratio of nonconformists to conformists artificially low and concluded that in computing the totals shown in the returns there is no evidence that the registry officials in the dioceses or those making the final totals deliberately falsified their results.[5]

Comparison of the returns of nonconformists made by the churchwardens and/or incumbents to the 1676 census with firstly, returns made by their predecessors and successors to the episcopal and archidiaconal visitations and secondly, those of the

1 Richards, 'Religious census'; Lyon Turner, *Original records* p.57; Chalklin, 'The Compton Census', pp.153-74; Hurwich, 'Nonconformists', p.185.

2 Peyton, 'Religious census', pp.100-4; Spufford, 'Dissenting churches', pp.67-95, esp. pp.94-5, 'Note on the Compton Census'.

3 See Whiteman's chapter above.

4 Whiteman, *Critical edition*, pp.xxix-xxx, xxxvi-xli.

5 See Whiteman's chapter in this volume; Whiteman, *Critical edition*, pp.lxxvii-lxxix.

constables to the quarter sessions, may allow us to detect evidence of deliberate under-reporting at the local level. This may be done particularly effectively for the parishes in the Archdeaconry of Exeter for which we have available both the quarter sessions and episcopal records for the whole of the 1670s and the archdeaconry records for the years 1670 to 1676. A comparison of the names of those prosecuted in each of these courts reveals surprisingly little overlap. Few individuals appear in more than one of these courts; any further presentments were most likely to be in the same court, and it was unlikely that an individual would be presented in another, except after a considerable lapse of time. Therefore it is important in any comparison of the census totals and other presentments for nonconformity to have available the records of all the courts to which nonconformists could be reported. The Exeter records are far more complete than any previously used for the purpose of comparison, comprising the act books of the vicar general's court, containing records of the 1671, 1674 and 1677 episcopal visitations, including some churchwardens' presentments for 1671, archdeaconry act books for the years up to 1676, constables' presentments and quarter sessions order books throughout the decade and records of convictions under the 1670 Conventicle Act. One can also refer to the licences for meeting houses issued under the 1672 Declaration of Indulgence.[6]

Of the 145 parishes in the archdeaconry of Exeter, eighty-seven had at least one nonconformist according to the Compton census, whereas the local records over the 1670s show the presence of nonconformists in 109 parishes (see Appendix to this chapter). The census discloses a total of 1,582 nonconformists in the archdeaconry whereas the other records name only 940 in the 1670s.[7] The former set of figures would lead us to suspect that

6 Devon Record Office [hereafter given as DRO], Vicar General's Court Act Books, C771, C772; Churchwardens' Presentments [hereafter given as CP] Boxes 1-14; Quarter Session [hereafter QS] Order Books 1/10, 1/11; QS 74 Conventicle Act Papers; QS 15 Constables' Presentments; Exeter City Records [hereafter ECR] Conventicle Act Papers; Exeter Cathedral Library [hereafter ECL] Archdeaconry of Exeter [hereafter AE] Act Books 1/1, 1/2; *Calendar of State Papers, Domestic* 1671-72, 1672, 1672-3.

7 In the Appendix to this chapter I have only counted those in column B for the 1670s on the grounds that those prosecuted for absence from church were more likely to have corresponded to those who 'obstinately refuse or wholly absent themselves' rather than the group who were charged with not receiving the sacrament who presumably were otherwise conformable and were attending church. For further discussion of the implications of these figures for the pattern of nonconformity prosecutions in the 1670s and 1680s see Jackson, 'Nonconformists', pp.122-49.

some under-representation occurred in the Compton census, while the latter would tend to the opposite conclusion.

Clearly the figures deserve closer scrutiny. The totals from the local records reveal a wider geographical distribution of nonconformity; thirty parishes are shown to have had nonconformists who were not indicated in the census, while the census indicates nonconformity in eight parishes where no dissenters appear in other records. Of these eight parishes, four show evidence of nonconformity in the 1660s or the 1680s, and another, Venn Ottery, was a tiny parish, usually united with the neighbouring parish of Harpford for which nonconformists appear in the records but not in the census. This leaves only three parishes, Stockleigh English, Combe Raleigh and Feniton, where nonconformists are indicated in the census but nowhere in the local records. Prosecution in the 1670s then appears to have extended to virtually all parishes in which nonconformity was visible in 1676. That it had extended even further is not surprising, since if it had any measure of success, it is not unlikely that there were some parishes where the prosecutions of the early 1670s had produced conformity by 1676.

In the thirty parishes where nonconformists are recorded in the local records but not in the census, virtually all the local instances of prosecutions are recorded in the first half of the 1670s. Of course one must allow that a few of the sixty-eight individuals concerned may have died or moved to another area by 1676. Detailed consideration reveals that four of these parishes had houses licensed for Presbyterian meetings in 1672 and one for a Congregational meeting. This is the only evidence we have of nonconformist activity in the 1670s in three of the parishes: Sheldon, St John's in Exeter and Hemyock. Sheldon was the venue for a Presbyterian conventicle held in the parish church in 1670 and Hemyock had two licensed Presbyterian meetings. The presence of a licensed meeting house, while evidence of a nonconformist interest within a parish, does not seem to have been taken as sufficient to require notice in the Compton census. Of course, even the owners of a house used for meetings might not measure up to the criterion of those who 'obstinately' or 'wholly' absented themselves from church. Presbyterians were frequently partial conformists. Amongst the other nonconformists in these parishes were nine conventiclers, eight Presbyterians and one of unknown denomination; the rest had been presented for absence either by constables or churchwardens. We know the outcome of the proceedings of thirty-three of the cases which came before the ecclesiastical courts involving these individuals; nineteen ended in excommunication, nine appear to have ended with an unsuccessful *viis et modis* citation, two of the accused had fled and three produced a certificate of conformity and were dismissed. It would not appear then, that many of those involved were conformable, even in the face of court prosecution.

One is left with the strong suspicion that in at least some of these parishes the presence of nonconformists was ignored when the Compton census returns were prepared. It is difficult to see how churchwardens and ministers were able to miss nonconformists such as those of Dunsford, particularly William Crusie, a labourer, and probably a Baptist, who was repeatedly presented for absence and conventicling between 1668 and 1675.[8] Also presented in the parish were Crusie's wife and three other men each of whom had been excommunicated for absence from church in either 1674 or 1675. One explanation might be that by 1676 Crusie had moved from the parish of Dunsford.[9] Also ignored in the census was Henry Smeath of Down St Mary who was excommunicated for absence from church in 1674 and 1675 and remained excommunicate until at least 1681.[10] On the other hand there were probably a number of those in the local records similar to the Clarke family of Upton Pyne who made their one major appearance as nonconformists in 1670 when they attended a Presbyterian conventicle in the neighbouring parish of Newton St Cyres.[11] The head of the family, Richard Clarke, was also presented by the churchwardens in November 1668 for not receiving the sacrament, but in reply protested that he was 'otherwise conformable' and would certify to his conformity before the year's end.[12] No doubt, despite their attendance at the Presbyterian conventicle, the family remained conformable and were counted as such in the Compton census.

8 DRO, Churchwardens' Presentments, Box 4, 8 Sept. 1668; DRO, QS 74/31/1, 22 May 1670; DRO, C771, 4 March 1671/2; ECL, AE 1/1, 16 Dec. 1669; ECL, AE 1/2. 20 Nov. 1675.

9 DRO, C771, 4 March 1671/2; ECL, AE 1/2, 4 July 1674, 20 Nov. 1675.

10 ECL, AE 1/2, 20 June, 3 Oct. 1674, 26 Jan. 1674/5, 27 Nov. 1675, 29 Jan. 1675/6; ECL, AE 1/3, 4 June 1681.

11 DRO, QS 74/32, 13 June 1670, conviction of Richard, Mary and Judith Clarke and their servant John Roberts.

12 DRO, PR/D/6/56, 23 Nov. 1668.

The geographical distribution of nonconformity

Although the evidence is not entirely straightforward, it would appear that the census and local records agree reasonably well regarding the distribution of dissent. There is no evidence of widespread avoidance of reporting the presence of nonconformity, or that nonconformists in parishes in which their presence was reported in 1676 totally avoided prosecution. There remains the possibility, of course, that there were some parishes where the presence of nonconformity was not acknowledged in either prosecutions or census returns.

If then the distribution of nonconformity among the parishes of Devon indicated by the local records and the census coincide reasonably well, the substantial difference between the numbers of nonconformists reported in the census and known from local records would indicate that they were overestimated in the census, or that many remained unprosecuted in the courts. A closer examination of the figures supports both conjectures as far as the urban parishes are concerned. While the census records 1,177 nonconformists in the parishes with urban centres or major markets (that is, Thorncombe, Honiton, Axminster, Tiverton, Bampton, Bradninch, Cullompton, Ottery St Mary, St Thomas and the Exeter parishes), the local records show only 468 prosecutions. At Thorncombe, Axminster and Tiverton the number of nonconformists in the census could only have been obtained by an extremely complete return which included all the members of dissenters' families. The totals are larger than the number of dissenters from each town identified from all local sources over the whole period from 1660 to 1689. The under-representation of urban nonconformists in the local records may be attributable to the fact that boroughs such as Honiton, Tiverton, Bradninch and Cullompton held their own borough courts, at which nonconformists may have been prosecuted.[13] On the other hand, it may also indicate the favourable conditions which large urban parishes afforded to the nonconformists, enabling them to escape prosecution. The only urban centres which are exceptions to this pattern are Ottery St Mary, Bradninch and Exeter. The case for Exeter, for which the Compton census gives only 122 nonconformists whereas the local records include 140 names, is special in two ways: on the one hand, directly under the gaze of

[13] The records of these courts unfortunately have not survived.

the bishop, it may provide one of the few examples where the numbers of nonconformists were systematically underestimated; on the other, most of the parishes (twenty in all) were small or very small, so that it should have been possible for the incumbent and churchwardens to know what was going on.[14]

The low number of prosecutions in Exeter for absence from church or conventicling in the 1680s might, however, indicate that vigorous measures in the 1660s and early 1670s had had their effect. In the 1680s proportionately more Exeter dissenters, apart from Quakers, were being charged with offences, such as not partaking of communion, rather than absence from church. This perhaps suggests a growth in partial conformity resulting from the campaign of prosecutions by the Exeter magistrates and the preaching of Presbyterians such as Robert Atkins and George Trosse urging dissenters not to weaken the Church of England.[15]

At Bradninch, the presence of a fervently anti-dissenter justice and a strong Quaker congregation probably ensured the maximum number of prosecutions. However, the fifteen nonconformists recorded in the census were probably less than the Quaker strength in the parish, which may have stood at between twenty and thirty during the 1670s. The parish also contained some Presbyterians. At Ottery St Mary the virulence of the campaign against the Presbyterian minister, Robert Collins, probably resulted in a particularly high number of people being convicted for conventicling. The likelihood is that the prosecutions were particularly thorough and netted a number whose nonconformity was partial or temporary and who would have probably escaped prosecution had they lived elsewhere. With these possible exceptions then, it would appear that in the urban parishes of Devon, the number of nonconformists was not likely to have been understated. It is, of course, difficult to feel much confidence in the accuracy of such an estimate as the 500 nonconformists listed for Tiverton, but it should be noted that it was a very large parish.[16]

A completely reversed relationship appears if we consider the figures for the rural parishes alone. In them, the census indicates

14 See chapter by Whiteman above.

15 Calamy, *Account*, p.215; Trosse, *Life of Trosse*.

16 On the controversy concerning the population of Tiverton parish in the seventeenth century, see Whiteman, *Critical edition*, p.269, fn.2.

a nonconformist population of 408, while the local records show 469. In the Honiton, Dunkeswell, Tiverton and Dunsford deaneries and in a high proportion of parishes the figures obtained from the two sources agree fairly well. However, in Plymtree, Kenn, Aylesbeare and Cadbury deaneries the discrepancies are larger. In Plymtree deanery the census figures appear too low for Buckerell, where we know of a large population of Presbyterians, whereas at Broadhembury and Silverton they are considerably higher than the numbers appearing in the local records. In Kenn deanery the census figures are consistently below those of the local records. This is also the case in Aylesbeare deanery, except in the parishes of Farringdon, Sidmouth and Woodbury, where the census numbers are slightly higher than the local records indicate. In Cadbury deanery there is a mixture of discrepancies on both sides, the largest being the census's under-representation of nonconformity at Thorverton and Cheriton Fitzpaine. It is, of course, impossible to offer explanations for all these discrepancies, although it is likely that slight under-representation in the census may indicate that some of the nonconformists prosecuted in the courts may have conformed for the occasion of the census. On the other hand – and this is a consideration of the first importance – some over-representation may be due to the requirement that all nonconformists be counted in the census rather than the number of families, whereas the courts tended to prosecute heads of households rather than whole families.

Quakers in the Compton census

On the whole it would appear that, with a few exceptions, most of the known Quakers were counted (Devon had few Baptists). They appear in the figures for parishes such as Thorncombe, Honiton, Axminster, Membury, Upottery, Churchstanton, Holcombe Rogus, Burlescombe, Cullompton and Colaton Raleigh. Indeed, in most cases where a sizeable number of nonconformists are recorded in rural parishes they are almost certainly Quakers. On the other hand, it is equally clear that substantial numbers of Presbyterians and Independents were counted. They can be positively identified in some parishes where we are fairly sure that few or no Quakers or Baptists lived, such as Buckerell, Halberton, Loxbeare and Nether Exe. More often they appear in the census in ones or twos in individual parishes rather than in groups like the Quakers. Broadly this corresponds with the pattern of prosecutions of nonconformists in Devon. Although the Presbyterians were undoubtedly the most numerous sect it is always the Quakers who are the most obvious in official records. The Quakers were certainly the most keenly-felt thorn in the side of ecclesiastical and civil officials in Devon between 1660 and 1689 and beyond. They were the group most resistant to the sporadic official campaigns against dissenters which netted large numbers of Presbyterians and Independents, as well as Quakers, in the early 1670s and early 1680s. As the resolve of the mainstream nonconformists dwindled and more resorted to partial conformity, it was the Quakers who bore the brunt of official prosecution.[17]

Conclusion

Overall one can say that in rural Devon the criteria which the churchwardens and incumbents used to decide who to count as a nonconformist for purposes of the census appear to be fairly close to the criteria upon which prosecutions for absence from church and attendance at conventicles were based. Yet in the urban areas of Devon the situation is more uncertain. In other words these figures do not provide any evidence of systematic or gross distortion of the number of nonconformists.

17 See Jackson, 'Nonconformists', chapter 4.

Appendix

NONCONFORMITY IN THE ARCHDEACONRY OF EXETER

A comparison between the Compton census and local records of nonconformity.

A) Rural parishes

Parish	1676 Compton census	1660s Prosecutions for absense	1660s Other prosecutions	1670s Prosecutions for absence	1670s Other prosecutions	1680s Prosecutions for absence	1680s Other prosecutions
	Number of nonconformists						
Honiton Deanery							
Offwell	-	1	-	4	-	-	4
South Leigh	-	1	1	2	-	2	-
Gittisham	-	1	-	2	-	3	1
Kilmington	5	-	-	6	-	13	7
Musbury	1	5	-	1	-	5	-
Membury	13	4	-	18	-	31	40
Combpyne	-	1	1	1	-	10	-
Axmouth	3	1	-	1	-	2	-
North Leigh	2	-	-	3	1	5	-
Seaton	3	13	-	1	-	10	12
Widworthy	-	-	-	-	-	-	-
Uplyme	2	5	-	4	-	28	6
Farway	-	-	2	2	-	-	11
Cotleigh	6	-	-	1	3	-	3
Totals	35	32	4	46	4	109	84
Dunkeswell Deanery							
Awliscombe	1	4	-	4	2	4	3
Dunkeswell	-	-	-	-	-	-	-
Upottery	13	3	2	9	1	2	20
Sheldon	-	-	-	1	-	-	-
Yarcombe	5	2	-	3	-	4	4
Clayhidon	1	1	-	3	-	2	11
Hemyock	-	-	-	2	5	5	4
Combe Raleigh	1	-	-	-	2	-	-
Luppitt	6	6	-	5	1	9	2
Churchstanton	10	-	-	11	-	19	-
Totals	37	16	2	38	11	45	44

Parish	Number of nonconformists						
	1676	1660s		1670s		1680s	
	Compton census	Prosecutions for absense	Other prosecutions	Prosecutions for absence	Other prosecutions	Prosecutions for absence	Other prosecutions
Tiverton Deanery							
Halberton	68	3	3	26	-	34	11
Bickleigh	2	-	-	-	-	1	-
Willand	5	-	1	3	-	1	-
Sampford Peverell	9	3	-	12	-	30	1
Uplowman	6	-	-	3	-	9	-
Huntsham	-	-	-	1	-	-	-
Loxbeare	2	-	-	17	-	1	-
Morebath	1	-	-	1	-	-	-
Hockworthy	-	-	-	-	1	2	-
Calverleigh	3	-	-	3	-	-	2
Holcombe Rogus	13	1	-	20	-	17	-
Burlescombe	13	1	-	25	-	20	-
Clayhanger	-	-	-	3	-	-	2
Washfield	10	7	-	11	-	6	1
Totals	132	15	4	125	1	121	17
Plymtree Deanery							
Buckerell	25	15	2	34	-	2	5
Plymtree	1	2	-	1	13	7	-
Clyst Hydon	-	-	-	1	8	-	-
Payhembury	3	1	1	4	-	5	8
Kentisbeare	6	1	1	8	-	13	2
Broadhembury	25	5	-	9	-	20	19
Talaton	7	4	17	4	-	-	8
Feniton	2	-	-	-	-	-	20
Silverton	13	5	6	2	2	2	15
Rewe	2	-	-	3	28	10	-
Butterleigh	1	-	-	1	1	9	-
Clyst St Lawrence	1	-	-	1	-	-	-
Totals	86	33	27	68	52	68	77
Kenn Deanery							
Kenton	2	2	-	8	-	3	16
Ashcombe	-	-	-	-	-	1	1
Exminster	3	-	-	4	-	3	-
Dunchideock	-	-	-	1	3	15	8
Trusham	-	-	-	-	-	3	-
Alphington	3	1	-	5	5	-	1
Shillingford	-	-	-	-	-	-	-
Kenn	2	1	2	3	3	-	8

Parish	Number of nonconformists						
	1676	1660s		1670s		1680s	
	Compton census	Prosecutions for absense	Other prosecutions	Prosecutions for absence	Other prosecutions	Prosecutions for absence	Other prosecutions
Shaldon	-	-	-	-	-	-	-
East Ogwell	-	-	-	-	-	-	-
West Ogwell	-	-	-	3	-	-	-
Stokeinteignhead	-	-	-	-	-	-	3
Combeinteignhead	-	-	-	-	-	2	1
Powderham	-	-	-	3	-	-	-
Mamhead	-	-	-	1	6	-	3
Totals	10	4	2	28	17	27	41
Aylesbeare Deanery							
Lympstone	5	-	1	12	7	-	25
Sowton	-	2	-	-	2	2	-
Aylesbeare	2	10	-	5	2	2	3
Clyst St George	-	1	-	2	-	-	-
Broadclyst	2	10	2	6	1	1	16
Pinhoe	3	1	2	7	-	3	6
Rockbeare	3	1	-	5	-	1	-
Whimple	-	-	-	4	2	-	1
Huxham	-	-	-	-	-	-	2
Farringdon	11	1	-	7	-	-	3
Poltimore	-	-	-	1	-	-	-
Clyst St Mary	-	-	-	-	-	-	-
Withycombe Raleigh	-	-	-	-	-	2	-
Sidmouth	14	4	-	11	-	8	12
Venn Ottery	1	-	-	-	-	-	-
Harpford	-	1	-	2	-	-	-
Colaton Raleigh	6	8	-	15	10	3	2
Bicton	-	-	-	-	-	-	-
East Budleigh	-	-	-	1	-	5	-
Otterton	2	-	-	7	-	2	-
Woodbury	10	1	-	6	-	4	-
Totals	59	40	5	91	24	33	70
Cadbury Deanery							
Poughill	-	-	-	1	-	1	6
Cadbury	1	2	-	1	2	2	-
Newton St Cyres	1	-	-	1	-	4	9
Cadeleigh	1	-	3	1	4	7	9
Down St Mary	-	1	-	2	-	2	4
Upton Hellions	-	-	-	-	-	-	1
Shobrooke	5	2	-	2	14	3	15

Parish	Number of nonconformists						
	1676	1660s		1670s		1680s	
	Compton census	Prosecutions for absense	Other prosecutions	Prosecutions for absence	Other prosecutions	Prosecutions for absence	Other prosecutions
Nether Exe	-	1	-	2	-	-	20
Thorverton	9	3	2	19	-	3	14
Upton Pyne	-	-	2	3	2	1	1
Cheriton Fitzpaine	1	12	-	5	-	-	1
Brampford Speke	-	-	-	1	4	-	1
Stockleigh English	2	-	-	-	-	-	5
Stockleigh Pomeroy	2	2	-	4	8	-	9
Totals	22	23	7	42	34	23	95
Dunsford Deanery							
Drewsteignton	6	3	1	6	-	4	7
Christow	8	-	4	6	-	2	4
Holcombe Burnell	-	-	2	-	1	-	-
Tedburn St Mary	3	-	-	1	-	5	-
South Tawton	1	-	-	-	-	3	-
Hittisleigh	-	2	-	-	3	1	-
Spreyton	-	-	2	-	-	-	-
Ashton	-	-	-	-	-	-	-
Cheriton Bishop	4	2	-	9	-	3	5
Gidleigh	-	-	-	-	-	-	-
Bridford	5	-	-	2	-	2	-
Throwleigh	-	-	-	-	-	-	-
Chagford	-	-	-	-	-	-	-
Doddiscombsleigh	-	-	2	-	1	-	-
Dunsford	-	1	-	5	-	-	-
Whitestone	-	1	-	2	1	-	-
Totals	27	9	11	31	6	20	16
Rural total	408	172	62	469	149	446	444

B) Urban parishes

Parish	1676 Compton census	1660s Prosecutions for absense	1660s Other prosecutions	1670s Prosecutions for absence	1670s Other prosecutions	1680s Prosecutions for absence	1680s Other prosecutions
Thorncombe	162	29	1	34	2	48	8
Honiton	36	6	3	12	-	22	42
Axminster	175	-	-	5	-	68	7
Tiverton	500	3	5	67	6	109	5
Bampton	74	22	-	23	1	54	42
Bradninch	15	36	1	55	8	33	13
Cullompton	60	19	-	38	8	102	40
St Thomas	17	-	-	26	-	33	14
Ottery St Mary	16	13	-	68	4	28	2
Deanery of Christianity (Exeter)							
St Sidwell	34	-	-	13	-	12	2
St Olave	-	-	-	1	-	1	3
St Mary Steps	2	-	-	-	-	1	3
St Stephen	-	-	8	7	5	1	-
St John	-	-	-	1	-	-	30
St George	12	1	-	3	-	-	18
Holy Trinity	18	-	1	43	1	-	8
St Mary Major	8	-	-	10	-	1	3
St Edmund	-	-	-	5	-	-	2
St Pancras	-	-	-	-	-	-	-
St Martin	3	-	-	-	-	2	-
St Petrock	6	1	-	5	1	5	7
St Lawrence	-	6	-	-	-	-	24
St Paul	8	-	1	1	-	10	-
All Hallows on the Wall	-	-	-	-	-	-	-
St David	21	-	-	43	12	9	22
All Hallows Goldsmith Street	2	-	-	3	-	2	-
St Mary Arches	-	-	-	3	-	-	6
St Leonard	4	-	-	-	-	-	-
St Kerrian	4	-	-	2	-	2	13
Exeter Total	122	8	10	140	19	46	141
Urban Total	1172	136	20	468	48	543	314

Number of nonconformists (columns above).

Source: For the sources of this table see footnote 6 of this chapter.

Part II

Poll taxes & the Marriage Duty Act

INTRODUCING THE DOCUMENTS

The principal sources that are examined in the second part of this volume are the assessment lists created by the various Poll taxes and the Marriage Duty legislation. As with the Hearth tax, the format of these surviving documents is highly variable, and consequently their usefulness to the historian is governed as much by the conscientiousness of the local officials responsible for their creation as by the intention and wording of the relevant legislation. The latter, together with the administrative framework, is described in some detail in the following chapter by Tom Arkell. This section, therefore, simply provides a brief guide to the general physical appearance of these lists, in terms of format and structure.

Clearly, the appearance of such lists varies from place to place. One of the most detailed Poll tax lists known to have survived is the one for Kettlewell Ward in King's Lynn, Norfolk, for the first quarterly Poll of 1692 (Illustration 2.1). This remarkable list is rich not only in nominal information, with the names of children and servants, but also in recording occupations and the ages of those under twenty-one. The compiler of this list was exceptionally meticulous in his task so that the detail included here enables one to determine the beginning and end of each household, even though they have not been indicated, and also to identify, for example, the two step-children of Samuel Soames. Interestingly only one person in the illustration given here, the tanner Matthew Markant, was liable to pay more than the basic poll of one shilling a quarter.

A later list for Kettlewell Ward, that of 1694 (Illustration 2.2) is, however, more representative of the norm for a fuller Poll tax list. No ages are recorded and there is less consistency in the recording of names, so that here, for instance, unlike in the previous example, it would be difficult to determine the precise relationship between Thomas and widow Platfoote. It is important to note that the alterations and additions made to both lists illustrate the fact that they were dynamic working documents recording the changes relevant to four collections during the course of a single year. Both illustrations contain several alterations, indicating a change of circumstance. At the foot of one page it can be seen that an entry for a servant was crossed out with the note 'gone into Lincolnshire', while in the earlier list the entry for Robert Platfoot has been scratched out and changed to read 'Widow Platfoot'. Reference to the subsequent list shows that the new entry was amended accordingly. Clearly, this relatively rare opportunity to compare subsequent listings over time can greatly enrich the information given in a single document, a point forcefully demonstrated in the chapter by Sheila Cooper below.

The earlier assessment list of 1678 for Wellesbourne Hastings, Warwickshire (Illustration 2.3) is equally thorough, but for the demographic historian the names are arranged in a less useful order than is the case for King's Lynn. In this Warwickshire example each of the first nineteen entries gives relatively detailed information about the members of the more substantial families living in the constabulary. Only the first three, headed by a baronet, a gentleman and the vicar, were liable for more than the basic poll of one shilling per head and, since the entry for the last was amended subsequently, it appears as if the vicar may have attempted initially to avoid paying his surtax. However, it is impossible to determine the composition of each household because the thirty-three servants who worked for these families are listed separately, with the male servants being followed by the females. The reason for this, as explained in chapter 8 below, is because the servants had to pay a graduated tax on their wages in addition to the basic poll. The second page of this list, which is not illustrated, concludes in strict social status order with nineteen separate entries for the labourers and their wives or widows. However, unlike in King's Lynn, their children together with everyone receiving poor relief were exempt from the tax and consequently omitted from the list.

In general most of the lists that survive for the earlier Poll taxes cover rural areas, while those from the 1690s are mainly urban. It is also important to stress that many of the lists that survive record far less nominal and occupational information than those illustrated here. It must also be realised that because of the exemptions from the taxes, which varied considerably between the different Poll taxes, none provides a complete enumeration of the community or parish in question.

In contrast the best of the Marriage Duty assessment lists were virtually complete local censuses arranged by household. The one for the parish of St John, Southampton, for 1695 (Illustration 2.4) is a particularly good example of such a document. Each residential unit is bracketed together in the margin and, except for wives, the names of all its members are given as well as their status in the household – children, relatives, servants or boarders. The five columns on the right-hand side record the various duties for which these enumerated people would become liable if they died, got married or had children during the subsequent twelve months. As a consequence only the widowed and unmarried of marriageable age were listed as being liable for the marriage duty and the married for the birth duty. On this page of the document Thomas Hobs alone was liable to pay the tax on bachelors aged twenty-five or over and widowers without children – and this detail was added as an afterthought. Altogether only two boarders in widow Etheridge's household (as sons of a gentleman) were liable to pay a surcharge above the basic rates. No one was recorded here as having an income of £50 per annum or a personal estate worth at least £600, but interestingly in the following year both Richard Taunton senior and junior were included in this category.

Much more exceptionally, a return also exists for all the duties that were actually collected in St John, Southampton for the year May 1695 to April 1696 (Illustration 2.5). It is interesting to note in this return the abbreviation of '7ber', '8ber' for September, October and so on, but of far greater importance is the relatively small number of burials (9), births (11) and marriages (3) that were taxed during the year in this parish. Because the parish of St John was quite small in terms of population, numbering just under 150, it is therefore plausible that the list equates to the 'real' total of events, but unfortunately a cross-check with the contemporary parish registers for St John is not possible. However, the results of a similar exercise conducted for London are presented in the chapter by Jeremy Boulton.

The assessment list of 1702 for the Bristol parish of All Saints (Illustration 2.6) is more representative of the norm for most Marriage Duty assessments because the residential units are not clearly delineated. Consequently, the identification of household boundaries must depend on implicit rather than explicit information. This is possible when the relationships and status of all the individuals are recorded, but if boarders and lodgers, for example, are not specified explicitly it becomes impossible to tell if they might not have been the heads of separate small households or, in this list, whether Mrs Mary Roberts headed her own household or belonged to that of George Chard and his sister. Unfortunately, such uncertainties make lists like this too problematical for a detailed analysis of household structure along the lines undertaken by Kevin Schurer below.

The assessment of 1697 for Braybrooke, Northamptonshire (Illustration 2.7) demonstrates the extent to which other lists can be even less informative on the crucial issues of residential groups, relationships and status. Family groupings clearly do exist here, as the names suggest, yet it is impossible to determine where one household ends and the next begins, let alone who were servants, boarders or the like. Unfortunately, a list such as this is, therefore, of very limited use for historical research.

Lastly, it is interesting to note that among the virtually complete collection of Marriage Duty assessments that have survived for the City of London (see chapters 9 and 11 below) that for St Benet, Paul's Wharf in London for 1695 (Illustration 2.8) contained the household of Gregory King listed among the Herald's Office. From this we can discover that he was taxed as an Esquire and that one of his servants was aged over twenty-five. In the assessment for the following year his houshold also contained a female servant (see Peter Laslett's chapter above). These were the servants who, no doubt, ministered to King and his wife while he wrestled with the various drafts of his *Natural and Political Observations*, his Scheme for 1688 and most of the calculations recorded in his *Burns Journal*. The extent of under-enumeration in these lists together with the revenue gained from both the Marriage Duty and the Poll taxes was, indeed, one of the issues which much concerned King and also forms the core of the discussion in the chapter which follows.

Illustration 2.1 Poll tax – Kettlewell Ward, King's Lynn, Norfolk, 1692

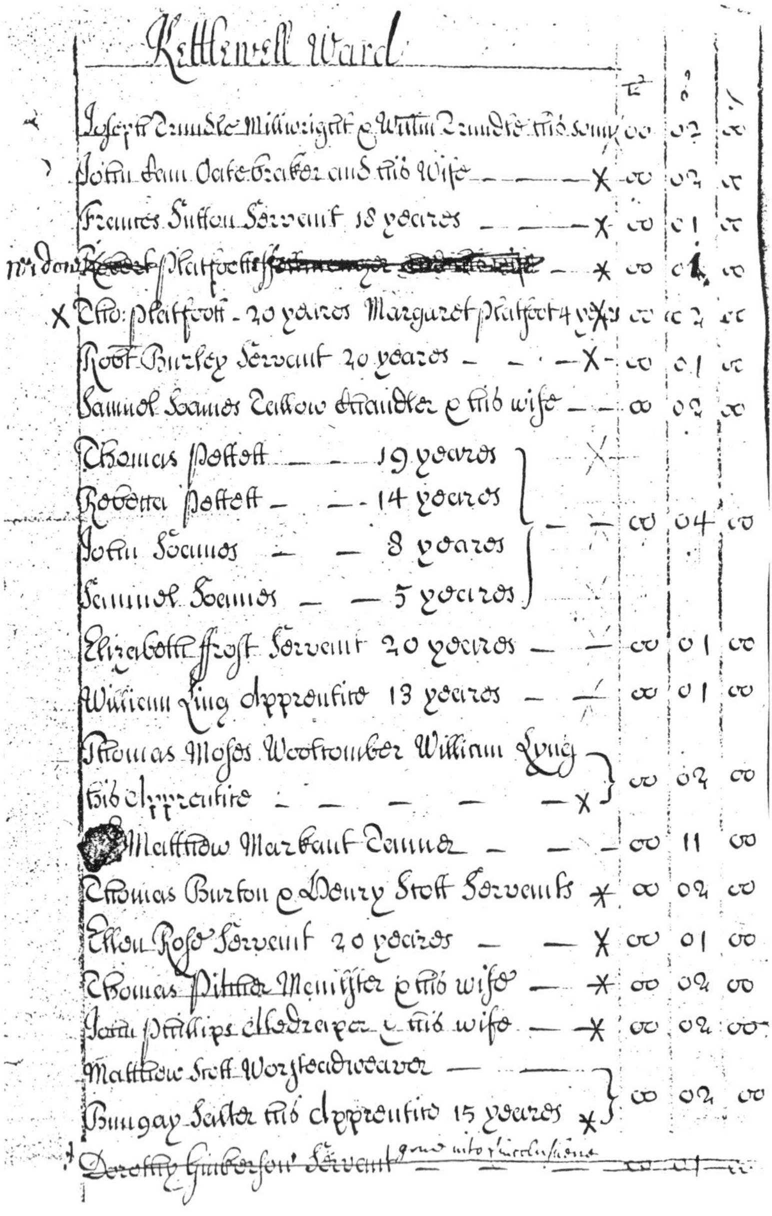

Kettlewell Ward

		li	s	d
	Joseph Trundle Millwright & Willm Trundle his sonn	00	02	00
	John Fenn Oatebraker and his Wife — X	00	02	00
	Frances Sutton Servant 18 yeares — X	00	01	00
widow	[struck] Plattfoott [struck] — *	00	01	00
X	Tho: Plattfoott - 20 yeares Margaret Plattfoot 4 yeares X	00	02	00
	Robt Burley Servant 20 yeares — X	00	01	00
	Samuel Seames Tallow Chandler & his wife	00	02	00
	Thomas Pottott 19 yeares; Roberta Pottott 14 yeares; John Seames 8 yeares; Samuel Seames 5 yeares	00	04	00
	Elizabeth Frost Servant 20 yeares	00	01	00
	William King Apprentice 13 yeares	00	01	00
	Thomas Moses Woolcomber William Lyng his Apprentice — X	00	02	00
	Matthew Marchant Tanner	00	11	00
	Thomas Burton & Henry Stott Servants *	00	02	00
	Ellen Rose Servant 20 yeares — X	00	01	00
	Thomas Pitcher Minister & his wife — *	00	02	00
	John Phillips Woolendraper & his wife — *	00	02	00
	Matthew Stott Worstedweaver; Bungay Salter his Apprentice 15 yeares *	00	02	00
	[struck] Dorothy Gimberson Servant — gone into Lincolnshire	[struck] 00	01	00

Illustration 2.2 Poll tax – Kettlewell Ward, King's Lynn, Norfolk, 1694

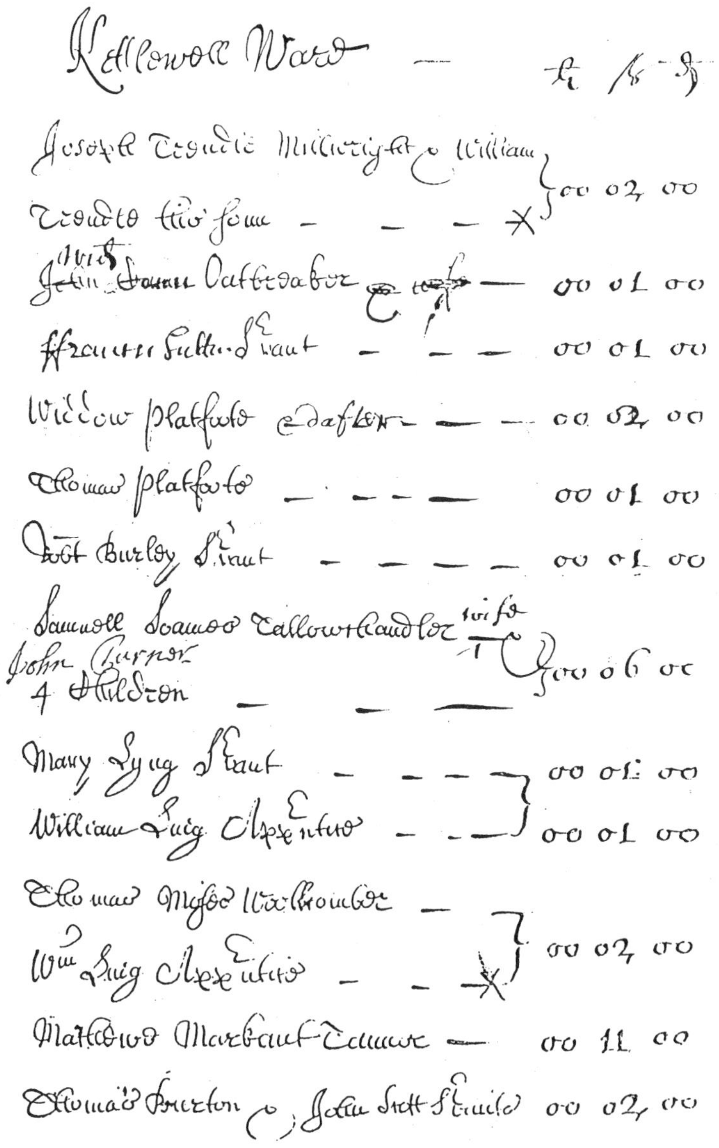

Kettlewell Ward — li s d

Joseph Trendle Millwright & William Trendle his sonne — X } 00 02 00

~~John~~ Anne ~~Danne~~ Oatbreadbaker ~~& wife~~ — 00 01 00

ffrancis Sutton Servant — 00 01 00

Widdow Platfoote & daughter — 00 02 00

Thomas Platfoote — 00 01 00

~~Robt~~ Burley Servant — 00 01 00

Samuell Seames Tallowchandler wife John Turner 4 children — } 00 06 00

Mary Lyng Servant — } 00 01 00

William Lyng Apprentice — } 00 01 00

Thomas Myles Watchmaker —

Wm Lyng Apprentice — X } 00 02 00

Matthew Marchant Tanner — 00 11 00

Thomas Burton & John Stott Servants 00 02 00

Illustration 2.3 Poll tax – Wellesbourne Hastings, Warwickshire, 1678

Hastings — A Certificate for ye Raising Money by ye Poll of all ye Names Sirnames Qualities & Degrees of Every person dwelling within the Constablry of Wellsborne Hastings viz

		£	s	d
Imps —	Sr Jno Mordant Kt & Bart	13	01	00
	Jno Nikolls Gent his wife & one Child	1	03	00
	Mr Robt Jones Vicar his wife & 2 Children	0	04	—
	Leonard Hawkings Husbandman his wife & 3 Children	0	05	00
	Jno Nason husbandman & Eliza: his sister	0	02	00
	Rich Rose husband & 3 Children	0	04	00
	Robt Hopper Husband his wife & 2 Children	0	04	00
	Nath Jackson his wife & one Child Husband	0	03	00
	Tho Yorke husband his wife & 2 Children	0	04	00
	Jno Hopper husband his wife & 1 Child	0	03	—
	Tho: Yorke Jun his wife & 2 Children Husband	0	04	00
	Tho: Jackson Sen: Husbandman	0	01	00
	Susanah Jackson Widdow & 5 Children	0	06	00
	Sam Jackson husband his wife & 2 Children	0	04	00
	Ellinor Tyler Widdow & 1 Child	0	02	00
	Tho: Jackson husband wife & 1 Child	0	03	00
	Tho: Jackson Jun his wife & 1 Child	0	03	00
	Rich Newcombe Carrier his wife & 2 Child	0	04	—
	Tho: Hyman Innkeeper his wife & 4 Children	0	06	00
Servant Men	Tho: Parker his wages and Poll	0	04	00
	Robt Moore	0	04	00
	Jno Salmon	0	03	00
	Jno Jones	0	04	00
	Sam: Carlis	0	04	00
	William Edwards	0	04	—
	William Clarke	0	03	00
	Edward Marshall	0	04	—
	John Cox	0	04	00
	Thomas Dun	0	02	00
	William Hall	0	04	—
	William Ward	0	04	00
	William Blunt	0	04	—
	Tho: Hyarne	0	04	—
	Sam: Martin	0	04	00
	Rich Baskeke	0	02	00
	Tho: Wellings	0	04	—
	Robt Nutt	0	04	00
	Steph: Downes	0	03	—
	~~William Ellings~~	0	0	00
Servant Maids	Dorothy Phipps her wages & Poll	0	02	00
	Mary Sharsham	0	02	—
	Mary Maycocke	0	02	—
	Mary Terrill	0	02	—
	Jane Cross	0	02	—
	Elizabeth Gregg	0	02	—
	Mary Horton	0	02	00
	Ann Houte	0	02	00

Illustations 2.4 Marriage Duty assessment – St John, Southampton, 1695

You are to collect the severall sumes on each person in the parish of St John's according to their degree, as appears in these collums, as Batchelor, widdowers and Births, and Burialls, Marridges & such as are of 50£ per annum – and also for all those on whom any thing hath come due according to the Act, by birth, buriall, or marridge from ye 1st of may 1695	for those of 50£ or more or 600£ 20	for Widdowers & Batchelors yearly 1	Births 2	Burialls 4	Marridges 2.6
Rich Taunton Senr	00	0	02	4	0–0
his wife	00	0	0	4	0–0
Rich: Taunton Junr	00	0	02	4	0–0
his wife	00	0	02	4	0–0
Children: Rich Taunton	00	00	0	4	0–6
John Taunton	00	00	0	4	2.6
Mary Taunton	00	00	0	4	2.6
Neece Ann Tampton	00	00	0	4	2.6
Servant: Thomas Hobbs – batchelor	00	00	0	4	2.6
Servant: Martha Kelley	00	00	0	4	2.6
Mrs Elleredg widow	00	00	0	4	2.6
Children: William Elleredg	00	00	0	4	2.6
Edward Elleredg	00	00	0	4	
Eliza: Elleredg	00	00	0	4	
Borders: Lazarus Cole	00	00	0	4	2.6
Robert Cole	00	00	0	4	2.6
Edward Barton the sonn of a Gentleman	00	00	0.0	1.4	1.2.6
Charles Barton the sonn of a Gentleman	00	00	00	1.1.6	1.2.6
Servant: John Hunt	00	00	00	4	0.2.6
Servant: Mary Knight	00	00	00	4	0.2.6
Mr Paul Conradt	00	00	02	4	00
his wife	00	00	00	4	00
Children: Ann Conradt	00	00	00	04	2.6
John Conradt	00	00	00	04	0.6
Eliza: Conradt	00	00	00	04	
Servant: Jeane Bibley	00	00	00	04	2.6
Elizabeth Hustel widow	00	00	00	04	2.6
Children: William Hustell	00	00	00	04	
Mary Hustell	00	00	00	04	
Sarah Swiar widow	00	00	00	04	2.6
Children: Thomas Swiars	00	00	00	04	
Sarah Swiars	00	00	00	04	
her mother Sarah Furr-bush widow	00	00	00	04	2.6
Joan Fryar widdow	00	00	00	04	2.6
Child: William Fryar	00	00	00	04	
Rich: Smith	00	00	00	04	
his wife	00	00	00	04	
Children: Rich: Smith	00	00	00	04	
Joseph Smith	00	00	00	04	
Daniel Smith	00	00	00	04	
Rebekka Smith	00	00	00	04	
her mother Susana Ballett	00	00	00	04	
Mr John Harwood	00	00	00	04	
his wife	00	00	00	04	
Servant: Joan Fryar	00	00	00	04	2.6
Mary Lannum widdow	00	00	00	04	2.6
Children: Mary Lannum	00	00	00	04	
Elizabeth Lannum	00	[illegible]	[illegible]	[illegible]	

Illustration 2.5 **Marriage Duty Act – List of duties collected for St John, Southampton, 1695-6**

1695	St Johns Parish in Southampton	Burialls s: d	Births s: d	Marridges s: d	Widdowers s: d	Batchelors s: d
18 May	Buried Sisly ye wife of Wm Gibbings	4:0				
30 ditto	Buried Eliz: ye Daught: of Wm Gibbings	4:0				
11 June	Buried Jean Hullett	4:0				
28 June	Maried Geo: Amey & Mary Rummy			2:6		
6 July	Born Eliz: ye Daughter of Walt: Taylor		2:0			
21 Augu:	Born Mary ye Daught of Tho: Huckland		2:0			
8: 7ber	Born Eliz: ye Daught: of Jon Dennis		2:0			
3: 8ber	Buried Jean ye Wife of Jon Lives	4:0				
24: ditto	Born Margart ye Daught: of Jon Sibberell		2:0			
15: 9ber	Buried Jean ye Wife of Tho: Combs	4:0				
21: ditto	Married Wm Gibbings & Eliz: Arnold			2:6		
24: ditto	Born Lucey ye Daught: of Christ: Corminess		2:0			
1: 10ber	Born Ellioner ye Daught: of Wm Henry		2:0			
20: ditto	Buried Mary ye Daught: of Tho: Huckland	4:0				
26 ditto	Born Jon ye Son of Jon Pyas		2:0			
1 Janr	Born Eliz: ye Daught: of Edw: White		2:0			
10 Janr	Born Benjam: ye Son of Jon Shirley		2:0			
21 ditto	Married Jon Goldring & Sarah Buckland			2:6		
6 Febru:	Buried Amey ye Wife of Geo: Wilshear	4:0				
10 ditto	Buried Jon ye Son of Rich: Panton Junr	4:0				
12 Aprill	Buried Rich: Speed	4:0				
12 ditto	Born Martha ye Daught: of Mattw James		2:0			
20 ditto	Born Eliz: Amey ye Daught of Geo: Amey		2:0			
	Tho: Hedges Widower				1:0	
	Tho: Hobbs Batchelor					1:0
	Wm Manners Batchelor					1:0
	£ 03:08:06					

Illustration 2.6 Marriage Duty assessment – All Saints, Bristol, 1702

A Rate and Assessment Made on ye Parish of all saints in the City & County of Bristoll by Virtue of an Act of Parliamt for granting to her Majesty Certaine Rates & Dutys upon Mariadges Births & Burialls And upon batchellors & Widdowers for ye yeare 1702

	Burialls	Births	Marriages	Batchelors & widdowers
	li s d	li s d	li s d	li s d
Mr Thomas Hendy				
Grace his wife	0:4:0	0:2:0		
two servants				
Mr John Cure 600 man				
Eliz his wife & 1 child ...	1:4:0	0:12:0		
three servants	0:14:0			
Mr Tho: Hopper	0:4:0			
Ann his wife & 5 children	0:4:0	0:2:0		
Mrs Rodwood his mother				
two servants				
George Chald & sister	0:4:0			
Mrs Mary Roberts widdo 600				
Two servants	0:14:0			
Mrs Dorothy Horne wido 600	0:4:0			
Charles her son	0:14:0			
one servant	0:14:0	0:0:0	0:12:6	
Mr Edw: Thornhill 600	0:4:0			
Eliz his wife & Edw: his kinsman	1:4:0	0:12:0		
Two servants	0:14:0	0:0:0	0:12:6	
Mr Peter Wakely widdower	0:4:0			
Joseph Wakely	1:4:0	0:12:0	1:2:6	0:6:0
three servants	0:4:0	0:0:0	0:2:6	
Mr Frances Exley				
Mr Chauncy & 2 children	0:4:0	0:2:0	0:2:6	
two servants				
Mr Whitchurch Phippen 600				
Mary his wife & 2 children	0:4:0	0:12:0		
Three servants	0:14:0			
Maddam Hicks wido of alderman Hicks	0:4:0			
Mr Henry Combs 600	0:4:0			
Mary his wife & 2 children	1:4:0	0:12:0		
one servt	0:14:0			
Mrs Eliz: Jackson widdo	0:4:0			
Mrs Mary Wm & Sarah Jackson her daughters	0:4:0	0:0:0	0:2:6	
one servant				
Mr Andrew Warren				
Mary his wife & 2 children	0:4:0	0:2:0		
two servants				

Illustration 2.7 Marriage Duty assessment – Braybrooke, Northamptonshire, 1697

Northampton [illegible]

Braybrook assessment by vertue of an act of Parliament made in the sixth & seventh year of his Majestys Reign intituled an act for granting to his Majesty certaine Rates & Duties upon Marriages Births & Burialls and upon Batchellors & Widowers for the terme of five years for carrying on ye Warr against France with Vigour.

Name	Burialls			Births			Marriages			Widowers/Bachelors		
[illegible] King				0	2	0	0	2	6	[illegible]		
Elizabeth King	0	0	0	0	0	0	0	2	6	0	0	0
Matthew King	0	0	0	0	0	0	0	0	0	0	0	0
Sarah King	0	4	0	0	2	0	0	0	0	0	0	0
Jno Staggs	0	0	0	0	0	0	0	2	6	0	0	0
Will Clipsham	0	0	0	0	2	0	0	0	0	0	0	0
Frances Clipsham	0	0	0	0	0	0	0	2	6	0	0	0
Elizabeth Clipsham	0	0	0	0	0	0	0	0	0	0	0	0
Elizabeth Witt	0	4		0	0	0	0	0	0	0	0	0
Robt Spencer	0	4	0	0	2	0	0	2	6	0	0	0
Mary Spencer	0	0	0	0	0	0	0	0	0	0	0	0
Edward Spencer	0	0	0	0	0	0	0	0	0	0	0	0
John Spencer	0	4	0	0	2	0	0	2	6	0	0	0
Ann Spencer	0	4	0	0	2	0	0	2	6	0	0	0
John Bosworth	0	4	0	0	0	0	0	0	0	0	0	0
Mary Bosworth	0	0	0	0	0	0	0	0	0	0	0	0
Samuell Bosworth	0	0	0	0	0	0	0	0	0	0	0	0
Wm Robinson	0	4	0	0	2	0	0	2	6	0	0	0
Elinor Robinson	[illegible]			[illegible]			[illegible]			[illegible]		
Elizabeth Robinson	[illegible]			0	0	0	[illegible]			[illegible]		
Will Robinson	0	4	0	0	2	0	0	2	6	0	1	0
John Page	0	4	0	0	2	0	0	2	6	[illegible]		
[illegible] Underwood	0	4	0	0	4	0	0	2	6	[illegible]		
Alice Underwood	[illegible]			[illegible]			[illegible]			[illegible]		

Illustration 2.8 **Marriage Duty assessment – St Benet, Paul's Wharf, London, 1695 (including the household of Gregory King)**

	Burials	Births	Marriages	Widowers and Batchelors
Marth Minnell cook Servt	1.4.0	– –		
Anthony } Sonnes Batchelors	1.4.0	– –	1.2.6	6
David }	1.4.0	– –	1.2.6	6
John Russell } Servts 1s	0.4.0			
Mary Tilley }	0.4.0			
Bridgett Lloyd Spinster	0.4.0	– –		
John Parker a Mason	0.4.0	2 –		
Hester his wife	0.4.0			
child unchristened	0.4.0	0.2.0		
Heraulds Office				
Sr Henry St George Knt	10.4.0	5s.2 –		
Dame Elizt his wife	10.4.0			
John Gibbs } Servts 1s	0.4.0			
Phillis Downer }	0.4.0			
Mary Jones }	0.4.0			
Richd Elliott }	0.4.0			
Gregory King Esqr	5s.4.0	1.2 –		
Anne his wife	5s.4.0			
Saml Stoppins } Batchrs Servts 1s	0.4.0	– –	0.2.6	6
Chris. Jarvaise }	0.4.0			

8

An examination of the Poll taxes of the later seventeenth century, the Marriage Duty Act and Gregory King

TOM ARKELL

The Poll taxes of the later seventeenth century

Parliament approved the imposition of eight main Poll taxes on England and Wales during the second half of the seventeenth century.[1] Although these may now appear in retrospect as a kind of series, stretching from 1660 to the end of the century and stemming from an earlier one in 1641, at the time they were levied they were regarded as specific and almost one-off measures for raising desperately needed revenue for military purposes. These Poll taxes form a very complex subject to study because continual changes meant that the terms of no two Poll taxes were the same and substantial elements of additional Poll taxes were also contained within the Marriage Duty Act, levied from 1695 to 1706, and two other contemporary land taxes.[2] Nevertheless, it will be argued that when these are studied in combination they can provide considerable insight into many problems posed by the Poll taxes and also into the computations of Gregory King that culminated in his well-known Scheme for England in 1688.[3]

The Poll tax of 1660 was a direct descendant of the one raised in 1641 to enable Charles I to pay off the Scottish army that had occupied the northern counties and from which the inhabitants of Northumberland and Durham were consequently excused.

1 I am grateful to Gerald Aylmer and Keith Wrightson for their helpful comments on an earlier version of this chapter.

2 See the appendix to this chapter for the main details of the relevant acts. Wherever possible the dates used in the text are those for the collection of each tax and not its approval. The appendix also gives in brackets the dates recorded in the *Statutes of the realm*. These are, of course, in the old Style (when the year changed on 25 March) and refer to the year when the relevant parliamentary session began and not when the particular act was passed. All the other dates in this chapter are given in the usual compromise of New Style for the year and Old Style for the day and month. This will explain such apparent paradoxes as that William and Mary's first acts of parliament were dated 1688, but their accession did not occur until 1689.

3 See table 1 of Laslett's chapter in this volume (chapter 2).

However, the ancestry of this first seventeenth-century Poll tax remains shrouded in mystery, in comparison to the family tree which sprang from it. Its successor was passed within three months of the restoration of Charles II in 1660 and was one of several measures designed to enable the Cromwellian army and navy to be disbanded by raising sufficient money to pay off the arrears that were owing to them.

Chandaman has shown that the format of these early Poll taxes cannot be understood properly if they are divorced from the general context of later Stuart taxation. Contemporary belief regarded indirect taxes on consumption as the appropriate sources for the funding of the government's regular expenses and direct taxes on wealth and property as being suitable only for contributing to its extraordinary expenses, notably war. In 1660 the main direct tax used to pay off the forces of the Commonwealth was the monthly assessment. Despite its unpopularity as a parliamentary innovation, it was very efficient from the government's point of view because its proposed yield was divided into county quotas based on their presumed wealth, and then each county was forced to produce its apportioned assessment. In theory both an individual's personal and real estates were liable for these assessments, but in practice they fell almost exclusively on land and were paid primarily by the tenants.[4]

The monthly assessment was much more unpopular than the other main property tax, the subsidy, which was a percentage tax whose burden fell most heavily on the wealthiest men. The subsidy imposed a much higher rate on personal wealth than on real estate, the former being taxed on its capital rather than annual value. It also obliged the taxpayers to pay the largest sum for which they were liable under only one, not both, of these headings and permitted them to make their own valuations, after first deducting their debts and 'other necessary expenses'. Not surprisingly, therefore, those factors which made the subsidy so much more popular to most taxpayers led directly to declining yields for the government and so, when it had to raise money urgently in the summer and autumn of 1660, the new government was forced to continue with the much more efficient monthly assessment.

[4] Chandaman, *English public revenue*, pp.138-95. The discussion of the taxes of Charles II's reign in this chapter draws heavily on his work.

Table 1 The Poll taxes 1641-1699

Categories of taxation

Basic rate

1 Adults (aged 16 and over)
M = married, S = single, A = additional to other surcharges;
2 Children (under 16)

Exempt

1 Adults receiving alms;
2 Adults exempt from paying rates to church and poor;
3 All children;
4 Children of parents receiving alms;
5 Children of parents exempt from paying rates;
6 Children of day labourers and servants in husbandry;
7 Children of parents with four or more children and estate worth £50 cv or less

Double rate

1 Popish recusants;
O = who have not taken oaths of allegiance etc.;
2 Aliens;
3 Those who have not taken oaths of allegiance and supremacy;
A = adults, G = gentlemen and above

Lords

1 Lord temporal;
2 Duke;
3 Marquis;
4 Earl;
5 Viscount;
6 Baron;
7 Eldest son of: duke;
8 marquis;
9 earl;
10 viscount;
11 baron;
12 Younger son of: duke;
13 marquis;
14 earl;
15 viscount;
16 baron

Table 1 Contd.

	1641	1660	1667	1678	1689-90	1690	1692-3 quarterly	1694-5 quarterly	1698-9 quarterly
Basic rate									
1	6d.	6d. **M** 1s. **S**	1s. **A**	1s. **A**	1s. **A***	1s.	4s. **A**	4s. **A**	4s. **A**
2			1s.	1s.	1s.	1s.	4s.	4s.	4s.
Exempt									
1	X	X	X	X	X	X	X	X	X
2						X	X	X	X
3	X	X							
4			X	X	X	X	X	X	X
5			X	X	X	X	X	X	X
6				X	X	X	X	X	X
7				X	X	X	X	X	X
Double rate									
1	X					X **O**			
2			X						
3						X **A**	X **G**	X **G**	X **G**
Lords									
1							£40	£40	£40
2	£100	£100	£50	£50	£50	£50			
3	£80	£80	£40	£40	£40	£40			
4	£60	£60	£30	£30	£30	£30			
5	£50	£50	£25	£25	£25	£25			
6	£40	£40	£20	£20	£20	£20			
7		£60	£30	£30	£30	£30			
8		£50	£25	£25	£25	£25			
9	£40	£40	£20	£20	£20	£20			
10	£35	£35	£17-10s.	£17-10s.	£17-10s.	£17-10s.			
11	£30	£30	£15	£15	£15	£15			
12				£25	£25	£25			
13				£20	£20	£20			
14				£15	£15	£15			
15				£13-6s-8d.	£13-6s-8d.	£13-6s-8d.			
16				£12	£12	£12			

Table 1 The Poll taxes 1641-1699

Categories of taxation

Knights

1 Baronet or Knight of Bath;
2 Knight bachelor

Gentry

1 Esquire or reputed esquire (21 and over to 1667; 16 and over from 1678)
 B = inc. barrister at law;
2 Above the rank of gentleman, but not a lord;
3 Former or present JP, sheriff, deputy lieutenant, MP etc;
 E = estate of £300+ cv;
4 Gentleman or reputed gnetleman with estate of £300+ cv (aged 16 and over);
5 Former or present alderman below an esquire;
6 Doctor of Physic;
7 Doctor of Law;
8 King's sergeant at law;
9 Sergeant at law

Women

1 Widow: one-third of former husband's rank etc;
 E = except ecclesiastical;
2 Widow: estate of £1000+ cv or income of £100+ pa;
3 Spinster: estate of £1000+ cv

Estate

1 Real and personal estate: graduated tax on annual value of £5+ pa;
2 Personal estate: capital value of ready money and debts;
3 Personal estate: £300-£600 cv;
4 Real and personal estate, excluding lords: £600 cv and above

Religious

1 Lord spiritual;
2 Archbishop;
3 Bishop;
4 Dean;
5 Canon;
6 Prebend;
 R = except sole prebendary rated at £30 and below;

Table 1 Contd.

	1641	1660	1667	1678	1689-90	1690	1692-3 quarterly	1694-5 quarterly	1698-9 quarterly
Knights									
1	£30	£30	£15	£15	£15	£15			
2	£20	£20	£10	£10	£10	£10			
Gentry									
1	£10	£10 **B***	£5	£5	£5	£5			
2							£4		£4
3						£5	£4 **E***		
4			£1	£1	£1	£1	£4		£4
5	£5	£5							
6	£10	£10	£5	£5	£5	£5			
7	£10	£5	£5	£5	£5	£5			
8	£25			£20	£20	£20			
9	£20	£20		£15	£15	£15	£15		
Women									
1	X	X	X E	X E	X E	X E			
2							X		X
3							X		X
Estate									
1	1%-5%	2%							
2			1%	1%	0.5%	0.5%			
3								£2	
4								£4	
Religious									
1							£40	£40	£40
2			£50	£50	£50	£50			
3	£60		£20	£20	£20	£20			
4	£40		£10	£10	£10	£10			
5	£20		£2-10s.	£2-10s.	£2-10s.	£2-10s.			
6	£10		£2-10s.**R**	£2-10s.**R**	£2-10s.**R**	£2-10s.**R**			

Table 1 The Poll taxes 1641-1699

Categories of taxation

Religious (contd.)

7 Archdeacon;
8 Other ecclesiastical officials;
9 Doctor of Divinity with benefice;
10 Anglican clergyman with two or more benefices worth:
A = £150+ pa; **B** = £120+ pa;
11 Anglican clergyman with one benefice worth:
C = £100+ pa; **D** = £80+ pa; **E** = £60+ pa; **F** = £50+ pa;
12 Anglican clergyman with benefice etc worth:
G = £300+ cv;
13 Dissenting preacher or teacher with:
A = £150+ pa; **G** = £300+ cv;
14 Dissenting preacher or teacher with:
D = £80+ pa; **E** = £60+ pa; **H** = no income limit

Trade

1 London merchant not freeman of city;
2 English factor living in London;
3 Tradesman, artisan etc living in house worth £30+ pa in London;
4 Those practising physic or surgery in London;
5 Range of London officials, members of companies etc;
6 Merchant and merchant's broker;
7 Tradesman, shopkeeper, vintner with estate of £300+ cv;
A = artificer, not vintner

Aliens

1 Alien merchant;
2 Alien merchant of the degree of a knight;
3 Alien merchant trading overseas;
4 Alien merchant trading in England;
5 Alien tradesman, craftsman etc heading a household;
6 Jew (1690: aged 16 and over);
7 Jewish merchant;
8 Jewish broker

Offices

1 Office-holder under king receiving £10+ pa (except household servant);
2 Those with pension, annuity etc from king of £20+ pa;
H = no income limit;

Table 1 Contd.

	1641	1660	1667	1678	1689-90	1690	1692-3 quarterly	1694-5 quarterly	1698-9 quarterly
Religious (contd.)									
7	£15		£2-10s.	£2-10s.	£2-10s.	£2-10s.			
8	(5)								
9			£5	£5	£5	£5			
10				£5 **B**	£5 **B**	£5 **B**	£8 **B**		£8 **A**
11	£5 **C**	£2 **C**				£1 **F**	£4 **E**	£4 **D**	£4 **E**
12					£1* **G**		£4* **G**		
13					£1* **G**				£8 **A**
14						£1 **H**	£4 **H**	£4 **D**	£4 **E**
Trade									
1	£5	£10		£10	£10	£10			
2	£2	£2							
3				10s.	10s.	10s.			
4						£2-10s.			
5	(20)	(22)							
6							£4	£4	£4
7					£1* **A**		£2		£2
Aliens									
1				£10	£10	£10			
2	£40	£40							
3	£10	£10							
4	£5	£5							
5	5s.	10s.							
6					£10	10s.			
7						£20			
8						£5			
Offices									
1	£10	£10							
2			15% **H**	15%	15%	5%			

Table 1 The Poll taxes 1641-1699

Categories of taxation

Offices (contd.)

3 Income from public office, employment etc (except armed forces);
4 Income of public officers etc taxed in monthly assessment;
5 Income of public officers etc not taxed in monthly assessment;
6 Income of lawyers etc and physicians;
7 Range of various legal and related officers;
8 Various lawyers and legal officers etc

Miscellany

1 Servant's money wages, not including board wages;
  V = under £3 pa;
2 Servant's money wages: £3+ pa;
3 Capital value of shares in East India and Guinea Cos;
  H = and Hudson Bay Co;
4 Annual value of shares in New River Co;
  O = and three other water Cos and one printing Co;
5 Those liable to find horse and horseman for militia (for each horse or proportionately);
6 Others who did not find a horse for the militia but kept a coach, chariot or calash;
7 Each hackney coach;
  S = or stage coach

Notes: * = contained in revising act etc; (figures) = number of posts, i.e. officials etc. with own specific poll; cv = capital value

The Poll tax of 1660

The Poll tax of 1660 was a graduated one based mainly on social status, which was partly intended to tax alternative sources of wealth to those tapped by the monthly assessments. These included different ranks of the nobility and gentry, lawyers, officers of government departments receiving £10 per annum or more; merchants, members of the London companies, clergymen with an income over £100 per annum; doctors and keepers of hackney coaches. Widows were required to pay one-third of the rate charged for their former husband's rank or degree. The diverse nature of this tax's coverage reflects the belief of many contemporaries that, in comparison to landowners, office-holders, merchants and some professional people did not pay an equitable

Table 1 Contd.

	1641	1660	1667	1678	1689-90	1690	1692-3 quarterly	1694-5 quarterly	1698-9 quarterly
Offices (contd.)									
3				10%		5%			
4			3.33%		5%				
5			10%		15%				
6			6.67%	10%	15%	15%			
7	(27)	(55)							
8					£1*		£4	£4	£4
Miscellany									
1			5%	5%	2.5% **V**				
2					5%				
3				1%	2% **H**	2% **H**			
4					10%	10% **O**			
5							£4	£4	£4
6							£4	£4	£4
7		10s.					£5 **S**		

proportion of the national taxation. A detailed breakdown of the assessment, together with the Poll taxes of other years, is given in Table 1.

Two further provisions spread the net of this Poll tax much more widely. All those with yearly incomes of £5 per annum or more from land (assessed at its 'true and full yearly value'), leases, money and stock were to pay two per cent of their annual value, with personal estates being assumed to produce an annual income of five per cent of their capital value. In addition single people aged sixteen and over were to pay one shilling, while six pence was to be paid by 'every other person of what estate or degree soever he or she be' who was above sixteen, not receiving alms and not otherwise rated for the Poll tax. This rather confusingly worded clause was lifted directly from the tax of 1641, when it was not preceded by the double rate for single people so that its meaning was then very clear. The influence of the subsidies on this 1660 Poll tax is apparent in the clauses which permitted payment under only one heading. However, although this was intended to be the greatest proportion for which the taxpayer was charged, because some aspects of the tax, such as rank or degree, were so much easier to assess than the proportion of a person's estate, many must have paid for the former even when the latter was higher.

The Poll tax of 1667

The Commons attempted to abandon the monthly assessment in 1663 when they replaced it with four subsidies which included a small Poll tax on aliens and popish recusants of eight pence per head. However, the attempt failed because of its very disappointing yield so that the Second Dutch War was financed primarily from 1665 to 1667 by a series of assessments. This humiliating reversal of policy placed a very heavy taxation burden on land and rents, which parliament tempered slightly by reviving another Poll tax early in 1667. This was a greatly revised format because it was deliberately designed to be a supplementary tax to the assessment; the yield of the previous Poll tax had been unsatisfactory and the attempt to tax people mainly according to their status had caused problems, especially in London where there was considerable confusion over many individuals' precise social standing. It was also the first measure which contained the word 'Poll' in its title.

In 1667 the basic poll was raised to one shilling for married as well as single people and was also applied to children under 16, except for those whose parents were exempt from paying rates to the church and poor on grounds of poverty. The shilling was also made additional for those who had to pay higher rates. The graduated part of the poll was drastically curtailed and the contributions from the nobility and higher ranks of the gentry were halved. This time no tax was levied directly on land or real estate, but gentlemen whose property had a capital value of £300 or more paid a flat rate of one pound instead. However, a graduated poll was revived for the restored higher ranks of the clergy.

The most innovatory part of this Poll tax was its attempt to milk the more elusive forms of personal wealth that had eluded the monthly assessments, especially incomes from offices and substantial sums of money. This wide-ranging percentage section of the 1667 Poll tax now incorporated one basic principle of the subsidy, which was to tax the capital value of personal estate and not its annual value. Thus the 1 per cent levy on the capital value of all the ready money and sperate debts of individuals and corporate bodies was effectively a 20 per cent tax on their annual value because of the traditional assumption that capital value gave a 5 per cent yield. This was therefore some ten times higher than the 2 per cent on the annual value of real and personal estates which was levied by the previous Poll.

The rest of the percentage taxes constituted a form of flexible income tax. After allowance had been made for their expenses, all office-holders and others in public employment, apart from the forces, had to pay 3.33 per cent of their annual income if they were taxed already in the monthly assessment and 10 per cent if they were not. Similarly physicians, sergeants-at-law, attorneys, solicitors and other legal officials had to pay 6.67 per cent. Servants were taxed on their cash (but not board) wages at 5 per cent and all government pensions, annuities etc. had to pay the highest rate of 15 per cent. This attempt to tap the less tangible forms of personal wealth without the services of professional tax collectors can be counted as either a partial failure or a partial success, since it raised about half of the rather optimistic original estimate.

The Poll tax of 1678

An eleven-year gap separated this Poll tax from the next in 1678, the final year of a bitter war between the French and the Dutch, when popular pressure was trying to force Charles II to declare war on France. In the interim the Commons had tried in 1671 to breathe new life into the subsidy, by basing it on real values rather than notional ones and by bringing within it money, goods and offices. However, it still failed to produce even half its estimated yield so that the subsidy was abandoned again until after the Revolution. These innovations in the subsidy were influenced in part by the Poll tax of 1667, but they appear not to have influenced the next Poll tax of 1678, which was modelled very closely on that of 1667.[5]

5 Chandaman, *English public revenue*, p.169 claims that 'the distributive provisions of the 1678 Poll' were 'tempered in some respects by the experiences of the new Subsidy'. Yet such influences have not been detected.

Like its predecessor, the Poll tax of 1678 was conceived essentially as a tax on personalty to supplement an assessment that had been approved in the previous year. And so the 1 per cent levy on personal estates of debts and ready money was extended to cover the capital value of shares in the East India and Guinea companies. The percentages levied on people's incomes were also simplified and rationalised. The rate for servants' wages remained unchanged at 5 per cent, but now no allowances were made for the expenses of those office-holders, lawyers and physicians who had previously enjoyed them. This time all their incomes were subject to a standard levy of 10 per cent, together with those of judges and other judicial officials. The highest rate of 15 per cent was again confined to those with royal pensions or annuities, but now with the new proviso that they had to exceed £20 per annum.

Exemption from the basic poll of one shilling was extended to the children aged under sixteen of day labourers and of servants in husbandry as well as to all those whose parents had four or more children and estates with a capital value of less than £50. The graduated poll was extended to include special tariffs for the younger sons of the nobility, while the age limit for esquires was lowered to sixteen and wealthier clergymen with more than one benefice were also included. In addition, London and foreign merchants who had previously been charged in 1660 were now restored to the tariff together with sergeants-at-law and a new category was introduced for Londoners engaged in a trade or manual occupation and who occupied a house worth at least £30 per annum.[6]

William III of Orange

After 1680 neither Charles II nor James II required any further direct taxation, but following the accession of William and Mary in February 1689, the new political situation disrupted this temporary stability in the national finances. William of Orange straightaway seized the opportunity to harness English resources to his lifelong struggle against the hegemony of Louis XIV of

[6] Chandaman's extremely reliable analysis of these Poll taxes was marred by one small error (*English public revenue*, p.170) which ascribed exemption to the parents and not the children of those with four or more offspring. In addition, for London tradesmen etc. with houses worth £30 per annum, I have interpreted 'holding' to mean occupying and not possessing as Chandaman did.

France, which precipitated a war in Europe of nearly nine years that started immediately with an unwanted diversion to win back control of Ireland from James II. During William's reign public expenditure in England shot up nearly threefold from under £2 million to over £5 million a year. Altogether between 1689 and 1702 government expenditure totalled more than £72 million, and less than one-tenth of what was then regarded as this huge sum was raised by long-term borrowing. The Commons obstinately refused to accept that the war would be either long or expensive and so they tried to finance it in the traditional way with a series of short-term loans pegged to specific taxes, which invariably compounded their problems because, all too often, their estimated yields proved unrealistically optimistic.[7]

Various familiar, revised and new taxes were required to raise all this money and the government's continuing financial embarrassment gave unprecedented opportunities to projectors and speculators to devise and advocate new taxation schemes, as well as precipitating a 'financial revolution'.[8] The main source of direct taxation was described rather vaguely on most occasions as an 'Aid' and was normally a revision or combination of the monthly assessment and subsidy, which came to be known by the end of the decade as the Land tax. A determined effort was made from 1693 to use the percentage principles of the subsidy of 1671 for taxing personal wealth at a rate of four shillings in the pound, but its yields soon declined so that parliament resorted once more to using county quotas from 1698.[9] In this context the Poll tax was merely one of several measures used to tap more personal wealth in what had become the traditional manner.

7 Dickson, *Financial revolution*, pp.46-7.

8 Brooks, 'Political arithmetic', pp.34-5.

9 Identification of the first Land tax is almost as elusive as of the first prime minister and depends partly on definitions. The first act to contain the phrase 'Land Tax' in its title was 8 & 9 Wm. III c.6 (1696-7), levied in 1697-8 with a supplementary Poll tax, but 'Land Tax' did not re-appear in the title of another act until 1702 (1 A. c.6). According to Chandaman's definition that 'the Land Tax represented a unique fusion of the Subsidy and assessment principles' (*English public revenue*, p.195) the first one should be 9 Wm. III c.10, levied in 1698. However, the Four Shilling Aid raised in 1693 by 4 Wm. & M. c.1 (1692) is normally regarded as the first of the series and is accepted as such by Beckett, *Land tax*, p.12. In contrast, for Brooks the Land tax seems to have been initiated at the start of William and Mary's reign; see Brooks, 'Public finance', pp.281-300. See also the chapter by Alexander below for a detailed discussion of the 4s. Aid of 1693.

The Poll taxes of 1689 and 1690

The first of William and Mary's Poll taxes was levied in July 1689 specifically for the 'reducing of Ireland'. Even though it was a replica, with only minor variations, of the previous one imposed in 1678, serious problems may have arisen over its collection because later in the year parliament passed a review in which it was claimed that many had avoided assessment either as esquires or gentlemen, or for their ready money and debts or for the basic one shilling poll. As well as chasing these defaulters, the new act also introduced a few additional categories to the Poll tax for collection in May 1690.

In the original act the rate on personal estates of debts and ready money was reduced to half a per cent of their capital value. However, an increased levy of 2 per cent was imposed on the capital value of the East India and Guinea companies' shares and also applied to those of the Hudson's Bay company, while a 10 per cent tax was introduced on the annual value of the New River company's shares. In 1689 two differential rates were introduced for servants' wages and also revived for office-holders who had contributed to the monthly assessment. In addition, Jews were taxed specifically for the first time. Some confusion may have been created by this act's failure to confirm that the basic shilling poll was applicable to everyone liable to a surcharge because this was not clarified until the review. This revising act also imposed an additional levy of one pound on all tradesmen, shopkeepers and artificers with an estate worth at least £300 capital value, as well as on various clerics and a range of legal officers.

The next full Poll tax of June 1690 followed so hard on the heels of the review that it omitted virtually all these later additions, including the clarification over the basic poll. On this occasion one pound was levied only on Anglican clergymen with benefices worth £50 per annum or more and on all dissenting preachers and teachers. The difficulties of collecting the previous poll were reflected in the decision to extend exemption on adults to those who were not liable to contribute to the rates for church and poor because of poverty (one of the three exemption clauses of the recently-abandoned Hearth tax). The attempt to tax servants' wages was also abandoned and the rate for those with incomes from offices or royal pensions reduced to five per cent. The other changes were less fundamental. The definition of an esquire was extended to embrace, for example, past and present MPs and JPs. The 10 per cent tax on the annual value of shares was also applied to several other water companies and one printing company. A new levy was imposed on those practising physic and surgery in London and a differential rate introduced for the Jews. The political situation was reflected most overtly in the new double rate that was devised to punish those papists and others who had not taken the oaths of supremacy and allegiance to the new regime.

The quarterly Poll taxes of 1692-9

The next Poll tax of 1692-3 contained more radical departures from the terms of its predecessor than even the one in 1667. For a start it was levied quarterly at three-monthly intervals. In addition, all attempts to tax a percentage of people's wealth were abandoned, almost certainly because they were now incorporated in those incipient Land taxes, which parliament called 'Aids'.[10] In this new Poll tax widows were no longer taxed according to their husband's former status, but on their own estate or income, and some wealthy spinsters became liable for the first time.

Furthermore, in 1692-3 the graduated Poll was reduced to a few broad categories, with all peers being grouped together and no distinction being made between esquires and gentlemen, who were charged at the same four pound rate as merchants, legal officers, many clergy and all non-Anglican preachers and teachers. Tradesmen, shopkeepers and vintners with a minimum estate of £300 now became liable to a levy of half this rate, which was a much simpler and more practical approach to tapping commercial wealth. Almost the sole part of this Poll tax that remained unchanged was the different categories of exempt from the basic poll, which was now raised to four shillings and was clearly made additional to the higher rates. Anyone who contributed to a horse and horseman for the militia or, if not, who kept a coach, chariot or calash was also charged extra and so were keepers of hackney and stage coaches.

Despite such relative clarity another review was considered necessary to encourage those to pay up who had so far avoided being assessed or taxed in full or in part. No doubt this reflected

[10] See chapter by Alexander below for a detailed comparison of this 1692-3 Poll tax and the 1693 4s. Aid.

some confusion among the taxpayers as well as some resistance to the increasing frequency with which the Poll taxes were now being levied. This revising act also took the opportunity to extend slightly the definition of those who were liable to pay the gentlemen's rate of four pounds and fixed an additional date in June 1693 for the final collection.

The second quarterly Poll of 1694-5 did not follow this pattern, but the third one of 1698-9 did, reverting to it with very few amendments. These included a rise in the value of the benefices of pluralist clergymen and in the estates of dissenting preachers and teachers and the omission of the additional levy on hackney and stage coaches. This was because hackney coaches in London had been taxed separately through a system of licences since 1694.[11]

The Poll tax of 1694-5 came closest to taxing people below the peerage according to their wealth rather than their social status. This second quarterly Poll had two simple main rates for the commoners. The higher one of four pounds comprised those with either a real or personal estate of at least £600 capital value to which were added a wide range of legal officers, merchants and their brokers and the better-off Anglican and dissenting clerics. The lower rate of two pounds was confined to those whose personal estates had a capital value of between £300 and £600. Because women as well as men were subject to these rates, the only additional elements in the Poll of 1694-5 were the equine surcharges for those who contributed to the militia or kept private coaches. The stark simplicity of this second quarterly Poll tax contrasts very sharply with the bewildering diversity of those pioneering graduated Polls of 1641 and 1660, but its simplicity could no more ensure repetition than the previous complexity.

Supplementary Polls: the Land taxes of 1697 and 1702

Between 1695 and 1702 three other taxes were introduced which contained significant Poll-tax elements. The Marriage Duty Act of 1695, which is discussed in more detail later, included a Poll tax on some bachelors and widowers. Then the declining yield from the early percentage Land taxes led to a decision to reduce the rate from four to three shillings in the pound in 1697 and to supplement it with a poll. After this failed and the government

11 Dowell, *History of taxation*, vol. 2, pp.52-3.

had reverted to the well-tried assessment principle of county quotas, the final Poll tax was tacked on to such Land tax legislation in March 1702, just after the death of William III at the start of the War of Spanish Succession.[12]

The Poll-tax element of the 1697 Land tax, which is sometimes known as the capitation tax,[13] bears little relation to the quarterly Polls of the same decade. Exemption was given to those in receipt of alms and to the wives and children of those who paid the basic poll. This latter totalled 4s 4d and was paid in thirteen lunar monthly instalments (of twenty-eight days) from February 1697 to January 1698. In addition, a range of percentage taxes on income stemmed from both the Poll taxes of 1667-90 and from the previous percentage Land taxes of 1693-6, but also contained some novel features. These Land taxes were quarterly and, in addition to income from land, had taxed personal estates, on the assumption that their annual value was 6 per cent of their capital value, and income from public employment, apart from the forces. They also left untouched royal pensions and servants' wages.

The levy on servants' wages that was re-introduced in 1697 embraced journeymen and others hired for the year who received wages of at least four pounds a year, with three different rates for those whose wages were £4-£8 (5.42 per cent), over £8-£16 (12.5 per cent) and more than £16 per annum (21.67 per cent). This highest rate of 21.67 per cent was also imposed on all royal pensions, annuities etc, regardless of their value and without any lower limit, and on the incomes of a very wide and precisely-defined range of office-holders together with those of lawyers, merchants' brokers, physicians, surgeons and 'persons exercising any other professions whatsoever'. All these percentages were additional to the basic poll and had to be paid in the same thirteen lunar months.

Although the levy on personal estates covered the same period, it had to be paid rather inconsistently in twelve instalments by calendar months. For the purpose of this tax personal estate was divided into three separate categories. Ready money and debts

[12] Cooper's detailed work on King's Lynn (see chapter 10 below) has clearly exposed the fallacy of Dowell's claim that 'the Poll tax of 1698 was the last', *History of taxation*, vol.2, p.46. See also Reed, 'Ipswich', pp.111-2 for an analysis of the 1702 Poll tax for Ipswich.

[13] Dowell, *History of taxation*, vol. 2, p.45.

accruing interest were taxed at the rate of 1.25 per cent of their capital value, half that of the levy on the stock of traders and shopkeepers at 2.5 per cent of their 'full, true and real' capital value. (Alternatively these rates can be seen as 20.83 per cent and 41.67 per cent of their annual value.) Since 1693 the previous Land taxes had rated both these categories at 1.2 per cent, but had left the third one totally untouched. And so this land or capitation tax of 1697 introduced an unprecedented levy of 0.6 per cent on the capital value of the livestock owned or tended by farmers and graziers.[14] The terms of this tax were never repeated and its failure may have owed as much to their complexity as to the relative ease with which the full and real values liable to the tax could be evaded.

The final supplementary Poll tax was paid quarterly and was attached to the Land tax for the year beginning 25 March 1702. On this occasion the exemptions and the basic poll of four shillings reverted to the pattern of the other quarterly polls, but the graduated categories for peers and below were not restored. Instead this poll retained a series of percentage rates that were similar to those of the supplementary poll of 1697, but by no means identical. The levy of 1.25 per cent on the capital value of personal estates was applied only to debts and investments that attracted interest, but not to ready money. The goods or stock of all traders, merchants and shopkeepers was again double-rated at 2.5 per cent of their capital value, but the cattle or stock of farmers was exempted specifically. Servants' wages were also omitted and the levy on royal pensions and annuities reduced to 20 per cent. Because the main body of this Land tax for 1702 had already imposed a levy of 20 per cent on the incomes of most office-holders, the more precisely-worded Poll tax section of the act imposed on them only another 5 per cent. However, the incomes of those lawyers, merchants' brokers, physicians, surgeons, dissenting preachers and teachers and other professional people which had been unaffected by the relevant clause of the Land tax were all subjected in the poll section to a 20 per cent tax.

14 Davenant claimed misleadingly in his *Essay* that in the second quarterly poll of 1694-5 the tax on those with estates worth £300-£600 'seems to take in stock of all kinds', but then he also thought wrongly that it applied to real as well as personal estate; Thirsk and Cooper, *Seventeenth century*, p.799.

After 1703 the government no longer resorted to raising money by the temporary expedient of a Poll tax because it had developed the capacity to undertake substantial long-term borrowing and had also greatly increased the regular yield from the Land tax. In time, therefore, the concept of a Poll tax became thoroughly discredited in the nation's popular memory.

Collecting the Poll tax

One of the main attractions of the Poll tax for the government was the speed with which it could be collected, at least in theory. In practice, however, it took much longer than anticipated for much of the money to reach the Exchequer. This was primarily because the administration of the Poll tax was not handed over to professionals appointed by the king, as happened with the collection of the excise and of most Hearth tax returns, but, like other direct taxes, was kept firmly under the control of independent property owners.[15]

Parliament appointed numerous commissioners to supervise the collection of the Poll tax in each county, city or other administrative area identified in the relevant act. These commissioners were then responsible for subdividing their areas into appropriate hundreds, wards, townships, parishes, etc, where they appointed a few leading inhabitants to act as assessors. The duties of these assessors were to draw up for the commissioners certified lists of all those inhabitants who were chargeable for the Poll tax, together with the relevant details of those who were liable to the additional surcharges. Normally people were assessed for the place where they lived at the time when each poll was levied, but to avoid double taxation of those who owned more than one house, the commissioners were empowered to give certificates of discharge that recorded any sums which had been paid elsewhere. The commissioners also had the power to examine, challenge and alter the details of any particular assessment as well as to hear appeals from those who disputed their own.

From 1667 onwards the process of collection was organised quite separately from the assessment. In 1660 it followed a similar procedure to the initial one of 1641. Originally the collectors for each parish or local area were appointed by the commissioners and returned the money to them by an agreed date. The

[15] Chandaman, *English public revenue*, pp.171-4.

commissioners then paid these sums to the sheriffs for each county, who passed them on to the treasurers responsible for the Poll tax. From 1667 the parishes or equivalent areas nominated 'two or more able and sufficient persons' of their own to act as collectors. They were responsible for returning the money they had collected to a head collector in 1667 and to a deputy of the receiver general for each county from 1678 onwards. These middlemen had to ensure that this money reached their receiver general, who then transmitted it to the Exchequer. To enable them to check the totals when the money arrived, the commissioners were also responsible for providing the receivers general and the Exchequer with duplicates of the total sums charged for each rated place 'without naming the persons'.

The assessors were unpaid, but those involved in the various stages of collection were eligible for a small commission on their receipts. In 1660, for instance, the collectors received one penny in the pound, two pence in 1667 and three pence from 1678 onwards, while the receivers general were entitled to two pence in the pound from 1667. The commissioners' clerks were rewarded from 1667 with a similar allowance of two pence in the pound.

The yield of the Poll taxes

It is usually assumed that the yield to the government from these Poll taxes fell significantly short of the sums which it ought to have received, but unfortunately this cannot be either proved or disproved from the current evidence. Table 2 reveals that the yields from the four single Polls of 1667-90 were quite similar, but the continual changes in their rates and terms may mean that the differences should have been much greater. In comparison there was a progressive decline in the product of the quarterly Polls in the 1690s, although it is not possible to isolate the capitation from the Land tax element in the total of £613,000 for 1697.[16] Altogether it appears as if there was increasing resistance to paying the quarterly Polls, but there may also have been an increased failure for the money that had been collected to reach the Exchequer.

Contemporaries often made over-optimistic estimates for the yield of their taxes, including the Polls. This is well demonstrated by comparing the estimates for 1667 and 1678, which should have

[16] Dowell, *History of taxation*, vol. 2, p.45.

Table 2 Net yields from the Poll taxes

	Single Polls
1667	£246,000
1678	£261,000
1689-90	£288,000
1690 review and additional Poll	£23,000
1690	£240,000
	Quarterly Polls
1692-3	£579,000
1693 review	£6,000
1694-5	£486,000
1698-9	£321,000

Source: Chandaman, **English Public Revenue**, pp.181, 188; Dowell, **History of Taxation**, vol.2, p.45.

been reasonably comparable but were apparently reduced from £500,000 to a more realistic £350,000. The main reason for such uncertainty stems from contemporary ignorance of the number of people living in England and Wales, of the proportions comprising their different ranks and occupations and above all of their relative wealth. Consequently, even the best-informed, such as Petty, King and Davenant, could make only intelligent guestimates, which we now know were quite unreliable. Davenant, who published in 1695 the total yields by county of the 1689 and 1692 Polls, was particularly keen to discover by how much these had fallen short of their targets. However, since he assumed that England had some 1.3 million houses with a mean household size of about six, his estimated yield of £800,000 for the first two quarterly Polls is highly suspect.[17]

The Marriage Duty assessments of 1695-1706

The so-called Marriage Duty Act was another product of the government's desperate need for money in the 1690s. Gregory King believed that the idea for this tax originated with one Richard Frith, who was probably a London property developer who had several associations with King.[18] The act which instituted the tax granted 'to his majesty certain rates and duties upon

[17] Thirsk and Cooper, *Seventeenth century*, pp. 798-803.

[18] Brooks, *Political arithmetic*, pp.42-5.

Table 3 Marriage Duty rates, 1695-1706

Burial	Birth	Marriage	Bachelor over 25 & Childless Widower	Category of taxation	
4s.	2s.	2s-6d.	1s.	Basic Rate (additional to surcharges)	
£50		£50	£12-10s.	Duke†	Peers
£40		£40	£10	Marquis†	Peers
£30		£30	£7	Earl†	Peers
£25		£25	£6-5s.	Viscount†	Peers
£20		£20	£5	Baron†	Peers
£30	£30	£30	£7-10s.	Eldest son of Duke†	Eldest sons of Peers
£25	£25	£25	£6-5s.	Eldest son of Marquis†	Eldest sons of Peers
£20	£20	£20	£5	Eldest son of Earl†	Eldest sons of Peers
£17-10s.	£17-10s.	£17-10s.	£4-7s-6d.	Eldest son of Viscount†	Eldest sons of Peers
£15	£15	£15	£3-15s.	Eldest son of Baron†	Eldest sons of Peers
£25	£25	£25	£6-5s.	Younger son or unmarried daughter* of Duke†	Younger sons and daughters of Peers
£20	£20	£20	£5	Younger son or unmarried daughter* of Marquis†	Younger sons and daughters of Peers
£15	£15	£15	£3-15s.	Younger son or unmarried daughter* of Earl†	Younger sons and daughters of Peers
£13-6s-8d.	£13-6s-8d.	£13-6s-8d.	£3-6s-8d.	Younger son or unmarried daughter* of Viscount†	Younger sons and daughters of Peers
£12	£12	£12	£3	Younger son or unmarried daughter* of Baron†	Younger sons and daughters of Peers
£15		£15	£3-15s.	Baronet, Knight of Bath†	Knights and Gentry
£10		£10	£2-10s.	Knight bachelor†	Knights and Gentry
£20		£20	£5	King's sergeant at law	Knights and Gentry
£10				Wife or widow of King's sergeant at law	Knights and Gentry
£15		£15	£3-15s.	Sergeant at law	Knights and Gentry
£7-10s.				Wife or widow of Sergeant at law	Knights and Gentry
£5		£5	£1-5s.	Esquire or reputed esquire†	Knights and Gentry

Table 3 Cont'd

Burial	Birth	Marriage	Bachelor over 25, etc.	Category of taxation	
£1		£1	5s.	Gentleman or reputed gentleman†	Knights and Gentry
£5§	£5	£5§	£1-5s.§	Eldest son of Baronet, Knight of Bath, or Knight bachelor†	
£1§	£1	£1§	5s.§	Eldest son of King's sergeant at law, sergeant at law, esquire, reputed esquire, gentleman or reputed gentleman†	
£1	£1	£1	5s.§	Younger son or daughter* of Baronet, Knight of Bath or Knight bachelor†	
£1	£1	£1	5s.§	Younger son or daughter* of King's sergeant at law, sergeant at law, esquire, reputed esquire, gentleman or reputed gentleman†	
£50		£50	£12-10s.	Archbishop	Clergy and Professions
£10				Wife or widow of Archbishop	
£20		£20	£5	Bishop	
£5				Wife or widow of Bishop	
£10		£10	£2-10s.	Dean	
£2-10s.				Wife or widow of Dean	
£2-10s.		£2-10s.	12s-6d.	Archdeacon, canon or prebendary	
£1				Wife or widow of Archdeacon, canon or prebendary	
£5		£5	£1-5s.	Doctor of Divinity, Law or Physic	
£1				Wife or widow of Doctor of Divinity, Law or Physic	
£1	£1	£1	5s.	Son or daughter* of Archbishop, canon, prebendary, doctor of divinity, law or physic	
£1		£1	5s.	Person with real estate of £50+ p.a. or personal estate of £600+ cv.	Others
10s.				Wife or widow of person with real estate of £50+ p.a. or personal estate of £600+ cv.	
10s.	10s.	10s.	2s.6d.	Son or daughter* of person with real estate of £50+ p.a. or personal estate of £600+ cv.	

Notes: † For these categories, the wife or widow of someone in the category was also liable for surcharges on burial duties and relevant birth duties. * Daughters were subject only to the relevant burial and birth duties. § Denotes information omitted from the text of 6 & 7 Wm. & M. c.6. These data have been taken from Gregory King's broadsheet on the Marriage Duty rates reprinted in Glass, 'Introduction', pp.xi-xii.

Marriages, Births and Burials and upon Bachelors and Widdowers for the term of five years'. It was approved by parliament in April 1695 and came into force on 1 May 1695.[19] Two years later it was renewed for an additional six years so that it ran eventually from 1695 to 1706.[20] During these eleven years the act's principal terms remained unchanged, its amendments tackling only various administrative weaknesses.

The Marriage Duty Act of 1695

This Marriage Duty Act had two distinct parts: charges on vital events as and when they occurred, which was essentially a tax on families, and annual payments by both bachelors aged over twenty-five and childless widowers, which was essentially a Poll tax on single independent males. The latter partly reflected the double-rating of single adults in the Poll tax of 1660 and was paid in half-yearly instalments at Michaelmas (29 September) and Lady Day (25 March), like the recently-abolished Hearth tax. Both aspects of the Marriage Duty Act were profoundly influenced by the Poll taxes and a detailed study also provides rather unexpected confirmation for Frith's claim that he originally devised the Marriage Duty scheme some six years previously.[21] The Duty Act's graduated surcharges for the births, marriages and burials of males with the rank of gentlemen and above, which are set out in Table 3, were identical with their rates in the 1678 and unrevised Poll taxes of 1689, but not with those from 1690 onwards. In addition, the annual charges for almost all bachelors and widowers were a quarter of those levied in 1678 and 1689.[22]

Only one new category was devised for the relatively wealthy people who were not gentry: those with a real estate of at least £50 annual value or a minimum personal estate of £600 capital value. All these surcharges were additional to the basic rates, but those who were liable for two or more surcharges had to pay only the highest.

19 See footnote 3, chapter 1 above for a detailed discussion of the inception of the Marriage Duty Act.

20 The excellent summary of the Marriage Duty Act contained in Glass, 'Introduction', stated incorrectly (p.xiii) that the renewal was for five years only. This repeated the error that was contained in Glass, 'Two papers on Gregory King' (p.171), although the note on p.172 gave the correct date.

21 Brooks, *Political arithmetic*, p.42.

22 Dowell, *History of taxation*, vol.2, p.544 recorded the bachelor tax for the younger sons of baronets and Knights of the Bath incorrectly.

Husbands were responsible for paying the duties on marriages and the heirs or executors the burial duties of those who died aged over twenty-one. Fathers, mothers or guardians (in that order) were liable for the burial duties of deceased minors and also for all duties on births. Exceptionally, when the widow of a peer or of the son of a peer remarried and had children by a husband of a lower rank, the couple became liable to pay birth duties appropriate to her former husband's rank.

Although members of families in receipt of alms were exempt from all aspects of this tax (as in the Poll taxes on which they were modelled), their parish was responsible for paying their burial duties. In large towns and cities with more than one parish, this financial burden of burying the deceased poor was intended to be shared evenly among all their parishes. The only other people who were excused from paying any of these duties were the fellows and students of Oxford and Cambridge colleges, who were exempted from duties payable by bachelors, celibacy being a compulsory condition that was imposed upon them at that time.

Administration of the Marriage Duty Act

The administration of the Marriage Duty Act was similar in outline to that of the Poll taxes, because it taxed relatively unpredictable events – births, burials and marriages – but it was also more complex.

Initially the commissioners responsible for administering the first year of this act were the same as those who had been appointed already to supervise the collection of the 1695 Land tax.[23] In subsequent years they were replaced as commissioners by the JPs for their county, borough or relevant administrative area, apart from 1698-9, when the JPs were supplemented by the commissioners for that year's Land tax, which was the first to revert to county quotas.[24] From 1698 onwards the commissioners were instructed to meet at least once every three months to review the operation of the act in their area.

23 Glass, 'Introduction', p.xvii referred to the right Land tax act, but stated rather misleadingly that it related to tonnage and poundage duties. In fact the commissioners appointed by this act (s.5) were responsible only for the administration of the Land tax and it was a much later part of the act (s.75) that was concerned with the payment of tonnage and poundage.

24 These changes stemmed from the fact that the Land tax was granted only annually; see Brooks, *Political arithmetic*, p.32.

As with the Poll taxes, the commissioners determined the subdivisions of their territory into hundreds, townships, parishes etc. and the appointment of assessors from among the principal inhabitants. For the Marriage Duty Act, these assessors had to draw up for the commissioners complete certified lists of everyone living in their area, including their full names, 'estates, degrees, titles and qualifications', together with the sums for which they were or would be liable under each of four headings relevant to the act: burials, births, marriages and unmarried.[25] If the commissioners suspected that someone had been underassessed or omitted from a list, they could interview him or her and alter the assessment accordingly, as well as hear appeals from those who claimed they had been overassessed. Because servants and lodgers were required to be taxed where they lived, these assessments or certificates, as they were called officially, were planned as a complete annual nationwide household enumeration.

Onerous though the task of assessment was, collection of the duties probably posed more problems because, as parliament subsequently recognised, many were 'casual in their natures'.[26] Initially the assessors recommended that 'two or more able and sufficient persons' act as collectors for their parish, constablewick or local area for one year. Subsequently these collectors nominated their own successors. They were instructed to return the money which they collected within twenty days to a deputy of their appropriate receiver general. The commissioners were responsible for providing the receivers general with a duplicate copy of each assessment so that they could check their receipts before passing on the relevant money at half-yearly intervals to the Exchequer and their accounts annually to auditors. Allowances of two pence in the pound were paid to the receivers general and three pence (raised in 1698 to five pence) to the collectors. Again, the assessors who drew up the original lists in 1695 were unpaid unless they also acted as collectors. At the end of each year the collectors had to return an amended and updated list of their inhabitants to the commissioners, who in their turn were instructed to scrutinise it carefully before passing it on to the collectors for the next year. Until 1698 the parsons were also required to read out these newly-revised lists in church after morning service to give people an opportunity to appeal.

25 These lists were normally written out by hand, but in 1696 six of the eighteen assessments for Bristol were returned on printed forms; see Ralph and Williams, 'Introduction', p.xviii.

26 9 Wm. III c.32, s.9.

The Anglican clergy were also instructed under the Marriage Duty Act to extend the scope and increase the reliability of their parish registers and to make them available freely to the collectors and other interested parties. From 1698 the clergy were enjoined to record in their registers details of individuals' rank and quality relevant to the graduated duties for burials, births or marriages, together with the names and addresses of all those who were responsible for paying the duties on burials and births and the address of the bridegroom for marriages.

Initially some confusion was created over the division of responsibility for recording births between the collectors and the Anglican clergy. From the outset incumbents were instructed to include births as well as christenings in their registers, but at first parents were required to report all births and stillbirths to their collectors within five days. Consequently, the Anglican clergy could not keep a complete register of all births and the requirement was altered in the following year when the births of all infants who were not christened by their local ministers had to be reported to them from June 1696 onwards by the parents who then became liable to pay six pence. Since the collectors were not mentioned in this amendment, in theory the parents should have continued to report all births to them, but this is unlikely to have happened in practice because the parochial registers were now intended to contain a complete record of all births and the collectors were given statutory access to them twice in every year.

Originally the clergy were instructed to record those burials which occurred not just in their own churchyard but also 'in such common burying-places as their respective parishioners are usually buried in'. However, the following year parliament tried to close a loophole in the Act concerning the burial of people in parishes different from those where they lived normally, sometimes involving a traffic in corpses.[27] In future, clergymen who conducted such funerals were required to report the details to the collectors of the deceased's 'home' parish within ten days.

From 1695 onwards the 'pretended marriages' of non-Anglicans such as Quakers, Roman Catholics and Jews 'or any other persons who shall cohabit and live together as man and wife' had to be reported to the collectors within five days and then charged as if

27 For an illuminating discussion of this traffic in corpses in London see the chapter by Jeremy Boulton below.

they were valid marriages even though payment of the marriage duty did not confer any such legality upon them. After a year parliament considered that the principal source of evasion from the duties on marriages stemmed from clandestine marriages that were conducted irregularly without banns or licence so that in future clergy, sextons or parish clerks who engaged in, or connived at, such marriage ceremonies became liable to heavy fines.[28]

Internal migration was another factor which disrupted the smooth working of the Marriage Duty Act and which was tackled in 1698 by the last major amending act. In the attempt to prevent those who moved from one place to another escaping from paying their duties, the commissioners were instructed to issue certificates of default to enable the commissioners for the areas to which such defaulters had moved to raise the money by distraining and selling their goods.

The yield from the Marriage Duty Act

These detailed amendments appear to have had very little impact on the yield to the government from the Marriage Duty Act. In its first five years a total of £258,000 was raised, giving an annual average of just over £50,000 a year, but these figures do not reveal whether it rose or fell during the quinquennium. The former seems unlikely because its annual yield slumped quite dramatically to under £3,000 per annum in subsequent years, when the complexities of its administration appear to have combined with its unpopularity to undermine the Act.[29] The final revision to the act in Anne's reign appears to have partly recognised the widespread hostility of the Anglican clergy to it, by acknowledging that several 'had not exactly observed' their directions and then indemnifying from the consequent penalties all those who had kept their registers incorrectly but whose parishioners had still paid their duties.

Even at its peak, the annual yield from the Marriage Duty Act was worth no more than about one fifth of the product of a single Poll or little more than was raised by one penny in the pound in the assessed land taxes from 1698 onwards. When one considers

[28] It should perhaps be stressed that numerous financial penalties were threatened for non-compliance with various aspects of the Marriage Duty Act so that it may be rather misleading to emphasise this one.

[29] Dowell, *History of taxation*, vol. 2, p.46; Brooks, *Political arithmetic*, p.33.

the large number of people who were engaged in the raising of such relatively paltry sums, it seems surprising that the experiment was not abandoned earlier. Alternatively, it could provide confirmation for those who have suggested that the government's prime interest in this tax was not fiscal but social control, which it planned to achieve through annual updated censuses of all its inhabitants, including those who had recently moved house, and the recording of all their births, marriages and burials.[30]

Towards a better understanding of King's computations

More than a generation ago Glass described with great skill and perception the tortuous nature of Gregory King's computations and explained how much they were influenced by the Marriage Duty Act.[31] However, as Laslett has argued in his chapter above, the extent of King's indebtedness to the Poll tax data has not been recognised so widely[32] and it will be suggested here in Laslett's support that a careful reading of King's *Burns Journal*, in combination with his *Natural and Political Observations*,[33] reveals that his work on the two sources was closely complementary and that his well-known Scheme for 1688 (reproduced as Table 1 in Laslett's contribution to this volume) appears to have been the product mainly of computations derived from the Poll taxes, supported by the Hearth tax.

Various drafts for the *Natural and Political Observations* are contained within the *Burns Journal*, which show very clearly one of the principal sources of King's motivation. He was determined to prove that Petty's and Graunt's estimates for the nation's population were too large.[34] He believed that these had misled Davenant and, more importantly, the House of Commons into overestimating seriously the potential yield of the Marriage Duty Act, Poll bills and other taxes and therefore England's ability to sustain a lengthy war against France. And so he argued that a sound analysis of the English economy could not be achieved

30 Glass, 'Introduction', p.xiii.

31 Glass, 'Two papers on Gregory King', pp.159-220.

32 For an earlier exposition of part of the argument developed here see Arkell, 'Poverty', pp.24-9.

33 Both are reprinted in Laslett, *The earliest classics*, and are discussed at greater length in his chapter 2 above.

34 King, *Burns Journal*, pp.1, 49, 53, 120, 121, 275. This whole issue is also discussed very perceptively in Holmes, 'Gregory King'.

without establishing first a reliable figure for 'the true number of people'.[35]

Some time before 1695 King became convinced that the population totalled no more than 5.5 million and possibly somewhat less, but his failure to settle on a final figure was caused in part by inadequate evidence, which drove him to undertake a variety of tortuously manipulative computations. Neither the Poll tax returns nor the Marriage Duty assessments were sufficiently complete on a national scale to enable King to resolve this uncertainty so that, in his analyses of both, he was forced to content himself with demonstrating that neither was incompatible with a maximum total of about 5.5 million in England and Wales.[36] King's uncertainty over the national population total also sprang from his inability to decide whether it was increasing or decreasing and, if so, at what rate. At first he appears to have believed the former, but then to have been converted to the view that because the war against Louis XIV was so damaging both the nation's economy and its population were in decline.[37] Unfortunately, however, because King never published any of this work, it is impossible to determine his final conclusions with any degree of certainty.[38]

Glass's seminal work made it abundantly clear that King had access to only a very small selection of Marriage Duty assessments, which often appear to have been communicated to him in an analytical form and on a personal basis.[39] He was obviously much better informed about the data for London where he lived, than for the rest of the country, although he did manage

35 *Burns Journal*, pp.241-2, 269; King, *Natural and Political Observations*, pp.31, 33.

36 *Burns Journal*, pp.61, 122, 159, 222, 276-7; King, *Natural and political observations*, pp.34-6, 39. It is therefore argued that the list of contents (p.32) gave a very misleading title to the first chapter of King's, *Natural and political observations*: 'The number of people in England and Wales, calculated from the assessments on marriages, births and burials'.

37 *Burns Journal*, pp.11, 48, 224; King, *Natural and Political Observations*, p.43.

38 The inconsistency of the national population totals contained in King, *Natural and Political Observations* belong to an unfinished draft rather than a final approved version. For example, it states on p.33 that in the 1690s the population was increasing by about 9,000 or perhaps 5,000 per annum but decreasing by 7,000 per annum on p.43.

39 Glass, 'Two papers on Gregory King' , pp.173-80, 197-201. Tiverton (Devon) could perhaps be added to Glass's table (p.199) of King's urban data.

to secure reasonably reliable information about the houses and population of all or part of a dozen towns, including his native Lichfield, Gloucester, Norwich and Exeter.[40] By comparison, King was disturbingly ignorant about the countryside, where some three-quarters of the people lived. Most of his rather sketchy knowledge seems to have been based upon some very limited information about one Norfolk hundred and five or six other parishes with an aggregate population of little more than 7,000.[41] His efforts to secure more information for about 75 parishes, constablewicks and so on in rural Devon and south-east Staffordshire were thwarted in part because the available data recorded only the sums of money that had been collected there at Michaelmas 1695, but King nevertheless made a determined attempt to squeeze as much as possible from the Staffordshire information.[42] And so, because at this stage King accepted the national total of about 1.3 million houses propounded by Davenant,[43] which Glass has already argued was inflated substantially,[44] King's series of estimated mean household sizes for the villages and hamlets of around four is doubly suspect.

Nonetheless, King did make intelligent use of the fragmented Marriage Duty data that were available to him to create soundly-based estimates of the birth and burial rates, age structure and sex ratios of various communities as well as of the variations in the marital condition of their inhabitants.[45] These then enabled him to take up with some confidence the challenge of estimating the Duty Act's potential yield, which he concluded eventually should have been about £81,000 per annum.[46] The depth of King's interest in the Marriage Duty Act is revealed further by the fact

40 *Burns Journal*, pp.58-60, 90-2, 97-100, 118, 124-9.

41 It is of course possible that this picture might be altered by other notebooks which have since disappeared. Unfortunately, the only details for Eynsford hundred (Norfolk) in the *Burns Journal* (p.141) were taken from two different Land taxes. It should also be pointed out perhaps that King altered the total number of houses for Widworthy (Devon) from 96 to a more realistic 51 (p.100).

42 *Burns Journal*, pp.79-80, 86-8, 103, 114. King's more detailed analyses of Harefield and Ringmore were undertaken only after he had finished these computations.

43 *Burns Journal*, pp.11, 120; Holmes, 'Gregory King', p.47.

44 Glass, 'Two papers on Gregory King', pp.202, 216-20.

45 *Burns Journal*, pp.30, 82-4, 93-100, 107-10, 132; King, *Natural and Political Observations*, pp.39-40, 70-1.

46 *Burns Journal*, pp.62, 110-6, 268; King, *Natural and political observations*, pp.58-9.

that his broadsheet summarising the different rates payable under the act was his sole demographic work published during his lifetime.[47] This interest culminated in his proposed amendments for increasing the act's yield in 1699, which would have transformed it virtually into a Poll tax, but they were never implemented by parliament.[48]

King's interest in the contemporary Poll taxes seems to have been just as strong, even though the *Burns Journal* contains far fewer calculations that relate directly to them. His interest was almost certainly aroused by the data published in 1695 in his friend Charles Davenant's 'Essay upon ways and means of supplying the war', which King thought contained flawed calculations of the potential yield of the first quarterly Poll. The Essay also included the total yields by county for the Poll taxes of 1689 and 1692 as well as a county by county breakdown of the number of 'houses' that Davenant claimed came from the Hearth tax of 1690, all of which appear to have been acceptable to King.[49] Davenant believed that the popularity of the new regime led to the first of William and Mary's Poll taxes being paid in 1689 'with great alacrity and affection' and so their returns could be used reliably to 'divide the people into such proper classes and ranks, as may in a manner show the wealth and substance of the whole kingdom'.[50]

However, it does not appear as if King had obtained any access to the detailed Poll tax assessments, even for London, as he had for some of the Marriage Duty lists, so that almost certainly his work that was derived from the Poll taxes used only the raw totals of their yields and not any detailed analyses for particular communities. He probably started his Poll tax work by wrestling with estimates of the number of people who had contributed to the main categories of those for 1689 and 1692, divided between greater London and the rest of the country, as Davenant had done.[51] Then he appears to have undertaken much more detailed computations for all the sub-categories of both these Poll taxes

47 Glass, 'Two papers on Gregory King', p.167.

48 Brooks, *Projecting*, p.40; *Burns Journal*, pp.120A-D.

49 Holmes, 'Gregory King', pp.46, 58-9; Thirsk and Cooper, *Seventeenth-century*, pp.798-803. In fact the Hearth tax was abolished in 1689; see Glass, 'Two papers on Gregory King', p.217.

50 Davenant, *Discourses on the publick revenues*, 1698, quoted in Stone, 'Some British empiricists', p.71.

51 *Burns Journal*, pp.66-7.

and the intervening single Poll of 1690, which he assumed had a net yield of £288,000 similar to its predecessor, but argued that it should have been £355,000.[52] These calculations were then used to support King's estimated total for the national population of about 5.4 million, dividing them between payable or solvent and the excused or insolvent.[53] The latter had been increased from 1690 onwards by the addition of all adults who were exempt from paying rates to church and poor because of poverty so that King's computations for all three Poll taxes were then fused together to yield one, two or occasionally three sets of alternative figures for the main Poll tax categories, with the solvent totalling either 2.4m or 2.55m and the insolvent 3m or 2.85m.[54]

Because King continued to accept without question Davenant's total of almost 1.32m 'houses', he experienced considerable difficulty in calculating the different mean household sizes for his main groups. In the end, his assumptions virtually forced King to reverse Davenant's estimates of 800,000 houses liable for the Poll tax and 500,000 exempt from it, by postulating initially 450,000 liable at 5.5 per house and 860,000 exempt at 3.5.[55] These were then transformed into an embryonic table for the well-known Scheme, which was not divided at this stage into solvent and insolvent, but which did record an excess of expenditure per head over income for those groups which were subsequently described as decreasing the wealth of the kingdom.[56] In his *Natural and political observations*, King revised his totals for 1688 to 511,000 at 5.25 for those increasing the wealth of the kingdom and 849,000 at 3.25 for the decreasers.[57] Given the data on which he had worked, such precision was deceptively spurious. Some unexpected further light is thrown on King's perception of these insolvent or decreasers by a marginal note in his *Burns Journal*. As has been demonstrated above, they comprised all who were exempt from rates through poverty as well as those who received alms, but only the former were liable for their own Marriage Duty payments, which King clearly considered to be inequitable. However, he did not argue that they should be excused from

52 *Burns Journal*, pp.70-5.

53 *Burns Journal*, p.159.

54 *Burns Journal*, pp.280-1.

55 *Burns Journal*, p.281.

56 *Burns Journal*, p.270.

57 King, *Natural and Political Observations*, pp.48-9.

paying all their charges, like those in receipt of alms, but suggested instead that they should pay half the basic rates.[58] In King's estimation, therefore, some do not appear to have been so insolvent that they should have been exempted from all taxes.

Finally, the possibility must be considered that King might have altered some of the details in his Scheme quite significantly had he started to question earlier Davenant's total for the number of houses. No record exists of any comment made by King on Houghton's more conservative total of 1.18m, which was published in 1693, but in a later discussion with Harley, King did suggest that the estimate by John Adams of 1.12m for 1680 should not be raised beyond a maximum of 1.24m for the mid-1690s and that Davenant had agreed that the total for 'inhabited houses' should be nearer 1.2m. At the same time King also admitted that his computations derived as much from such approximate totals drawn from the Hearth tax records as from the Marriage Duty assessments and other sources, which helps explain some of the further confusion that was caused by uncertainty over whether such figures applied to all or just inhabited houses, households or families.[59]

Conclusion

The better acquainted one becomes with King's work, the more one cannot help but admire its thoroughness, range and quality. Judged by any standards, he was an outstanding statistician and an amazing pioneer. But such admiration of his work must not exclude a realistic appraisal of its limitations. In fact his attempt to construct a coherent demographic and social superstructure for the whole of England and Wales suffered from the inadequacy of the materials that were available to him. Most of King's figures were the product of theoretical computations rather than direct empirical investigation and his highly plausible approximations required considerable massaging to obtain internal consistency and compatibility with such facts as were known to him. In

[58] *Burns Journal*, p.64. To help make up for the loss of revenue which would have ensued, King proposed an extra charge of 10s. upon those worth £100 and more and 5s. on their children in addition to the 4s. burial duty etc. Although his note is worded ambiguously, within the context of the Marriage Duty Act, King can only have intended it to apply to personal estates with a capital value of £100 and not per annum as Brooks, 'Political Arithmetic' (p.40) suggested.

[59] Glass, 'Two papers on Gregory King', pp.184-8, 217-9.

addition, their focus has been further blurred by King's failure to recommend unequivocally any final best buys. Nevertheless, despite continued sniping from modern academia,[60] no thrusting demographic developer has yet moved in with all the technology of modern scholarship to demolish King's imposing edifice and redevelop its terrain. If and when they do, they will have to use primarily those sources whose value was so clearly appreciated by King himself.

60 For a brief summary see Arkell, 'Poverty', p.24.

Appendix

DATES AND TITLES OF ACTS OF PARLIAMENT – THE POLL TAXES –

The first date or dates for each act or group of acts is in the New Style and records when the tax was due for collection. The dates in brackets are in the Old Style and are those for the parliamentary session of the particular act recorded in the *Statutes of the realm.*

1. 1641
16 Charles I c.9 (1640)
An Act for the speedy provision of money for disbanding the armies and settling the peace of the two kingdoms of England and Scotland.

2. 1660 September
12 Charles II c.9 (1660)
An Act for the speedy provision of money for disbanding and paying off the forces of this kingdom both by land and sea.

12 Charles II c.10 (1660)
An Act for supplying and explaining certain defects in an Act entitled An Act for the speedy provision of money for disbanding and paying off the forces of this kingdom both by land and sea.

12 Charles II c.28 (1660)
An Act for further supplying and explaining certain defects in An Act entitled An Act for the speedy provision of money for disbanding and paying off the forces of this kingdom both by land and sea.

3. 1667 March
18 & 19 Charles II c.1 (1666)
An Act for raising moneys by a Poll and otherwise towards the maintenance of the present war.

18 & 19 Charles II c.6 (1666)
An Act explanatory of the Act for raising moneys by a Poll and otherwise towards the maintenance of this present war.

4. 1678 May
29 & 30 Charles II c.1 (1677 & 1678)
An Act for raising money by a Poll and otherwise to enable his majesty to enter into an actual war against the French king and for prohibiting several French commodities.

5. 1689 July and 1690 May

1 William & Mary c.13 (1688)
An Act for raising money by a Poll and otherwise towards the reducing of Ireland.

1 William & Mary Sess.2 c.7 (1688)
An Act for review of the late Poll granted to their majesties and for an additional Poll towards the reducing of Ireland.

6. 1690 June
2 William & Mary c.2 (1689)
An Act for raising money by a Poll and otherwise towards the reducing of Ireland and prosecuting the war against France.

7. 1692 3 May, 3 August, 3 November, 1693 3 February and 1693 April
3 William & Mary c.6 (1691)
An Act for raising money by a Poll payable quarterly for one year for the carrying on a vigorous war against France.

4 William & Mary c.14 (1692)
An Act for review of the quarterly Poll granted to their majesties in the last session of this present parliament.

8. 1694 1 June, 1 September, 1 December, 1695 1 March
5 & 6 William & Mary c.14 (1694)
An Act for raising money by a Poll payable quarterly for one year for carrying on a vigorous war against France.

9. 1698 24 August, 24 November, 1699 24 February, 24 May
9 William III c.38 (1697-8)
An Act for granting to his majesty an Aid by a quarterly Poll for one year.

Supplementary Poll taxes

1. 1697 22 February - 1698 24 January (lunar and calendar monthly)
8 & 9 William III c.6, ss.1-9 (1696-7)

An Act for granting an Aid to his majesty as well by Land Tax as by several subsidies and other duties payable for one year.

2. 1702 24 June, 24 September, 24 December, 1703 24 March
1 Anne c.6, ss.1-7 (1702)
An Act for granting an Aid to her majesty by diverse subsidies and a Land Tax.

– THE MARRIAGE DUTY ACT AND ITS REVISIONS –

1695 1 May - 1706 1 August

6 & 7 William & Mary c.6 (1694)
An Act for granting to his majesty certain rates and duties upon Marriages Births and Burials and upon Bachelors and Widowers for the term of five years for carrying on the war against France with vigour.

7 & 8 William III c.35 (1695-6)
An Act for the enforcing the laws which restrain marriages without licence or banns and for the better registering Marriages Births and Burials.

8 & 9 William III c.20, ss.14, 16, & 17 (1696-7)
An Act for making good the deficiencies of several funds therein mentioned and for enlarging the capital stock of the Bank of England and for raising the public credit.

9 William III c.32 (1696-7)
An Act for preventing frauds and abuses in the charging collecting and paying the duties upon Marriages Births Burials Bachelors and Widowers.

4 & 5 Anne c.23, s.10 (1705)
An Act for laying further duties on low wines and for preventing the damage to her majesty's revenue by importation of foreign cut whalebone and for making some provisions as to the stamp duties and the duties on Births Burials and Marriages and the salt duties and touching million lottery tickets and for enabling her majesty to dispose the effects of William Kidd a notorious pirate to the use of Greenwich Hospital and for appropriating the public monies granted in this session of Parliament.

9

The City revealed: an analysis of the 1692 Poll tax and the 1693 4s. Aid in London

JAMES ALEXANDER

Introduction

Until recently London has been a neglected area of research for early modern historians. One particular lacuna is the lack of any detailed description of the economy of the central area of the metropolis occupied by the City.[1] Other areas of the City, especially the West End, are also in need of such research, yet for these areas evidence is not so plentiful as it is for the City. The most abundant period for records is the 1690s when Parliament was levying heavy taxation to finance the War of the Grand Alliance fought against France. As the introduction to this section clearly shows, numerous taxes were collected and it is the records that these left behind that form the foundation for this study. Use is specifically made of the 1692 Poll tax, known to contemporaries as the 'First Quarterly Poll Tax', and the 1693 '4s. in the £' tax or Aid. These, in particular, provide a most useful basis from which to describe and analyse the City economy and society. However, before proceeding with an examination of the economic and social structure of the capital, it is appropriate to detail the administrative system operating in the City for this was a complex monster, unlike those which characterised most other urban areas in this period.

Civil Jurisdictions and tax administration

The first point that needs to be made clear is that this study relates only to the City of London. By the end of the seventeenth century the metropolitan area of London had expanded far beyond the limits of the administrative City. Yet even so at this date the City accounted for some 120,000 people, around one-quarter of London's total population, a figure which meant that it was much

1 In this article the City of London refers only to that part of the metropolis under the jurisdiction of the Corporation of the City and not therefore to the City of Westminster or the urban parts of Middlesex and Surrey.

larger than any other town in England. In the City of London during the 1690s almost all national taxes were collected from the secular districts rather than the parishes. The boundaries of these districts were not primarily based on parishes but on a network of civil wards, divisions and precincts. The City's own administration was founded on these local jurisdictions. The City was often seen as being composed of two parts: the City 'within' the old walls, made up of ninety-seven parishes, contained about 70,000 people; the City 'without', consisting of thirteen parishes with over 50,000 people formed a thin strip around the outside of the wall. Both came under the jurisdiction of the Corporation.

In the 1690s the City was divided up into twenty-six wards. Twenty-one were wholly inside the line of the old walls and three were wholly outside. The remaining two included areas both inside and outside the walls, but the parts were often regarded as functionally separate. The wards were active in administering their own affairs, and elected a set of officials to carry these out. Each ward also elected a councillor or alderman to a senior Court of Aldermen, as well as electing a number of freemen to the lower Court of Common Council. The twenty-six official, or twenty-eight functional, wards could be, and indeed still are, of very irregular shapes. They were themselves internally divided into a number of varying sub-jurisdictions. Some were merely divided up into divisions, while others were further split into precincts. Some followed the boundaries of the parishes, some did not. Some local responsibilities were shared jointly with the parish while others were not. A Parliamentary inquiry in the early 1830s made it clear that there was no uniform pattern of organization by the local authorities and suggested that there were as many systems of internal government of wards as there were wards.[2]

Commissioners were appointed for each county and city of Britain to supervise the assessment and collection of the national Poll taxes. These commissioners then appointed individual assessors and collectors for each sub-district within their jurisdiction. There were over 200 districts or precincts within the City of London alone, each with its own set of tax officials. The assessors were appointed from within the local community and were listed at the back of each assessment, together with their signatures. The collectors were not always from the immediate locality and appear

[2] *British Parliamentary Papers, Second Report*, pp.138-54.

to have collected taxes for more than one district. They were entitled to receive a proportion of the revenue for their costs. These local tax collectors were in turn responsible either to the Exchequer in Whitehall for the handing over of the money, or to some intermediary, who then paid the funds to the government.

The fact that taxes were assessed locally, in often quite small sub-divisions, made it possible to collect data from over 200 separate and distinct areas within the City.[3] The assessors were under orders to make several copies of their assessments, one of which ended up in the Corporation archives. This was probably because the City Corporation's own Chamber, or treasury, was charged with gathering in the money from the individual groups of collectors and paying it into the Exchequer. A similar procedure may also have prevailed in a number of other corporate towns, such as Bristol, King's Lynn and Southampton which as a result also have records from this period.[4]

Sources and associated problems

As stated in the introduction to this chapter, an in-depth study of the City of London's social and economic profile in the 1690s has been made possible by the abundance of the surviving assessments for a variety of taxes levied in the 1690s to finance the war against France.[5] The Poll tax of 1692-3 was payable quarterly at a basic rate of four shillings per annum; but this was far from being a simple flat rate paid by all. Both the exemptions from the tax and an extensive set of surtaxes deriving from an individual's status or wealth are described elsewhere in this volume.[6] In the City only the two lowest levels of surtax occur with any regularity. The first was for tradesmen, shopkeepers and vintners whose estate or net wealth was assessed at over £300; they had to pay an additional £2 per year. The next level was for merchants, brokers to merchants, gentlemen with a real or personal estate of over £300 capital value and various professions; they had to pay an additional £4 per year. The assessments for

3 Data were collected on the basis of these 200 districts and used to plot a number of maps illustrating different facets of City life; for details see Alexander, 'Economic and social structure', in which further details substantiating other points made in this chapter can be found. See also Alexander 'Economic Structure'.

4 For details see Gibson, *Hearth tax* and the chapter by Cooper in this volume.

5 3 Wm. & M., c.6; 4 Wm. & M., c.1.

6 See chapter 8 above.

this 1692 Poll tax are especially important for a study of London because they survive for the whole of the City and also provide a high proportion of the householders' occupations.[7]

The Four Shilling Aid was chosen for detailed comparative study because of the numerous opportunities for linking households mentioned in both taxes created by the small time lag and because its assessments survive for all but one of the City's wards.[8] This tax was levied on two distinct features of a household's worth. All real property was to be taxed at four shillings in the pound (or twenty per cent) of its rack rent value. This was to be collected from the owner of the property or from the tenants on his behalf. It would appear from the assessments, which almost invariably listed the householder (whether owner or not), that the first responsibility for payment lay with the actual occupier of the property, although the ultimate responsibility rested with the landlord.

The second part of this tax was a levy of four shillings in the pound on the notional return or income from an individual's business wealth, or of 1.2 per cent on its capital value.[9] As the Act stated, this was to be based on his or her 'goods, wares, merchandises or other chattels or personal estate', apart from household possessions and stock upon land, and also on ready money and on all but his or her most hopeless debts. Theoretically the debts owed by the taxpayer were meant to be set against his monetary and non-monetary working assets. In effect, therefore, the Aid sought to tax net wealth, which made this part an ambitious prototype for the income tax. Because stock for business purposes was the most visible commodity covered by this aspect of the tax, it inevitably bore the lion's share. Like elements of the earlier Poll taxes,[10] the 4s. Aid attempted to tap an individual's wealth on a proportional basis rather than by merely placing the wealthier taxpayers in one of two or three different surtax categories, but this approach did provide considerable scope for evasion.

7 This was first pointed out by Glass, 'Socio-economic status', p.377.

8 4 Wm. and M., c.1. An assessment for the following 4s. Aid, 5 Wm. & M., c.1, was used for the ward of Cripplegate Within and for the precinct of St Martin Ludgate in the ward of Farringdon Within. In addition the later 4s. Aid was used for Portsoken since the Poll tax used for this ward was 9 Wm. III, c.38.

9 4 Wm. & M., c.1, s.1.

10 See chapter 8 above.

During the 1690s Charles Davenant wrote extensively about many of the contemporary taxes, including a discussion of the relative contributions of each county to various of them.[11] Despite the opportunities for evasion, Davenant believed that the Four Shilling Aid of 1693 was more effective at tapping the wealth of London than previous taxes had been. Later writers, such as Ward, have also tended to confirm the impression that it taxed London relatively effectively, especially when taking account of the problems which the city's 'densely packed but shifting population' posed for its mainly amateur administrators.[12] In general this Four Shilling Aid is regarded as one of the most successful levies of the 1690s and Beckett, for example, has concluded that 'for all its faults the 1693 4s. Aid raised £1,922,713, the largest amount ever collected from a single annual extraordinary tax'.[13]

Coverage of the taxes: comparisons between Marriage Duty and Poll tax data

The best measure available for determining the number of people and households in the City and for checking the coverage of both taxes are the first assessment lists made for the Marriage Duty Act in 1695, for which an almost complete set survives for the City of London. Except in the case of bachelors aged over twenty-five and childless widowers, these lists were not actual assessments for the tax, but only indicated the categories for which each inhabitant would have to pay if he or she died, got married or had a child during the coming year. These lists may therefore have been more reliable than most other assessments that were drawn up for immediate taxation purposes and are generally considered to have been one of the most complete census-type surveys conducted in early modern England.[14]

A comparison of the 1692 Poll tax lists with those for the Marriage Duty reveals that the former omitted many households

11 Davenant, 'Essay', pp.26-61.

12 Ward, *English land tax*, pp.39-41.

13 Beckett, 'Land tax', p.293.

14 Both King, contemporaneously, and more recently Glass, have considered the reliability of the assessment lists; see Glass 'Introduction', pp.xxviii-xxix. Their conclusions indicate that perhaps as many as ten per cent of the population were excluded, but no one can be sure. The lists should be regarded as giving a minimum figure rather than the exact number. See also chapter 8 for a summary of the Marriage Duty Act.

and people, particularly in the areas outside the walls.[15] In the City as a whole, nearly 80 per cent of the households were included in the Poll tax, with over 90 per cent in the area within the walls. Outside the walls approximately one-third of the households and just over half the individuals escaped assessment for the Poll tax. Most of these omissions will have been covered perfectly legally by the exemptions from the Poll tax. For example, a very large proportion of the missing individuals were certainly children, who were excused from the Poll tax by the provision exempting the offspring of day labourers. All these lists were consequently short of children and included very many apparently childless households. Compared with the mean of 1.38 children per Marriage Duty house found by Glass in a sample of forty parishes within the walls, the mean number of children per Poll tax household was 1.05 in the inner City and 0.66 in the outer areas.

In the Poll tax the mean number of persons per household was 5.2 within the walls and 3.8 without. This figure for the inner area bears some comparison with Glass's mean of 6.0 per house. Unfortunately, a more detailed comparison of the two taxes encounters the problem that parishes, which formed the basis on which the Marriage Duty was assessed, were not always coterminous with precincts. Constructing parishes out of a number of different precincts is a laborious task, especially when the precinct includes sections from more than one parish. In the cases where it was possible to delineate precincts straightforwardly and rebuild them as parishes a common pattern appeared. Parishes closest to the centre of the City had the highest proportion of Poll tax payers in their populations, whilst those towards the outside of the City had the least. These proportions ranged from a very low 25 per cent in the western precinct of Cripplegate Without and around 43 per cent for the whole ward of Portsoken (situated along the eastern edge of the City) to over 100 per cent for a handful of central parishes, including Allhallows' Bread Street where more people were listed as being liable to the Poll tax than to the Marriage Duty charges. The differing proportions for all households is set out in Figure 1.

The total number of households assessed for the 20 per cent tax on rents in the 4s. Aid was very similar to the number of

[15] This problem is frustrated by inconsistencies in the definition of households; see Glass, 'Introduction', pp.xxiv, (fn.1), xxx-xxxi.

Figure 1 The proportion of householders paying the 1692 Poll tax in the City of London

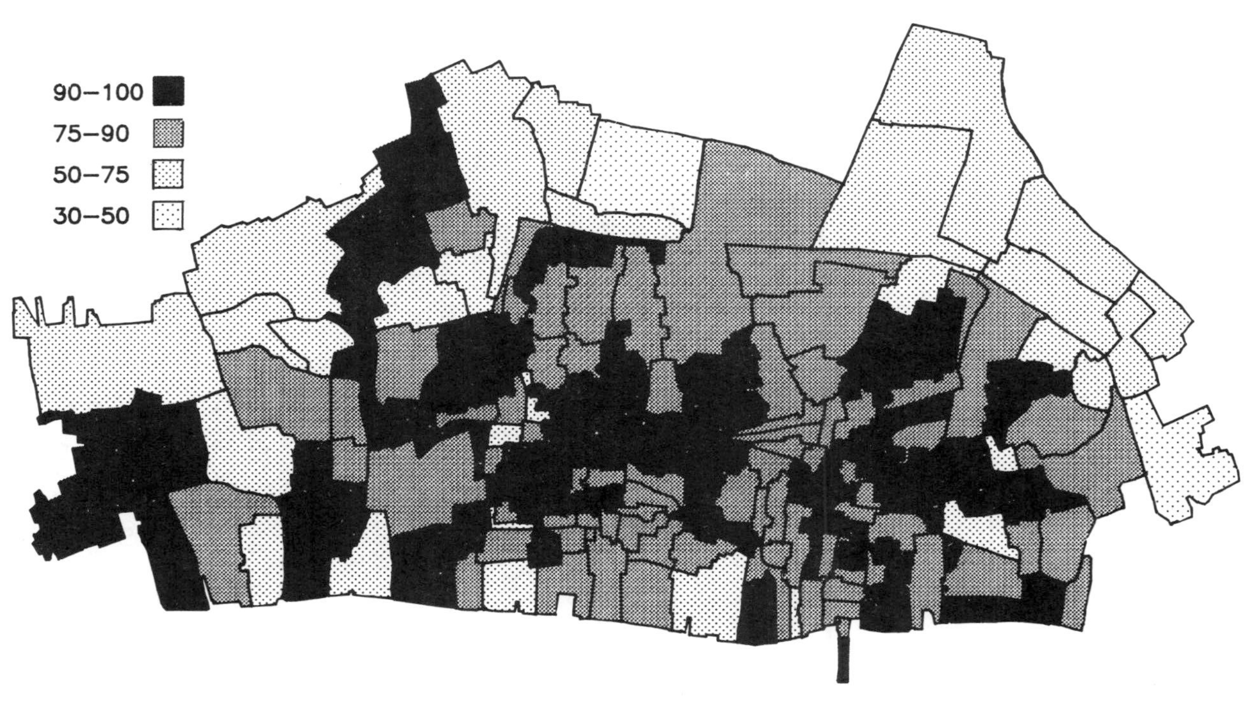

Table 1 Houses and people: the contrasting coverage of taxes in the City of London, 1692-95

Tax	City within the walls		City without the walls		All City	
	Houses	Persons	Houses	Persons	Houses	Persons
1692 Quarterly Poll	10,698	55,730	6,867	26,105	17,565	81,835
1693 4s. Aid						
rents	12,350	-	9,417	-	21,767	-
stocks	6,553	7,468	2,687	2,911	9,240	10,379
1695 Marriage Duty	11,501	69,733	10,537	53,346	22,038	123,079

households identified in the Marriage Duty assessments. However, this conceals the fact that, whilst the inner City had about a thousand more notional and actual rentpayers than households identified for Marriage Duty purposes, the outer area had several hundred fewer, as is demonstrated in Table 1. This is accounted for both by the difficulty of identifying the beginning and end of the various larger and more complex households in the inner areas and by the fact that, in the outer wards, the assessments for the 4s. Aid listed a number of householders as being responsible for the tax on more than one property.[16] In such cases the reliability of the total rental is not in doubt; only the number of individual households in each property, which inevitably adds a minor element of approximation to all calculations based on the total number of households for a particular area. There are also significant, but explicable, differences in the proportions who paid the various levels of surcharge to these three taxes. The smallest number of surtax payers was recorded by the Marriage Duty assessors who listed, in addition to the gentry and recognised professions, only those with a nominal worth of over £600 or an income from property of more than £50 a year. Next came the Poll tax, which surcharged those admitting to a personal estate of more than £300. The largest numbers were caught by the tax on business stock in the

16 Usually signified by the additional comment of 'tenants' or 'tenements'. This was particularly the case in the outer wards where smaller, poorer accommodation was more common.

4s. Aid, for which there was no specified limit, but in practice this surcharge seems to have begun when assessed wealth reached £12 10s.[17] Altogether well over half the householders within the City walls contributed to the extra levy on stocks and just over a quarter did so outside the walls.

Unfortunately, we know that evasion from these surtaxes was quite widespread, with many admitting to no more than nominal levels of wealth. Without a professional tax inspectorate and in a world where income and wealth were never strictly accounted, the problems of taxing wealth comprehensively, in particular such elusive commodities as ready money, debts and merchandise, could not be resolved. By comparison, land was a much more tangible and reliable unit on which to levy taxes, even in built-up areas like the City of London, so that eventually Parliament fell back on the Land tax as its main revenue raiser in addition to long-term borrowing. Nevertheless, support for the war was still very strong in London in the early 1690s and the 4s. Aid does appear to have tapped more unpropertied wealth there than any previous tax, so that the overall levels of assessment for most of these extra charges do seem to have been relatively high. Thus, if it could be established that the evasion levels from the surcharges for these taxes of the 1690s probably differed little across the City, then their validity for identifying differences in social composition will not be seriously undermined. The best opportunity for undertaking this task appears to be provided by a comparison between the surviving probate inventories and the different levels of business wealth or stock taxed under the 4s. Aid. The plethora of jurisdictions covering the City made the search for the former especially difficult, but a large enough sample of inventories was found eventually in the Prerogative Court of Canterbury, the Archdeaconry and Commissary Courts of London and the Orphans' Court.[18] The findings of this research are outlined in Table 2, which shows a significant positive correlation between the gross valuation of goods recorded in these inventories and the value of taxed stock. Consequently, it appears

17 This was the lowest rating found in the tax assessments. For the numbers in each band, see Table 1 in Appendix 3, Alexander, 'Economic and social structure', p.332.

18 Summaries of the Orphans' Court inventories can be found in The Common Sergeant's Book at the CLRO; the Canterbury inventories are held at the PRO; Archdeaconry and Commissary inventories are kept at the Guildhall Library Manuscripts Room.

Table 2 1693 4s. Aid tax on stocks matched with inventories

Taxed stocks £	Gross valuation Mean £	Gross valuation Median £	Taxed Stocks/'Wealth' Mean %	Taxed Stocks/'Wealth' Median %	n
A) Inventories from the Archdeaconry and Commissary Courts of London					
<25	96	43	-	-	22
25-49	124	73	20.2	34.2	13
50-99	529	261	9.5	19.2	8
100+	100	100	-	-	1
Total					44
B) Inventories from the Prerogative Court of Canterbury					
<25	424	198	-	-	28
25-49	173	120	14.5	20.8	6
50-74	651	453	7.7	11.0	22
75-99	226	226	33.1	33.1	1
100-149	1045	994	9.6	10.1	26
150-199	3066	3185	4.9	4.7	5
200-249	3583	3788	5.6	5.3	8
250-299	2014	2014	12.4	12.4	2
300-399	3954	3736	7.6	8.0	5
400+	9772	10175	4.1	3.9	3
Total					106
C) Inventories (gross valuation) from the Orphans' Court					
<25	1023	718	-	-	14
25-49	924	485	2.7	5.2	18
50-99	1068	846	4.7	5.9	31
100-149	3584	2000	2.8	5.0	47
150-199	3920	3671	3.8	4.1	18
200-299	5274	4012	3.8	5.0	30
300-399	5766	5565	5.2	5.4	12
400+	21845	15220	1.8	2.6	10
Total					180

quite appropriate to use data from the stock tax element of the 4s. Aid as a broad indicator of differences among the middle and upper levels of society in the City of London.

Patterns of rent, patterns of wealth: toward a social geography of the City

The social geography and structure of the City of London in the seventeenth century has been investigated by a number of previous studies, using three main sources. These were the Tithe survey of 1638, drawn up to establish the value to the Church of the individual parishes within the City, the Hearth tax returns of the 1660s and the Marriage Duty assessments for 1695. Emrys Jones and Roger Finlay mapped their own independently derived rental values from the 'moderated' ones of the 1638 survey, which were approximately four-fifths of the estimated annual rental values. Both showed a central area of the City of London with higher rents than the surrounding parishes, which was constricted into a narrow band running east-west, as well as spikes along London Bridge and in the west along Fleet Street.[19]

Important though these studies are, both are problematic because of their tendency to use rent levels as a proxy measure for 'real' wealth. Clearly, individuals seldom, if ever, pay a fixed proportion of their personal wealth on the property which they rent, the relationship between the two, rent and wealth, being far from evenly distributed within the population.[20] Equally, the mean number of hearths per household is an even more suspect measure of differential wealth between particular areas, especially since differing proportions of the smaller households were omitted from some individual returns.[21] Nonetheless, Power's study of London's social topography in the years immediately preceding the Great Fire suggested an almost identical pattern, despite his numerous reservations concerning the Hearth tax's limitations as a source. And yet he was still able to conclude that 'although there are some differences in the ranking of the parishes the overall picture of a central straggling core of wealthy parishes, surrounded by poorer parishes along the Thames and around the Walls, is the same'.[22]

In theory at least, the Marriage Duty assessment lists of 1695

19 Finlay, *Population and metropolis*, pp.70-82; Jones, 'London', pp.123-33; Jones and Judges, 'London population', pp.45-63; Glass, 'Introduction'.

20 Note the low correlation between rent tax and source tax in Table 2.06 in Alexander, 'Economic and social structure', p.35.

21 Power, 'Social topography', p.200. See also chapters 3 and 4 above.

22 Power, 'Social topography', p.206.

came closer to measuring wealth since people who had real estate that yielded an income of more than £50 per annum or personal estate of over £600 capital value were liable to pay the same surtaxes as gentlemen or reputed gentlemen. The map drawn by Glass, which was based upon the earlier work of Jones and Judges on these 1695 Marriage Duty data, showed the same basic pattern as revealed by the 1638 and mid-1660s studies.[23] A wealthy central area ran through the City, but apparently extended to include a larger area above and immediately to the west of the Bridge and to some areas in the north-west of the City. From this information alone one cannot tell whether this increased size of the wealthy area was due to a real increase of wealth in the areas outside the City's central core, to a change in the basis of the collection of the data since it caught more wealthy people as well as higher rentpayers, and/or to any post-fire rebuilding near the riverside. Such questions, however, can be answered in part by a comparative study of the relevant information contained in the surviving lists for the Poll tax and the Four Shilling Aid.

The information recorded in the 1692 Poll tax and the 1693 4s. Aid has two distinct advantages over the limitations of the other three sources discussed in the introduction to this chapter. Firstly, they make it possible to separate rent from wealth and to plot them independently of each other. In addition, due to the administration of these taxes, it is also possible to cover almost twice as many districts as the previous studies based on parish data and so provide a more sensitive guide to the contours of rent and wealth across the different areas of the City. Before undertaking this, however, one problem involved in drawing maps based on mean rental values must be considered briefly: the distribution of properties about the mean. When smaller districts contain one or two highly valued properties and several lesser ones, their mean rental value may be considerably higher than the median. This problem was manageable in this study, however, because the precincts were sufficiently large for the overall mean rental value to have been only slightly affected by one large property.[24]

23 See Glass, 'Introduction', p.xxiii; Jones and Judges, 'London's population', pp.45-63.

24 This and related problems are considered in Alexander, 'Economic and social structure', p.43.

The mean rents (or annual rental values) for each of the tax districts derived from the 4s. Aid assessments have been plotted in Figure 2. This material illustrates a similar distribution to those studies based on the 1638 tithe material, showing a large and undifferentiated area of higher rental values in the centre of the City. The distribution is also very similar to that derived from the 1695 Marriage Duty information, with the same broad spur of higher rent areas running southward to London Bridge as well as spreading north and west. As stated previously, however, rental values may not be a very good proxy for wealth. In comparison the amount of goods and money taxed under the 4s. Aid would seem to give a better indication of the relative levels of wealth, since it measures possessions rather than accommodation.

Figure 3 uses data from the stock tax element of the 4s. Aid to plot socio-geographical patterns within the City. This map again confirms the established belief that by the 1690s there was a fairly broad area across the centre of the City that was substantially wealthier than the surrounding areas, but it also reveals that this central area was in fact somewhat more variegated than had previously been thought. The most centrally located districts were not the most obviously wealthy districts. These districts covering the two main arterial routes through the City, the Cheapside and Cornhill east-west axis, and the route up from London Bridge northwards along Gracechurch Street and Bishopsgate, can now be seen to be somewhat secondary in terms of taxpaying wealth.

This same pattern is brought out even more clearly by plotting the mean stock tax paid by those who actually paid it as opposed to the mean stock tax for all households in a particular district. Figure 4 shows an even more pronounced pattern of wealth holding. The highest levels of wealth were definitely not concentrated on the main arterial routes, but were distributed around them in a number of specific pockets. Care must be taken with this map in case a small number of very wealthy taxpayers were engulfed by a large number of relatively poorer taxpayers who could distort the true wealth of a particular district as a whole.[25] The pockets of wealth in the suburbs disappear when the

[25] This effect was partly reflected by the apparent broader spread of wealth into some outlying districts of the City, such as the northern division of Bishopsgate Without, the High St precinct of Portsoken ward and the St Bartholomew the Great precinct in Farringdon Without ward.

Figure 2 Mean rental values in the City of London, 1693

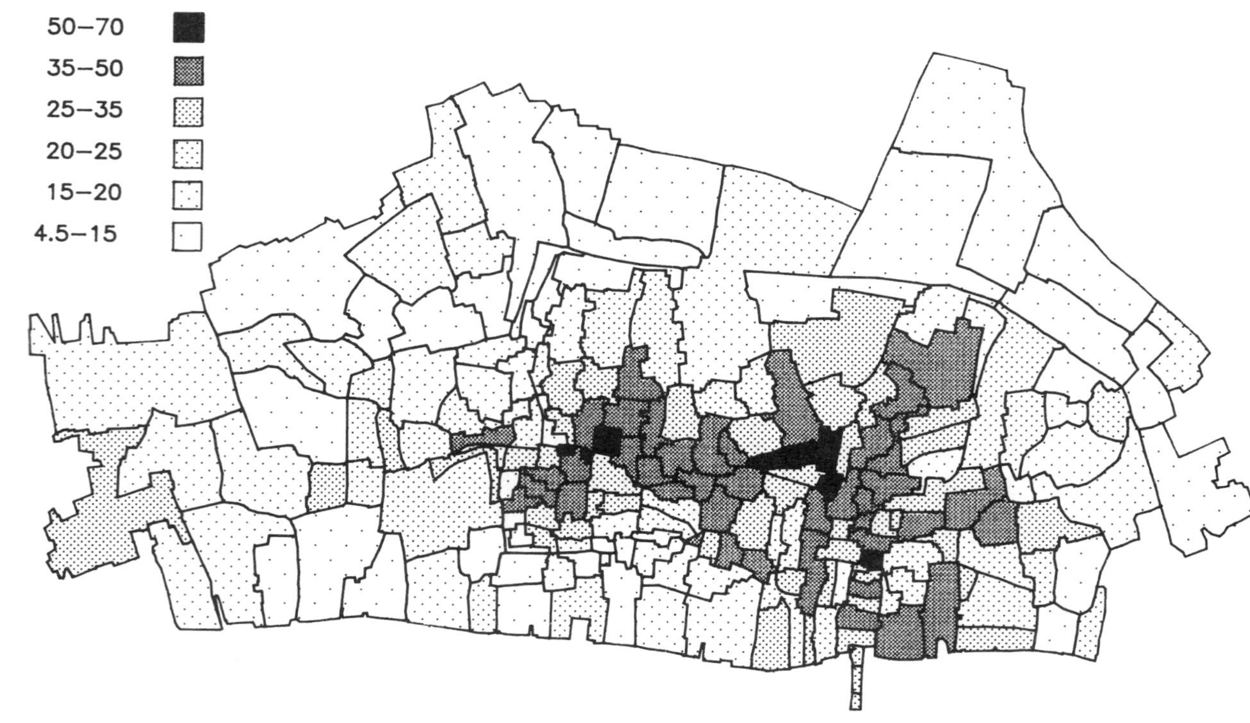

Figure 3 Taxed stocks in the City of London, 1693: mean assessment of all householders

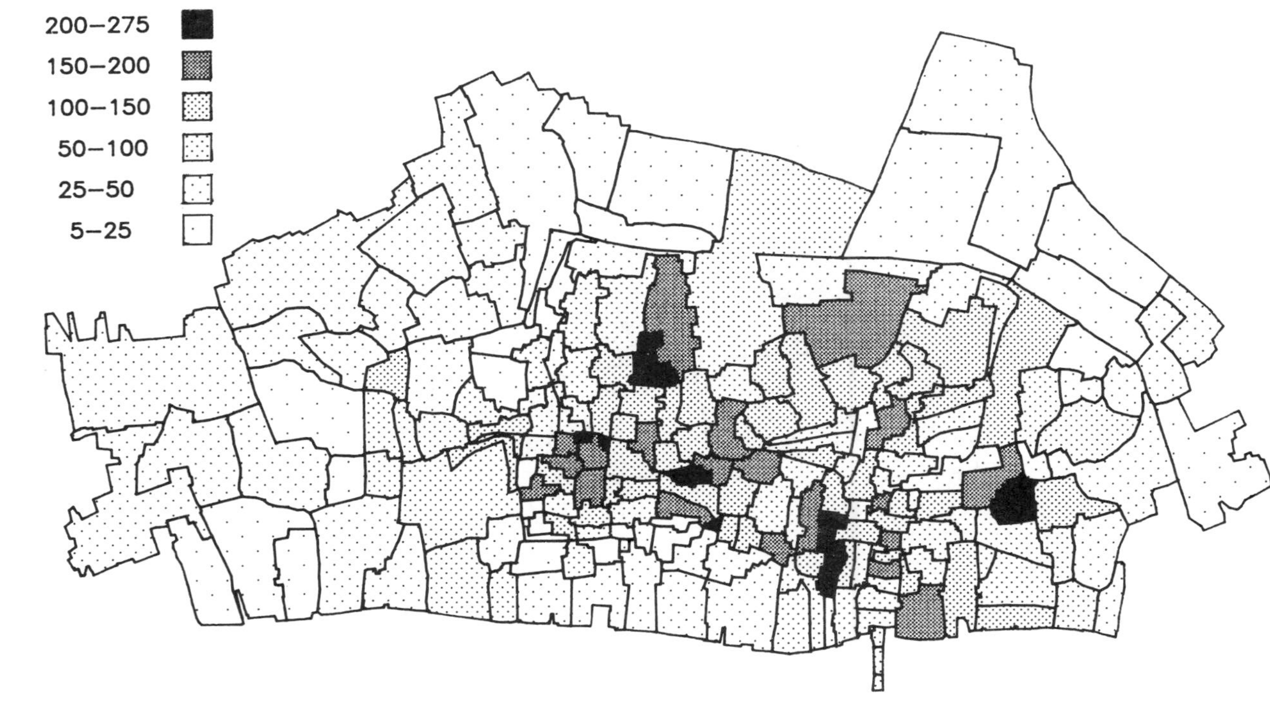

Figure 4 Taxed stocks in the City of London, 1693: mean assessment of tax payers

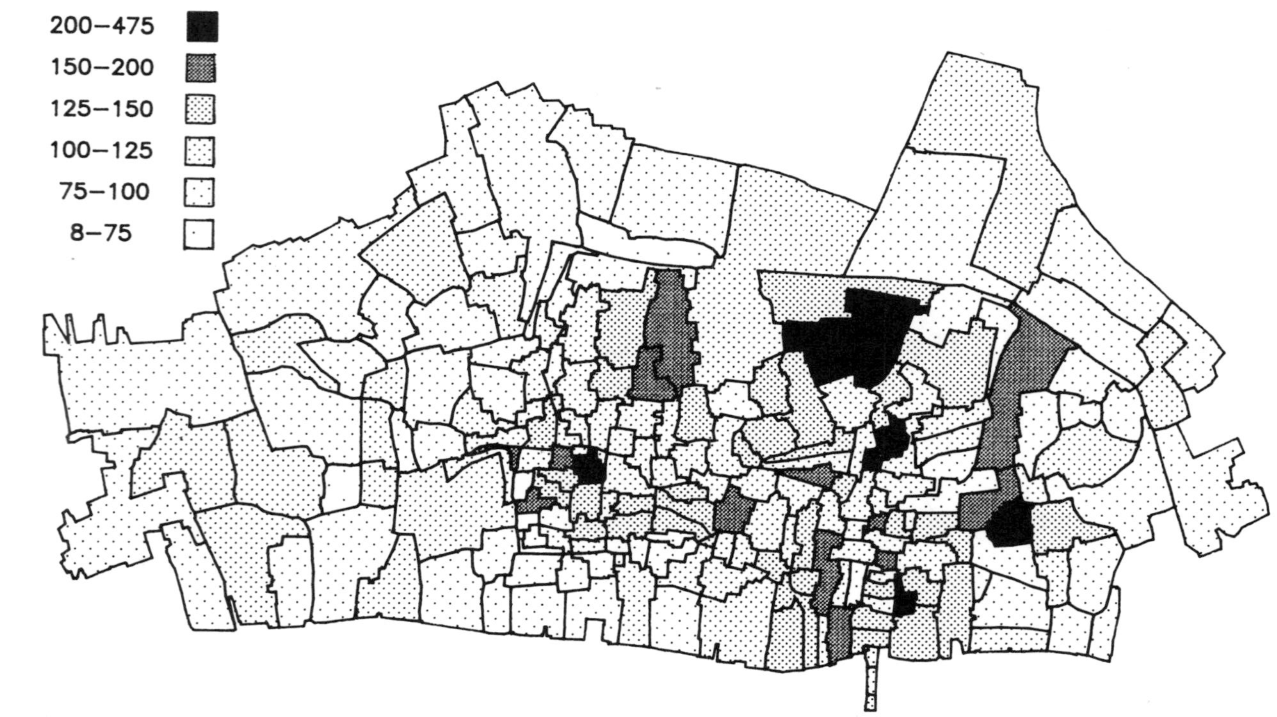

total taxed wealth of a district is divided by its total number of households rather than by only those considered wealthy enough to pay a tax on their stocks.

Another caution must also be registered. In the later seventeenth century the wealth of many householders would have been determined to a larger extent than today by the stage of the life-cycle at which they found themselves and by their health. The tax data unfortunately give no indication of age to shed light upon this factor, nor do they record the infirmity or otherwise of the heads of the households. Consequently, their age structure in the lower rent districts may have been biased upwards. However, such drawbacks do not prevent these sources from giving considerable insight into the spatial variations in the nature of society in the City.

Social structure

An analysis of the 1692 Poll tax lists in combination with the information from the 4s. Aid of 1693 also sheds new light on the overall social structure of the late seventeenth-century City. Out of a total of around 22,000 households, over 17,500 contributed towards the Poll tax. In addition nearly half, or 9,500, of these households was assessed for the tax on stocks, at a variety of different levels. It has been shown above that these were quite closely related to actual wealth, as measured by a sample of the probate inventories taken after some of them died.

Reference to Table 3 shows that at the very top of the social scale 3,250 households were considered wealthy enough to have had a member included in the surtax categories for the Marriage duties. These covered all the 1,682 householders who paid the higher, £4, surcharge in the Poll tax, as well as some of the 3,570 householders who paid the £2 surcharge. This group, comprising around 3,000 households, had, according to these two taxes, taxable wealth starting between £300 and £600 or property valued at more than £50 per year.[26] The evidence from the

[26] However, some conflict between the estimates of taxable wealth emerges from a consideration of the evidence of the 4s. Aid. This is because, whilst 1,000 of the top 3,000 householders taxed for stocks were assessed for stocks of £300 or above, a further 1,600 were assessed merely between £150 and £250. In theory all 3,000 stock tax payers should have been found paying for stocks of a minimum £300. This suggests that in practice the assessors of the 4s. Aid operated under different guidelines for assessing wealth in different taxes. Since we already know that their estimates were in any case well below the true value of the taxpayers' estates, the assessors would have had plenty of room for manoeuvre.

Table 3 A social table for the City of London in the 1690s

Class	Characteristics	Inventoried wealth	Number of households
I	Higher rate of poll surtax; some lower rate of poll surtax; most Marriage Duty substantial households; over £100 in taxed stocks	over £2,000	3,000
II	Most of the lower rate of poll surtax; remainder of the Marriage Duty substantial households; £25–£100 in taxed stocks	£100–£2,000	3,500
III	Basic rate of Poll tax only; £12–£25 in taxed stocks	£50–£500	4,000
IV	Basic rate of Poll tax only	£0–£50	7,000
V	Those not assessed for Poll tax but included in the Marriage Duty assessments	£0	4,500
			22,000

inventories clearly points to the conclusion that those with stocks taxed at £150 and above were significantly wealthy with gross estates running into thousands of pounds. In the inventories analysed, the median for those paying on taxed stocks of £150-£200 was over £2,500. Yet inventory evidence also suggests that significant numbers of individuals taxed for stocks of £50 and £100 were clearly under-assessed. It is valid therefore to move perhaps 500 of the 4,000 taxpayers out of that class and into the higher group. This brings the top social class, those householders who had estates valued at over £2,000 and in some cases up to £50,000-£60,000, to around 3,000 in all.

The next group consists of the bulk of those paying tax on stocks of £50 and £100. After moving 500 up to the higher category, there are over 3,500 householders left in this class. This group covered the majority of those who paid at the lower £2 surcharge in the Poll tax as well as those just below that level who had managed to pay only the ordinary rate. That this is a reasonable supposition is supported by the fact that it is possible, by linking the Poll tax listing to that of the 4s. Aid, to identify at least 400 householders who paid at rates of £100 and above in the stock tax, yet who did not pay towards the poll surtaxes. The inventory evidence indicates that this group had estates ranging from around £100 to over £1,000.

The top two groups together included some 6,500 households. It covered all of the 5,252 households headed by a person paying one of the poll surtaxes. It also included a number of households just below that surtax threshold or left out due to mistakes in assessment. This number represented over one-quarter of all City households. In addition, given the relatively large size of these households, at least one-third of the City's population would have resided in this comparatively wealthy sector.

In the lower middle bracket we can place the bulk of those who paid at the lower levels of the stock tax in the 4s. Aid, but paid no poll surtaxes. This group contains the 1,800 householders identified from the Poll tax who paid on taxed stocks of £12 and £25 in the 4s. Aid and also includes the 1,000 householders who were counted as paying the tax on stocks at these levels in the Aid but who could not be identified in the poll listing. The number also needs to be increased to include the households who successfully evaded both the tax on stocks and the Poll tax surcharges. This is very difficult to estimate but perhaps consisted of another 1,000 households out of a possible sample of 8,000 who paid the Poll tax but paid no surtaxes or taxes on stock. This would make this middling group around 4,000 households in all, representing a fifth of all households in the City. Together with the two higher social groups, this means that at least half of all the households in the City could be classed as comfortably off, with a range of inventoried wealth stretching from £50 to several thousands of pounds.

The evidence from the taxes also indicates that there was a substantial body of households well-off enough to pay the Poll tax, but no surtax or stock taxes. This would have meant that they would not normally have been considered for exemption from paying the poor rates. In 1692 this group contained about 8,000 households, of whom 1,000 have been placed in the higher class. This leaves a large group of around 7,000 households in an intermediate position between relative comfort and the classes outside the ordinary system of tax and ratepaying. It is difficult to find examples of inventories for those in these classes but the few that have survived indicate that they died with between zero and £50 wealth. Many were undoubtedly day labourers or casual workers.

The group at the bottom of this hierarchy, made up of those usually exempt from the Poll tax, were possibly on the poverty line. They were not all in need of relief since their exemption from the Poll tax was based merely on their inability to contribute to the parish rates, though they may well have been in need of occasional relief in bad years.[27] Yet it is also clear that many households were in need of permanent relief. Since there were 17,500 households paying at least the flat rate of Poll tax, approximately 4,500 remained in this bottom category.

Conclusion

On the whole the data derived from the 1692 Poll tax and the 1693 4s. Aid provide a rich picture of the social structure of the City of London. In particular they reveal not only the depth in wealth across the City, but also emphasise the diffusion of wealth and the absence of sharp discontinuities. Although super-rich households could be found only in certain areas, for example, large numbers of the middle orders were spread out across the City and lived even in the relatively poorer areas.

[27] A detailed study of such households can be found in Macfarlane, 'Studies in poverty'.

10

Household form and composition in King's Lynn: a reconstruction based on the Poll taxes of 1689-1702

SHEILA COOPER

Introduction

In the early 1990s the 'Poll Tax' became a much debated and fiercely contested issue. Although quite different in structure, Poll taxes are far from being a twentieth-century invention; they are not new to the 1990s, nor for that matter was the Poll tax new to the parliaments of the late seventeenth century. A number of infrequent and *ad hoc* Poll taxes have been implemented since Parliament passed the first direct tax of its kind, the Tallage of Groats in 1377, to meet the unusual and high costs of war with France. However, it was in the seventeenth century that the tax reached its zenith, both in terms of frequent use and attempts at extensive coverage. In the time of Charles I Poll tax revenues were used to disband the northern army. During the Restoration, Poll taxes helped first to pay off the forces and in 1667 to finance the Dutch War. The taxes of the later period – 1678, 1689, 1690, 1692, 1694, 1697, 1698, and 1702 – also financed military expenditures, for use against the French as well as the Irish.[1]

Despite their broad range through time every Poll tax after 1380 has shared a number of attributes. All exempted the poorest of the poor and none formed part of the Crown's regular support – military expenditure being a force behind all polls from the Tallage of Groats onward. Since 1380, all Poll taxes were

[1] The dates given are those of collection. Several of the tax bills were passed in the calendar year preceding their collection. Details of the various Poll tax Acts of the seventeenth century are given in chapter 8 above. I am grateful to Richard Wall of the Cambridge Group for the History of Population and Social Structure for much discussion and some tutelage on the Poll taxes during the preparation of this chapter. Although Stephen Dowell's standard *History of Taxation*, vol.2, p.46 and vol.3, p.6 claims that 'the Poll tax of 1698 was the last', a claim often repeated, Parliament passed a poll in conjunction with a Land tax in 1702; 1 Anne., c.6.

graduated in a number of ways relative to rank and wealth, a graduation that became more pronounced after the Restoration when Parliament attempted to use the apparatus of the Poll to tax income and personalty, thereby alleviating the burden on land.[2] Although the Poll taxes of the seventeenth century theoretically covered most of the population, reaching a much broader spectrum than did other direct taxes, an important feature of continuity of the Polls is that everyone did not pay them. It is important for the historian of the later Stuart period to realise that the lists prepared by assessors included differing proportions of the population at various times. Basically, three factors influenced the extent to which people were taxed. First were the exemptions incorporated by Parliament in the original bills which were extended most substantially in 1667 and 1690. Second were the economic conditions which helped determine how extensive the proportion of the population formally exempted in particular localities would be. And last there were unknown numbers of people from the Tallage of Groats through to the final instalment of the 1702 Poll who evaded paying the taxes. It seems perhaps ironic that despite the scope of the seventeenth-century Poll taxes, they never raised the revenue that was expected from them, while at the same time they inspired widespread dislike and consequently considerable evasion.

This chapter concentrates on an examination of a series of Poll tax lists which have survived for late seventeenth-century and early eighteenth-century King's Lynn, Norfolk. Although several Poll tax assessments have survived for other communities, the Lynn data are possibly unique because they form the longest and most complete series of such taxes, spanning the period from 1689 to 1702.[3]

[2] For a discussion of the attempt to use Poll taxes as a kind of incipient income tax see Chandeman, *English public revenue*, esp. p.147; Kennedy, *English taxation*, p.39.

[3] Surviving Poll tax returns for King's Lynn are catalogued at the Norfolk Record Office (NRO) and stored in the King's Lynn Record Office (hereafter KLRO). They include the Poll collected in 1689, KL/C47/10; four quarterly assessments and an extra fair copy for 1692, KL/C47/11-15; one quarterly assessment of 1694, KL/C47/16; and one of 1702, KL/C47/17-25. I am grateful to Susan Maddock, the NRO archivist who oversees KLRO records, for her considerable assistance. The law stipulated that duplicates of the collectors' tax records should have been deposited with the Exchequer without naming the persons, which explains why the present writer has found only total returns and some names of defaulters, not lists of taxpayers, in the Public Record Office; PRO, E179/154/698-9; E179/253/46; E182/686-7.

Payers and non-payers: estimating the coverage of the Poll taxes

In sheet after sheet, ward by ward, Lynn assessors inscribed the names of their fellow citizens and all others within each household liable to pay. Sometimes when the law directed they added information that indicated if an individual should pay a surtax. As stated already the assessors listed only those whom they deemed able to pay, those fitting the categories that Parliament designated in the Poll tax legislation. It is unfortunate from the historian's point of view that Parliament did not tax everyone, since, especially from 1690 onwards, these Poll tax lists largely identify what might be termed the 'middling sort', the wealthier citizens of the community – artisans, mariners, merchants and professional people – and their households, leaving out the least prominent, poorest, or most unskilled households of King's Lynn.

It is difficult to estimate the exact proportion of the population legally exempt either before or after 1690, when exemption was extended to those adults who were already excused from paying rates for the church and poor. In 1689, 3,581 individuals paid the Poll tax in King's Lynn. They doubtless formed a substantial portion of the inhabitants of Lynn, possibly around 85 per cent or more of the households. Lynn tax collectors clearly omitted excused alms-receivers, their resident children, and some others judged too poor to pay. Equally, the number of households without children listed indicate that the collectors taxed some poorer parents, such as day labourers and servants in husbandry, but not their children, resulting in an undercount of children. On the other hand, many of the children of the poor were taxed as servants in other households, which reduces the undercount somewhat. Also, it may be remembered that in this period late age of marriage and high infant and child mortality combined to keep families small.[4] Thus the additional exemption offered to those with four or more children under sixteen and without fifty pounds in goods probably touched relatively few families.

Lawful exemptions and some probable evasions aside, it would be useful to know the actual extent of coverage the Poll tax returns offer. Most seventeenth-century communities, like King's Lynn, have very little reliable data from which to infer population

[4] Wrigley and Schofield, *Population history*, pp.230-1, 249, 255.

figures. A few, however, have both Poll tax and Marriage Duty Act assessments extant and in these cases estimates of coverage can be inferred with fair certainty. Marriage Duty Act assessments, where they exist, usually cover the entire population and may be considered comparable to censuses.[5]

Assessments from All Saints within the Bar, a Southampton parish, exist for the 1689 and October 1692 Poll taxes as well as for the 1695 Marriage Duty Act.[6] The latter enumerated 402 people in the parish. In 1689, 352 parishioners paid the Poll, almost 88 per cent of the probable population in 1695. Gregory King estimated that 17 per cent of the population of late seventeenth-century Lichfield received charity, which would have left a maximum of 83 per cent of the population liable for a tax such as the Poll collected in 1689. Clarkson maintains that 'roughly' one-fifth of the population of late seventeenth-century England were paupers by contemporary standards,[7] consequently if Clarkson's paupers were synonymous with alms-receivers, his estimate for England would approach Gregory King's Lichfield figure, both being a little lower than the All Saints within the Bar evidence. At best the data from All Saints – one parish in all of England – are an indicator which, if we could examine such data for enough English taxation units, could help produce a reasonable range. At worst, the All Saints percentage provides a point of reference for figures from other 1689 tax returns.[8]

In the absence of Marriage Duty assessments one can derive approximations of the total population at risk to be recorded in a Poll tax list in a number of different ways. Some historians have used Hearth tax returns or the Compton census of 1676 to that end.[9] Alternatively one can apply crude rates of growth, derived

5 The Marriage Duty Act 6 & 7 Wm. & M., c.6, called for a population enumeration. Details are given in chapter 8 above.

6 Hampshire Record Office, SC 14/2/37B, SC 14/2/50b, SC 14/2/64.

7 Clarkson, *Pre-industrial economy*, p.233.

8 All Saints may have been a somewhat decayed parish at this time, regenerating in the eighteenth centuy. See Patterson, *History of Southampton*, pp.2-4. For a more detailed discussion of these issues see Arkell, 'Poverty', where it is argued that some 13-15 per cent of households appear to have been exempted from the Poll taxes of the 1660s, but because these households were relatively small they contained a somewhat lower proportion of the population. Also more children were exempt by 1689.

9 See, for example, Cressy, 'Education and literacy', p.377. Also note chapter 6 above.

from Wrigley and Schofield.[10] For example, the 1801 census records a population for Lynn of 10,096. Applying the rate of growth estimates calculated by Wrigley and Schofield to this figure backwards for 110 years produces a population of 5,745 for Lynn in 1691.[11] Informed by other sources, one can then adjust the Lynn estimate, allowing, for example, for epidemics and natural disasters such as the plague of the 1660s or the ship-sinking storms at the turn of the century.

Yet another estimate can be derived from baptismal register figures, either from the registers themselves or from John Rickman's 1801 collection of earlier parish register data.[12] The baptism numbers can be divided by a crude national birth rate to produce another estimate, which similarly can be adjusted to account for other known factors.[13]

The same methods of estimating the percentage of population taxed in 1689 can be used in later taxes, although because of the change in exemptions, the Polls taxed a considerably smaller population from 1690 on.[14] Gregory King thought that the 1692 Poll tax touched about 55 per cent of the English people, but his figure, cf course, represents a national mean that cannot necessarily be applied definitively to any one place.[15] Some percentages are lower; for example in Southampton's All Saints and Bristol's St John the Baptist parishes the numbers paying the 1692 Poll were about 42 and 40 per cent, respectively, of the numbers on Marriage Duty assessments for those parishes.[16] Other percentages are higher. In a sub-sample of a set of London

10 Wrigley and Schofield, *Population history*, pp.528-9.

11 Details of this calculation can be found in Cooper, 'Social structure in King's Lynn', pp.127-8.

12 John Rickman's 'Parish register abstracts' appear as a part of the 1801 census as *Abstract of the Answers and Returns made pursuant to an Act...Intituled An Act for taking an Account of the Population of Great Britain*. Parliamentary Papers VI. A discussion of Rickman's Abstracts appears in Wrigley and Schofield, *Population history*, pp.2-4.

13 Wrigley and Schofield, *Population history*, p.533. They estimate the crude national birth rate in 1701 at 34.2.

14 See chapter 8 above.

15 Clarkson, *Pre-industrial economy*, p.234; King, *Natural and political observations*, p.27.

16 HRO, SC 11/2/50b, SC 14/2/64; Bristol Record Office, St John Poll tax list 1692; St John the Baptist Marriage Duty assessment of 1697.

parishes, over 70 per cent of the number paying the 1695 Marriage Duty Act paid the 1692 Poll.[17]

In King's Lynn at least 2,162 inhabitants paid one of the four 1692 quarterly Polls, slightly more than 60 per cent of those who paid in 1689. If the 1692 taxpayers were 55 per cent of the Lynn population (King's all-England estimate) that population would have amounted to only 3,931 people, by most accounts a very low figure but one very close to the estimate derived using Rickman's figures and the crude birth rate for 1701.[18] Clearly, extrapolation from Gregory King's general estimate for any one community will be inadequate for a variety of reasons. One needs to take into account the apparent wealth or prosperity of the community in question, the age structure of the population, and the efficacy of the tax assessors or collectors. Without censuses or Marriage Duty Act assessments historians will have to depend upon the parliamentary acts to define who was included in the Poll and then have to match that information to documentary evidence and the economic structural peculiarities of the individual tax units. The study of Poll taxes and Marriage Duty Act assessments from a greater number of communities will no doubt eventually provide a more accurate idea of actual Poll tax coverage.

Because the exempt included alms-receivers and, from 1690 onwards, those excused from paying the church and poor rate through poverty, the economic conditions of the period clearly affected the Poll taxes' share of the total population and so the coverage of the Poll. One assumes that such poorer families were plentiful throughout seventeenth-century England, but their proportions nevertheless differed in individual communities, in part reflecting their economic structure and relative prosperity. Moreover, in trying to assess the extent of coverage of the Polls, one must consider other issues like sex ratios and the age structure of the population. These factors also have direct relevance to a study of the household composition of a particular community, such as King's Lynn.

[17] Glass, 'Socio-economic status', pp.217, 221. The seventy per cent is a crude estimate, based on a population of 9,200 for Glass's marriage duty sub-sample and 6,701 on the Poll tax return. The parameters of the groups were not, however, entirely identical. See also chapter 9.

[18] For details of estimates of the population of Lynn see Cooper, 'Social structure in King's Lynn', pp.124-9.

Evading the Poll taxes

Another problem encountered by a student of the Poll taxes is the fact that their coverage and yield were affected by evasion. By all accounts, moreover, evasion from the Poll taxes was extensive. The taxes collected never matched the revenue anticipated from them, and a number of times Parliament passed additional legislation to contain evasion and further increase the yield of a given Poll.[19] Evasion came in different forms and involved both failure to pay any part of the tax – the Poll itself and the surtaxes – as well as attempts to conceal titles, pensions, income, or other attributes that would have increased an individual's tax liability.

In his 1662 treatise on taxes, Sir William Petty, lauding the Hearth tax, noted that 'the number of Harths....remove not as Heads or Polls do'.[20] Marginalia on Poll tax rolls indicate a fair amount of mobility for what appear to be standard reasons. 'Gone to London', 'gone into the country with his daughter', 'joined the king's service', 'moved to Lincoln' are not unusual notations. But comments on separate lists of King's Lynn defaulters, which survive among Exchequer records, imply that some citizens chose removal as a method of evasion. These may have included Widow Margaret Sadler, who, among many others charged only for a poll, was 'not to be found'. Henry Windfield, his wife Frances, and their servant Helen Rowson, had 'gone out of town privately to parts unknowne' without paying, raising the spectre of people escaping the landlord by moving in the middle of the night. Equally, Mr Edmund Keene was conveniently 'out of town' in 1692, failing to pay his third quarterly tax on a thousand pounds' worth of stock. He could not be found, nor was there sufficient distress, that is to say goods that could have been seized in lieu of taxes.[21] Similarly, in 1667 Samuel Pepys noted the return of his fellow naval bureaucrat, John Creed, from Hinchingbrooke, where Creed had gone, Pepys thought, 'only to save his being taxed to the Poll

19 The 1667 Poll, for example, was followed later in the session by 'An Act Explanatory of the Act for raiseing Moneyes by a Poll', 18 & 19 Chas. II, c.6. The 1689 Act was extended by 'An Act for Review of the late Poll', 1 Wm. & M., s.2, c.7. The 1692 Quarterly Poll was reviewed later that year, 4 Wm. & M., c.14. Details are given in chapter 8 above. Each review tried to tighten the legislation and increase the revenue from it.

20 Petty, *A discourse of taxes and contributions*, p.71.

21 PRO, E182/687 pt. 1, E182/686. Many of those on these lists of 'defaulters' had died, and their servants had then 'gone'.

Bill'.[22] Pepys later taunted Creed, suggesting that 'a wise man', their mutual 'good friend', had claimed that Creed's excursion and his change of lodging on return to London were 'only to avoid paying to the pole bill'. A 'subtle false rogue', Creed blushed but did not deny the charge.[23]

In spite of considerable suspicion the collectors themselves offered no evidence that individuals who had moved had done so to evade taxes. Collector Thomas Robotham discovered in 1703 that Mr Williamson and his family had moved to Colbroke, where they paid all four quarters of the 1702 Poll. Others seemingly had left because of dire financial circumstances and possibly to avoid shame. John Turner, the bankrupt son of a prominent father, had gone from Lynn, 'he being failed', before Robotham could collect taxes on Turner's fifty pounds' worth of stock or the polls of his four children; 'no distress to be had'. Most defaulters probably left with few goods and, had they stayed, might not have been able to pay the tax. One of these, Francis Tooley, and his or her family were simply 'broke and gone'.[24] Some among the defaulters, however, did not flee. In May 1692 a frustrated collector noted that William Fincham's mother 'will not pay'. William paid for himself and continued to pay after his mother was dropped from the rolls. Mary Tourner, charged for two hundred pounds she had loaned at interest, stayed on in default. A saver, not a consumer, she had no goods for distress.[25]

The real problem with evasion from the Poll tax in all probability lay not with the basic poll itself but with the surtaxes, which were often ignored or underpaid. The moralistic Pepys was not above reproach in this area. Pleased that the 1660 Poll assessment listed him as a gentleman not a costly esquire, Pepys paid twelve shillings for himself and his two servants but feared, 'I shall not escape so, and therefore I have long ago laid by 10*l*: for them; but I think I am not bound to discover myself'.[26] Pepys saw no need to discover himself in 1667 either. 'I paid for my title as Esquire and place of Clerk of Acts, and my head and wife's, and servants' and their wages, 40*l*. 17*s*. 00*d*. And though this be a

22 Latham and Matthews, *Diary of Samuel Pepys*, vol.8, p.189.

23 Latham and Matthews, *Diary of Samuel Pepys*, vol.8, p.203.

24 PRO, E182/687 pt.1.

25 PRO, E182/687 pt.1.

26 Latham and Matthews, *Diary of Samuel Pepys*, vol.1, pp.315-6.

great deal, yet it is a shame I should pay no more; that is, that I should not be assessed for my pay, as in the Victualling business and Tanger, and for my money, which of my own accord I had determined to charge myself with 1,000*l.* money, till coming to the Vestry and seeing nobody of our ablest merchants, as Sir Andrew Rickard, to do it, I thought it not decent for me to do it; nor would it be thought wisdom to do it unnecessarily, but vainglory'.[27] In spite of Parliament's attempts to tap personal wealth, it was probably grossly undertaxed throughout the period of the surtaxes on the Polls, for many Englishmen and women must have felt, like Pepys, no need to 'discover' themselves. This fact, even more than the cautionary notes concerning general coverage, must clearly be taken into account in any analysis of the Poll tax returns.

The identification of households in the Poll tax lists

Poll tax lists from the Restoration and after bear a generic similarity. Assessors and collectors shared a basic set of organizing principles resulting in part from the Poll tax laws themselves, which held the household head responsible for the taxes of those within. Consequently, names of individuals appear clustered by household. Moreover, the lists present a mental or physical tour of the streets and lanes of the taxation unit. Dwelling by dwelling, the assessor listed names of the household head, spouse, children, other relatives, boarders or lodgers, apprentices and servants, almost always in that order. Usually relationships are indicated, although in Lynn, despite the tendency of the 1702 list to report everyone by name, they are less likely to report relationships. In 1694, 'Ezekial Goddard, wife, 3 children, servant' paid the Poll. In 1702, 'Ezekial Goddard, Elizabeth Goddard, Elizabeth Kendall, Jeffrey Goddard, and Sarah Hontzen, servant' were assessed. Was the first Elizabeth Ezekial's wife or daughter? Was the second a married daughter, a mother-in-law, a stepchild? The naming of relationships makes household analysis easier. The naming of persons facilitates mobility studies. The best lists name both.

In some lists assessors demarcate households with brackets, lines, a method of indentation, or extra spacing. But more often the households are not clearly delineated, and one must work at ascertaining where one household ends and another begins.

[27] Latham and Matthews, *Diary of Samuel Pepys*, vol.8, pp.152-3.

Because of the common method of listing, identification of servants, coming as they do at the end of the lists, serves as a household boundary and makes demarcation easier. When assessors list servants, they are generally labelled as such, sometimes with their wages stated. Lacking either of these indicators, however, the amount of the levy itself implies servitude, especially when taxation on servants' wages is in increments of sixpences.

Record linkage also facilitates household demarcation. If, as in the case of Lynn, a series of Poll taxes from the same period survive, expecially those of the 1690s, linking together the individuals and households in the records will serve to refine and substantiate the documents, although the accurate linking of the records is clearly of prime importance. Each pre-industrial English community will contain a number of people with identical surnames, and most communities will have at least a few such inhabitants with identical first names as well. Lynn had a plethora of John Turners: six of that name in the 1690s, three in one ward. Matching one of them from 1692 accurately with one in 1694 can present a number of problems. In addition, the vagaries of seventeenth-century orthography mean that Thomas Holly also appears as Hawley, Halley, and Holley. And proclivities for abbreviation abound turning, for example, Roger Hainesworth into Roger Haines.

Rules for linking individuals need to be made in advance of analysis and need to be applied rigorously. Because the tax lists are generally in street order, that order in itself can be enough to differentiate between namesakes as well as to link Hawley with Halley. In addition, the historian can match people at two different times by setting up a series of criteria including occupation (but not only occupation), title, relationship to another in the household, kinds of wealth, religion, resident ward or parish, etc. Consultation of parish registers, probate inventories, and probated wills offers additional information about lifespan and apprenticeship and freemen's records can help to verify membership in a given household.

Household structure in King's Lynn

In listing household members as a group, the Poll tax assessors made it possible in most cases to discern the shape or configuration of the household. As stated above, it is usual for members of the household other than the head to be listed by their relationship to the head, even if their names as such are not given. In most lists it is usual for taxpayers to be defined by one role only, their headship or their relationsip to the head. They are wife, child, son, daughter, kin, servant, pupil, ostler, apprentice, law clerk, or the like. These relationships can be used to group households into various classes.

In an attempt to facilitate discussion of household structures, Peter Laslett developed a six-category household typology, based on a scheme originally proposed by Louis Henry.[28] Trying to exhaust the possibilities of kinds of household structure, Laslett's model delineates the various household types on the basis of increasing complexity, concentrating on kin-related family members, excluding servants and apprentices from the classification. With this caveat the classification starts with solitaries or heads of households living by themselves. The second category, non-family units composed of co-resident individuals who do not share parent/child or spousal relationship, is somewhat more complicated. The next three types are based on conjugal family relationships and extensions thereof: simple-family households with a basically nuclear family relationship, that is, a conjugal pair, the pair and its unmarried progeny, or a single parent with unmarried child(ren); single-family households, where either a third generation or lateral relation is present in addition to the nuclear core; and multiple-family households of more than one married couple. The classification also provides an indeterminate group which allows for various combinations of the preceding types.[29]

From the figures given in Table 1 it can be seen that households in early modern King's Lynn were largely solitary in form, like that of widow Elizabeth Cubbage, who lived alone, or had a simple-family structure, like that of starchmaker Leonard Hutton, his wife, three children, and servant Joseph Starken. Over 94 per cent of the households on each tax list fell into these two categories and, in spite of the great variation in numbers of

[28] Laslett, 'Introduction', pp.28-32; L. Henry, *Manuel de Démographie Historique*, pp.44-6. For the scheme slightly modified, see Wachter, Hammel and Laslett, *Statistical studies*, p.40. For another example of application of the scheme, see Segalen, 'Family cycle and household structure', especially p.224.

[29] For a critique of the Laslett scheme, see Flandrin, *Families in former times*, pp.73-4.

Table 1 Household structure in King's Lynn, 1689-1702

Household type		1689 All Wards	1692 4th Quarter Six Wards	1692 4th Quarter All Wards	1694 All Wards	1702 Three Wards
Solitary	%	22.4	16.8	23.1	19.1	18.1
	n	289	55	166	125	41
No Family	%	1.1	1.3	1.1	1.6	4.7
	n	14	4	8	10	11
Nuclear (headed by married person)	%	64.5		64.7	66.5	69.5
	n	831		464	434	158
			80.4			
			261			
Nuclear (headed by one parent)	%	10.2		9.3	9.9	7.2
	n	131		67	65	16
Complex	%	1.8	1.6	1.7	2.9	0.5
	n	23	5	12	19	1
Totals	%	100	100	100	100	100
	n	1288	325	717	653	227

Notes: The complex category combines the two Laslett categories of extended and multiple.

households taxed from one period to the next, this percentage remained fairly constant. Even when one focuses on a single ward, the ratio holds. Indeed, the 1692 Kettlewell list of forty-four households shows that all of the ward's households were either solitary or single-family in form.[30] In a group of six wards where the assessors listed occupations for most male householders indicating that they knew their populations well and therefore that the data are reliable, the percentage still holds.[31]

Although in his analysis of a sample of English pre-industrial listings, Laslett has shown that the simple nuclear family household predominates, the proportions of Lynn households that

[30] The first quarterly Kettlewell list of 1692 gives ages of all young people so one can assume the assessors knew the population well. Kettlewell might be considered a control ward, but no one ward in Lynn was typical. Kettlewell had fewer taxpaying households and less general wealth than most other wards. See also p.130 above.

[31] Northend, Kettlewell, Paradise, Jews Lane, New Conduit and Stonegate Wards in the fourth quarterly list of 1692, as well as in preceding 1692 lists, have extensive occupational designations.

were either nuclear or solitary are somewhat higher than those in this pre-industrial sample.[32] The difference between Laslett's set and the Lynn percentages results possibly from the nature of Laslett's listings, which present complete populations, not solely populations of taxpayers. More probably, however, the difference reflects other possible differences between the two: age, gender or occupational and economic structures, for Lynn was an important port while Laslett's settlements were mainly rural.

In all but one of the Lynn lists, those households where the occupation of the head was known displayed a somewhat greater degree of complexity on average than the households overall. And the mean size of households where the heads' occupations were noted also tended to be larger. Thus when entire families, families headed by wage labourers and those not paying rates, were omitted from the tax lists, as they clearly were in the lists after 1689, one would expect the resultant percentages of simple-family and solitary households to understate those percentages among the population as a whole. In fact, the lowest percentage of simple-family and solitary households (94.8 per cent) did occur in 1702, when the highest percentage (56.3 per cent) of household heads had ascertainable occupations.

The absence from the 1689 list of the children of non-rate payers and day labourers whose parents were not exempt from the tax, might also contribute to an overcounting of simple and solitary households. This would be the case, for example, when the children of a poor young widow living with her parent(s) were not taxed. But when we arbitrarily add children to each household on the list, in effect restoring any children who might have been exempt, for the most part we succeed in making solitary households into nuclear family ones. Such an addition to every 1689 household changes only seven nuclear households into extended ones, eliminating households with no familial structure and raising the percentage of extended households from 1.8 to 2. At the same time such an addition raises the percentage of nuclear family households to 98, eliminating the solitary households. Thus the possibility that children might have been undercounted does not affect the finding that the household structure most common to pre-industrial Lynn was either the nuclear family or the solitary, with the addition of servants,

32 Laslett, *Family life and illicit love*, pp. 32-3.

apprentices and the occasional inmate of other kinds, but most definitely not of relatives. The addition of children to all households failed to result in extended-family structures because so few kin resided with the nuclear family.

Living alone in King's Lynn

The key feature of Lynn household composition lies not so much in the proportions of nuclear family households, but in the high percentages of solitary households, that is, households where the head lived by him- or herself or perhaps with servants and apprentices. Because many of the Lynn ward assessors did not clearly designate households, the attribution of singletons to separate establishments might be slightly inflated. The existence of multiple lists, which allow cross-checking, helps to reduce such a possibility. Again, the 1689 list, larger than the rest and more likely to exempt some children whose parents paid the tax, would thus be more likely to have an inflated solitary household count than the other lists, although, as we know, there were many conditions which limited the possible exemptions and thus mitigated their effect.

The percentage of solitaries in 1689, while high, was comparable to the other Lynn lists. The period under discussion, 1689 to 1702, came at the end of more than a half century of low gross and net reproduction rates and of the lowest rates of expectation of life at birth for pre-industrial England.[33] If Lynn mirrored the national experience then the low fertility/short life combination, along with the practice of putting adolescents into service, would have ensured a high proportion of solitary households.

Why Lynn in particular should have had such high proportions of solitary households merits further discussion. Some of the number would have resulted from the absence from single-parent homes of children who had gone to sea as well as into domestic service and apprenticeship.[34] Children in early-modern England – and Lynn

[33] See Wrigley and Schofield, *Population history*, pp.230-2, 530.

[34] Goose, 'Household size and structure', p.375, notes that analysis of five parishes of early-Stuart Cambridge shows a higher percentage of households with servants or apprentices than Laslett found in his study of one hundred English villages. Goose suggests that 'this difference might be expected of an urban population compared with a predominantly agrarian one' (p. 375). A similar situation in Lynn implies that the proportions of households with servants or apprentices would be positively correlated to proportions of solitary households.

was no exception – left their homes in sizeable numbers to enter domestic or agricultural service. The practice of sending young people into service in addition to the high level of mortality at the time and the constraints on fertility resulting from a high age at first marriage tended to keep the number of children resident in a family to fewer than four. The pervasiveness of apprenticeship and domestic servitude in Lynn indicates that these activities occupied the adolescent years of large groups of young people. Marriage did not take place until apprenticeship had ended, and there were no married servants that we know of, although the assessors recorded one servant as a widow. Thus many married couples, and wives especially, had served as servants, husbands also as apprentices, in a period before marriage.[35]

In addition, the extensive shipping trade removed both boys and men – some temporarily, some permanently – from the households of Lynn.[36] The removal of males would necessarily increase the number of households headed by solitary females. Equally, the skewed adolescent sex ratio might have led in the natural course of events to spinster-headed households like those of the three sisters by the name of Pennington, or those of Mesdames Sarah and Mary Stewart mentioned below. However the information presented in Table 2 suggests that the crucial element for Lynn adults in terms of whether they lived in solitary or simple-family households was not their gender but their marital condition. Unmarried women, or women whose spouses were not present in the household, were no more likely to live in solitary households than men of similar marital status. Unmarried men in solitary households, however, tended to live more often with servants and apprentices than did unmarried women.

35 One former apprentice was noted at the time he assumed his freedom in 1653 for marrying before his apprenticeship had ended; Millican, *Freemen of Lynn*, p.163. In Pound, *The Norwich Census of the Poor, 1570*, pp.48, 68, two men appear to be married servants.

36 Ships quite literally devoured men; see Scammell, 'Manning the Merchant Service', p.131. Disease, accident and desertion, as well as pirates, were major problems. In addition, the merchant seamen were subject to impressment. Andrews suggests that able mariners of the sixteenth century avoided the press; Andrews, 'The Elizabethan Seaman', p.247. But the wills of King's Lynn sailors serving their majesties at the end of the seventeenth century suggest that, ability aside, considerable numbers of mariners had either not avoided the press or had succumbed to the lure of the navy, where many of them 'crossed the bar'. See the indices in the Norfolk Record Office for lists of wills proved in the Prerogative Court at Canterbury, including wills of those lost or killed at sea.

Table 2 Solitary heads of household by gender in King's Lynn

	n	% Solitary
1689		
All Female Heads	212	71.2
All Unmarried Male Heads	156	67.3
1692		
All Female Heads	115	73.0
All Unmarried Male Heads	101	74.2
1694		
All Female Heads	84	61.9
All Unmarried Male Heads	88	71.5
1702, Three Wards		
All Female Heads	26	61.5
All Unmarried Male Heads	34	64.7

This difference between unmarried male and unmarried female householders could have resulted from wealth or occupation, or both. On average, men could more readily afford to hire servants, and they had greater occupational prestige which drew apprentices. They may also have had less ability to cope when on their own, a suggestion made at times when modern society's widowers are compared to its widows.[37] In Lynn males without spouses more often lived with kin or unrelated adults than did their female counterparts, a tendency that might add support to the hypothesis about differential coping on the basis of gender.[38] But the incidence in King's Lynn of non-solitary households without familial structure was very limited, regardless of the gender of the head.

If gender were not an important factor in contributing to the high percentage of solitary households in pre-industrial Lynn, the possibility remains that wealth may have been. Occupation could be an indirect indicator of wealth, for householders of substance – those who served as mayors and aldermen – received an occupational designation in the tax records. Not all those whose

[37] Wall, 'Women alone,' p.307, suggests that 'in a personal crisis situation (such as bereavement) men are more likely to become dependent on support of others than are similarly situated women'.

[38] In early seventeenth-century Cambridge, 'solitary widows were quite rare' but 'no solitary widowers were found in the lists'; Goose, 'Household size and structure', p.378. In three seventeenth-century town lists, Wall found no marked differences between widows and widowers in residing in non-solitary households; Wall, 'Women alone', p.312.

occupations were identified, especially when the information came from elsewhere than tax records, were particularly wealthy. But as a group those householders whose occupations we know, gleaned either from the tax lists or from freemen's records, were largely artisans or professional men, and several of these were wealthy enough to have to pay a surtax. Only three or four were women, whose designation, if unmarried, was generally that of widow. Only once on a tax list was a labourer identified as such.[39] However, occupation, or the lack of occupational designation, does not offer very much of an explanation for solitary households. The rates of males who were solitary householders were only slightly higher than the rates of solitary male householders with occupational designations. To the extent that wealth and occupation were linked, wealth or lack thereof does not seem to have been consequential to the solitary household form.[40]

In King's Lynn the large numbers of householders who lived by themselves or with servants or apprentices, or other non-related adults, were not primarily the result of considerations of gender or wealth. Rather, the decision – and decision seems perhaps too strong a word for what could have been a natural and expected progression in the life cycle – appears the result of marital status. Living alone was a widespread and accepted condition for those adults who by choice, mortality, or desertion had no spouse with whom to share a home.[41]

39 Wills and apprenticeship records allow identification of an additional few labourers. Occupational designations on tax lists exist for one-sixth to over half of all taxpaying household heads, depending on the list. Record-linkage yields a much higher rate of identification for those who appear on at least two records.

40 Wealth or status has been shown to be a consequential variable to size of household, that of the nobility having a much greater size, as one might expect; Laslett, *World we have lost – further explored*, p.96. In Stuart Cambridge 'a clear positive relationship existed between socio-economic status and household size'; Goose, 'Household size and structure', p.380.

41 Jack Goody notes that high rates of mortality and the small differences in ages of husband and wife at marriage 'ensured that both sexes were well represented in the bereaved'. Late age of marriage, he adds, 'meant a long generation, increasing the chances of orphanhood and of widow/widowhood'; Goody, *Development of the family*, p.189. While late marriage would increase the chances of orphanhood, chances of losing one's spouse by death were probably about the same fifty per cent they have always been. On the other hand, the relative proportions of an adult's life spent in a married *vis-à-vis* a widowed state could have been affected.

Toward a longitudinal analysis

The fact that the Lynn Poll tax records survive as a repetitive series from the end of the seventeenth to the early eighteenth-century allows us to trace both families and individuals longitudinally in addition to viewing people or households as cross-sectional groups. While many other records offer information on individuals, some of whom can be linked from document to document, such records tell us relatively little about the way people grouped themselves. Also the individuals whom such records feature are disproportionately male and quite often disproportionately wealthy. While the Poll taxes frequently fail to name men's wives, they do indicate that the women were there, and while many of the poor are missing from the taxes, these records dip much lower into the socio-economic scale than do most other surviving documents.

By linking together the information in the various Poll tax listings and other appropriate contemporary records it is possible to determine, for example, that Mary Skippon headed one of the largest households in King's Lynn in the 1690s, a household containing at times several females and several males, with four different surnames. Superficially resembling a latter-day commune, this group moved at least three times from their first appearance in the Lynn records, with some change in membership but no change in head, until 1702, when the last two survivors had become members of John Green's household.

As might be gathered by the discussion on household composition in the previous section, the Skippon household's configuration was unusual for Lynn. Although a few of the wealthier households of the Norfolk seaport approached or surpassed the size of the Skippon ménage, its odd membership makes this household group stand out in the surviving Poll taxes. Listed after Mrs Mary came Mrs Anne Skippon, then Luke and William Hainesworth, followed by others, including various persons surnamed Franklin and always a maidservant. While the household does not appear in the first Lynn tax list of 1689, the related Hainesworth family paid the 1678 Poll in West Lynn. The other surviving King's Lynn records all mention at least one Hainesworth (Luke), living with at least one Skippon (Mary), and both inhabit John Green's house in 1702.

Linked with other records, the Poll taxes provide a rather remarkable degree of information on household composition, occupation structure and mobility for a substantial segment of the Lynn population. In the case of Mary Skippon's household several linkages can be made. Roger Hainesworth, the West Lynn taxpayer, had received the freedom of King's Lynn in 1674-5 as the son of another Roger Hainesworth, who received the freedom in 1646-7 as the son, in turn, of Edmund Hainesworth, a mariner.[42] The younger Roger wrote his will in March of 1688/9, and it was proved in December. A widower, he left his late wife's jointure to his eldest son, yet another Roger, along with a silver tankard and a gold seal which had belonged to the boy's grandfather Skippon. To his other three sons – Luke, William, and Robert – Roger left all goods, chattels, plate, household stuff, rings, credits, lands and tenements to be shared equally after his debts were paid. If all the boys died without issue before they reached twenty-five the estate was to go to Hainesworth's 'sisters', Mary and Ann Skippon, to whose care his sons were entrusted.[43]

In September of 1689, his father probably already dead, the eldest Hainesworth son, Roger, became the apprentice of merchant Samuel Bridgeman, a Lynn alderman.[44] The boy was probably one of the two unnamed apprentices residing with Bridgeman when the 1689 Poll tax was collected. The youngest son, Robert, may well have died shortly after his father, for the tax lists of the 1690s report only Luke and William living with their aunts; and William, the third son, disappeared from the lists between 1694 and 1702. If not dead, William may have been apprenticed out of Lynn, for his name does not appear in the Lynn apprenticeship records, and his father had directed that his sons serve apprenticeships. In 1695, however, Luke, the second son, became the apprentice of John Green, a grocer who would serve as mayor of Lynn in 1709.[45] When the final Poll tax levied in England was collected in 1702, Aunt Mary Skippon had settled into the large Green household, along with the nephew she had fostered for so many years.

42 Millican, *Freemen of Lynn*, pp.185, 160.

43 NRO, Archdeaconry of Norwich Register of Wills, 1689, f.232. Mary and Ann Skippon were Hainesworth's sisters-in-law, sisters of the late wife.

44 KLRO, KL/C9/24. King's Lynn Register for Apprentices, 29 Sept. 1689.

45 KLRO, KL/C9/25, King's Lynn Register for Apprentices, 29 Sept. 1695.

Conclusion

The Poll tax records, then, provide a rich source for documenting the structure of contemporary households as well as their fluidity, mobility and stability. The records show that the Skippon household was unusual in some of these respects. As we have seen, most households in Lynn contemporary with Mary Skippon's held no kin other than the nuclear family, and very few held boarders or possible relatives like Mrs Frances Franklin and the other Franklins who moved in and out - Rebecca, Mary, Edward. But the Poll taxes also show the Skippon household appearing as the norm, both in having a servant as well as in the departure - well before adulthood - of the children of the family. Nor was the household unusual in its moves between Sedgeford Lane and Southgate wards, although its mobility was perhaps greater than one would have expected from a household headed by a woman known as 'Mrs'. Female-headed households, however, were often more mobile than similar male households, and the Skippon household demonstrated considerable longevity.

Using parish registers, one could perhaps trace Luke Hainesworth backward through his lineage to Edmund or beyond. Using apprenticeship and freeman's records, one can also trace Luke forward till he received the freedom of Lynn in 1703.[46] Using the longitudinal series of Poll tax records, however, we are able to place Luke within a familial context and place Luke's family and household within an expanded context, in that of neighbourhood, town and region.

Roger Hainesworth's will demonstrates the call upon kin that critical life (or death) situations could elicit.[47] But it does not reveal whether the response was met and, if so, in what manner or to what degree. Without the Poll tax records we would have missed the kind of households in which Luke lived and the certainty that his aunts had indeed served as substitute parents. A single Poll tax listing discloses that Mary Skippon had fostered Luke and William. The series demonstrates the commitment that lasted to and beyond apprenticeship and indicates superficially at least that the Hainesworth boys benefited from the foresight of a

46 Millican, *Freemen of Lynn*, p.210.

47 For a discussion of the role of kin in critical life situations see Anderson, *Family structure*, pp.136-61.

concerned father and the care of responsive aunts.[48]

This is just one example of the extent to which the picture of household and family development can be enriched by the amassing of longitudinal information. Several more could be given, but space prohibits this. Information such as this has become easier to obtain since the advent of modern data processing, as historians have increasingly turned to sources that their predecessors would have found unworkable. These sources have proved particularly rich for the social historian, whose insights have depended so heavily on records that necessarily projected a class bias because they were made by, and most frequently about, the upper classes. It is clear that sources such as the Poll tax lists permit historians to circumvent some, albeit not all, of this bias and also let us look at areas of historical life, like household structure, in a dynamic context – opening a window on society and allowing us a brief glimpse of the passers-by.

48 Examining the diary evidence, Pollock's *Forgotten children*, convincingly attacks the 'received view' of the history of English childhood, a view of indifference and neglect.

11

The Marriage Duty Act and parochial registration in London, 1695-1706

JEREMY BOULTON

The records generated by the so-called Marriage Duty Act of 1695 have proved of immense importance for historians interested in historical demography and household structure in the past.[1] As is explained earlier in this volume, in order to comply with the terms of the original Marriage Duty Act a complete enumeration of the total population was required.[2] Where such assessments survive they provide one of the most important sources for the study of population and household structure in England before the nineteenth century.[3] This chapter, however, explores the impact of the Act and its subsequent amending legislation on the quality of parochial registration in London at the end of the seventeenth century. It is hoped that this brief survey of the effects of the Act and the records it generated will suggest future lines of research to local historians.

The quality of Anglican parish registration

The quality of parish registers is central to their use by historical demographers working at either the national or local level. Allowances made for births, marriages or deaths that were not recorded as baptisms, marriages of burials in the Anglican parish registers can affect not only the trends of population growth

1 6 and 7 Wm. and M., c.6. Details of the legislation surrounding the Act are given in Arkell's chapter in this section of the volume (chapter 8). The Act was passed in the parliamentary session 1694-5 and came into force in May 1695. For this reason some writers refer to the 1694 Act while others refer to that of 1695, using the timing of the Act's introduction and passage.

2 Under clause XI the assessors appointed under the Act were to bring in to the commissioners 'their certificates in writeing of the names sirnames estates degrees titles and qualifications of all and every the persons dwelling or residing within the limits of those places... dividing them into several columns as they are in quality estate and qualification and the names of all other persons chargeable by this Act', 6 and 7 Wm. and M. c.6, XI; see Glass, 'Introduction', pp.ix-x.

3 A comprehensive listing of all Marriage Duty Act returns currently known to survive is contained in Christine Vialls, 'The Duty on Marriages'.

derived from aggregative analysis and all calculations based on that method, but also studies based on nominal record linkage, such as family reconstitution.[4] Under-registration may also indicate something interesting about local levels of religious dissent and the way in which nonconformists interacted with the Anglican registration system. Moreover, the various types of under-registration owe something to changing social customs that surrounded these vital events in the seventeenth century. The records and the registration system produced by the Marriage Duty Act allow historians to make independent checks on the accuracy and comprehensiveness of some late seventeenth-century parish registers.

There are two main classes of reason why the records of individuals' baptisms, marriages and burials may not be recorded in an Anglican parish register. The first of these is defective registration. This includes periods when pages from registers have been lost or events omitted and when times of political or religious upheaval disrupted register keeping. Defective registration results in obvious gaps or periods when the number of recorded events falls far short of the number expected. The second reason is the more difficult-to-detect under-registration. This second category refers to individuals not recorded in apparently well-kept Anglican registers, either on religious grounds or because changing baptism, burial or marriage customs made the Anglican registration system less comprehensive. The relative size and internal composition of under-registration changed over time and, as we shall see, probably displayed important regional variation in intensity.

The adequacy of Anglican parochial registration has, of course, been the subject of a number of studies.[5] To date, the most comprehensive is that described in Wrigley and Schofield's *Population History*. The estimates and allowances they made for both defective registers and under-registration underpinned their revolutionary reconstruction of English population movements.[6]

4 See, for example, the possible distortions produced by the growth of clandestine marriage in Colyton described by Wrigley, 'Marital fertility', pp.434-5. For the correction of under-registration by Wrigley and Schofield, see *Population History*, pp.89-154, 536-62.

5 See Krause, 'Changing adequacy', pp. 379-93; Levine, 'Reliability', pp.107-22; Wrigley, 'Births and baptisms', pp.281-312.

6 Wrigley and Schofield, *Population History*, pp.23-32, 89-154, 536-62.

Table 1 Components of under-registration in England 1630-1799

Date	Births				Deaths			
	Religious dissent (%)	Delayed baptism (%)	Residual (%)	Under-registration (%)	Religious dissent (%)	Delayed baptism (%)	Residual (%)	Under-registration (%)
1630-9	-	100	-	3.4	-	-	-	0.0
1640-9	3	90	7	3.9	50	-	50	0.2
1650-9	7	75	18	4.9	51	-	49	0.8
1660-9	10	64	26	5.8	52	-	48	1.2
1670-9	12	57	31	6.7	50	2	48	1.8
1680-9	13	52	34	7.7	43	15	42	2.5
1690-9	14	50	37	8.4	35	26	40	3.2
1700-9	14	48	38	9.0	28	35	37	3.7
1710-9	15	47	38	9.6	24	40	36	4.2
1750-9	15	47	39	12.4	12	59	29	6.7
1790-9	14	29	58	22.7	7	40	53	16.5

Source: Calculated from Wrigley and Schofield, **Population History**, p. 561.
Notes: The figures given under births and deaths indicate the relative proportion accounted for by each component for every 100 under-registrations in each decade. Numbers may not add up to 100 due to rounding up errors.

They argue that the incidence of defective registration, at relatively low levels after the Restoration in 1660, was reduced to negligible proportions by the effects of the Marriage Duty Act.[7] Regarding under-registration their estimates show, firstly, that under-registration of baptisms was always more serious than of burials and, apparently, marriages, and secondly that the beginning of religious and political conflict in 1640 marks the start of under-registration in burials and marriages and increases the tempo of that of baptisms. The levels of these fractions as calculated by Wrigley and Schofield are given in Table 1.

It is helpful to take each series in turn. Marriage totals are thought to have been exceptionally reliable in this period and the only allowance for under-registration made by Wrigley and Schofield is a small one for Quaker marriages.[8] In 1700, for example, 431 Quaker marriages unrecorded in Anglican parish registers are estimated to have taken place; only 1.03 per cent of the total for that year.[9] Such statements about the relative

[7] Wrigley and Schofield, *Population History*, pp.23-32.

[8] Wrigley and Schofield, *Population History*, pp.93-4, 562.

[9] Wrigley and Schofield, *Population History*, p.557, cols 5 and 6.

reliability of marriage registration in later seventeenth-century England are, however, greatly complicated by the growth of 'clandestine marriage' in this period. Marriages thought to have taken place irregularly, outside local Anglican parish churches, are now considered to have been responsible for as much as 14 per cent of all national marriages omitted from the Anglican marriage registers when the custom was at its height between 1680-1705.[10]

Table 1 sets out in simple percentage terms Wrigley and Schofield's estimates for the changing components of under-registration for burials and baptisms between 1630 and 1799. Anglican burials are not thought to have under-registered deaths at all until 1640. After that date allowance is made for the impact of religious dissent and also for residual non-registration; deaths that simply slipped through the Anglican registration system. For the period before the late eighteenth century Wrigley and Schofield estimated this latter figure to be 40 per cent of the comparable figure derived from birth under-registration.[11] From the 1670s registration of burials is thought to have been affected by growing numbers of children dying both unbaptised and also unregistered, although the relative numbers were small.[12] In order to convert totals of baptisms into totals of births they needed to make allowances for births of children dying before baptism took place, for the offspring of religious dissenters who deliberately opted out of Anglican ceremonial and finally for those who escaped from any form of registration at all. This latter residual under-registration was estimated from independent checks made from nineteenth-century census material. However, to quote Wrigley and Schofield, 'before the late eighteenth century the problem of residual escape from ecclesiastical registration becomes progressively less serious until in Tudor and Stuart times it was probably too slight to be a source of serious concern'.[13] For the period before the late eighteenth century Wrigley and Schofield chose to estimate residual non-registration as a constant factor of their allowance for religious nonconformity, basing this procedure on their observation that the same conditions (of urbanization,

10 Schofield, 'English Marriage', p.14. This is higher than the 10 per cent estimated originally in Wrigley and Schofield, *Population History*.

11 Wrigley and Schofield, *Population History*, pp.139, 561.

12 Wrigley and Schofield, *Population History*, pp.89-102, 136-43. See also Wrigley, 'Births and baptisms', pp.290, 310, n.36.

13 Wrigley and Schofield, *Population History*, p.103.

pastoral open parishes dominated by handicraft industry and poorly kept nonconformist registers) associated with high concentrations of dissenters also caused most residual non-registration. Before the last decades of the eighteenth century residual under-registration is taken to be 2.5 times that allowed for the direct effects of religious dissent.[14] Table 1 shows that before 1640 Anglican parish registers are thought only to under-record births by some 3.4 per cent, which was caused solely by infants dying before baptism. After 1640 allowance is also taken of the growth of religious nonconformity and associated residual non-registration. Under-registration of births continues rising slowly from around 4 per cent in the 1640s, to about 6 per cent in the decade following the Restoration and reaches 8.4 per cent in the last decade of the seventeenth century. The coverage of births continues to deteriorate slowly to 1750 and then degenerates rapidly in the late eighteenth century as the growth of religious dissent, rapid urbanization and an increasing tendency to delay baptism put greater pressure on Anglican parochial registration. In the last decade of the eighteenth century Wrigley and Schofield estimate that Anglican baptisms under-record births by nearly one quarter.

Overall, Table 1 shows that as the seventeenth century wore on and the extent to which Anglican baptisms under-registered births increased, albeit slowly, the proportionate share of the effect of delaying baptism declined as the effect of religious dissent and the problem of residual non-registration increased. In the last decade of the seventeenth century these latter factors were estimated to have been responsible for half of the 8.4 per cent under-registration. Conversely Wrigley and Schofield estimated that the non-recording of unbaptised children only caused a quarter of the small amount of death under-registration in the 1690s. The knowledge of such estimates is important since they form the background to our assessment of the effectiveness of the Anglican registration system and remind us that under-registration is multi-causal. The discovery of the size of one component of under-registration does not therefore preclude the existence of another. The records generated by the Marriage Duty Act enable us to reassess the validity of such estimates in particular regions.

[14] Wrigley and Schofield, *Population History*, pp.136-7.

The Marriage Duty Act and the registration of marriages, births, and deaths

When the Marriage Duty Act came into force in 1695 it had the effect of reducing the incidence of defective marriage registration to extremely low levels. That is to say the registers became better kept. Wrigley and Schofield have suggested, however, that it had no significant impact on the number of Quaker marriages that escaped Anglican registration.[15] In fact the Act and its subsequent amending legislation produced important effects on the number of marriages recorded in English parish registers. These effects were especially dramatic in London. The Marriage Duty Act taxed all marriages and its clauses were concerned to ensure that, as with births and burials, the collectors should have access to 'an exact and true account' kept by ministers of all persons married (as well as born and buried) in their parishes.[16] Under the Act bridegrooms were responsible for paying the marriage tax.[17] Quakers, Catholics and Jews, 'or any other persons who shall cohabitt and live together as man and wife shall and are hereby made lyable to pay...according to their respective degrees...as they ought to have paid by virtue of this Act if they had been married according to the Law of England' and were to notify the collectors within five days of the event.[18] Since parish paupers were exempt from the marriage tax a few parish registers record their marriages explicitly.[19] One effect of the Marriage Duty Act therefore was that a few ministers sought to record all unions in their parishes and not simply those solemnized in their own parish church. As with births and burials such records might be included in the marriage register proper or kept on more fragile separate sheets of paper.[20] The most celebrated marriage register

15 Wrigley and Schofield, *Population History*, pp.28-9, 92-4.

16 6 and 7 Wm. and M. c.6, s.20.

17 6 and 7 Wm. and M. c.6, s.6.

18 6 and 7 Wm. and M. c.6, s.57.

19 Glass, 'Introduction', pp. xi, xix, fn.1; see, for example, the Nottinghamshire parishes of Balderton, Farndon, and Ossington; Phillimore and Blagg, *Nottinghamshire*, pp.19, 132 and Blagg and Proctor, *Nottinghamshire*, p.84.

20 A few marriage registers in Nottinghamshire do, in fact, record Quaker marriages between 1695 and 1706. Note the marriages celebrated 'according to the Quaker's way of marriage' in Skegby, Notts; Phillimore and Bonser, *Nottinghamshire*, p.136. See also similar entries in the registers of Farnsfield and Kneesall; Blagg and Proctor, *Nottinghamshire Registers*, p.20; Blagg, *Nottinghamshire*, p.34. In South Collingham, Nottinghamshire, the incumbent recorded four marriages that took place in April 1702 which were regularizations of illicit consensual unions; see, for example, Phillimore

resulting from the 1695 Act is that of Tetbury, Gloucestershire, whose incumbent recorded all unions that took place between 1696 and 1699 among his parishioners, whether they occurred in the local parish church, in a neighbouring parish or were not in fact solemnized in an Anglican church at all.[21] Indeed evidence from the Tetbury register was the first to demonstrate the existence of substantial numbers of illicit or 'clandestine' unions in the countryside in the later seventeenth century.[22] As we have seen, so-called 'clandestine' marriage was a cause of serious under-registration of marriages in later seventeenth-century England.[23]

Collecting taxes on marriages was particularly difficult. This was known by contemporaries who seem to have recognised that it was, in fact, marriage duties that were being evaded most frequently.[24] In order to enable marriage duties to be collected, therefore, the Marriage Duty Act, together with its subsequent amending legislation, attempted to close down centres of clandestine or irregular marriage sited in parishes or precincts located in areas claiming exemption from ecclesiastical jurisdiction where large numbers of non-resident couples got married without licence or banns. Ministers breaking this law were liable to a heavy fine and, for a second offence, a three-year suspension.[25] By marrying in this way couples would avoid the attentions of the collectors of the tax. Moreover the clause had in mind, too, the Stamp Duty of 5s. payable on marriage licences or certificates of marriage which was also being avoided by such couples.[26] More extensive legislation was passed in the following year to suppress attempts to evade the provisions of the original Act. This amending Act placed heavy financial penalties on the

Nottinghamshire, p.20, 'John Wilsom marryed to Margaret Lund his Concubine, now his wife'.

21 Wrigley, 'Clandestine marriage', p.15-21. The Tetbury marriage register has been printed; see Phillimore, *Gloucestershire*, pp.90-2.

22 Wrigley, 'Clandestine marriage', p.15. Out of a total of sixty-eight recorded marriages 1696-9, fourteen (20.6 per cent) were explicitly described as 'clandestine'.

23 For the canon law of marriage and the various meanings of 'clandestine' marriage, see Brown, 'Fleet Marriages', pp.117-8; Ingram, 'Spousals', pp.37-40; Wrigley, 'Clandestine marriage', p.16.

24 Jones and Judges, 'London Population', p.49.

25 6 and 7 Wm. and M. c.6, s.47.

26 For the imposition of Stamp Duty, see 5 and 6 Wm. and M. c.21, s.1. See also a subsequent amending Act, 7 and 8 Wm. III c.35, s.1.

employment of clerical substitutes by ministers in clandestine centres and extended the fines for marrying without banns or licence to every offence, to other officiating officers and to the couple themselves.[27]

The legislative campaign against clandestine marriage initiated by the Duty Act seems to have had an immediate national impact. Following the Act there was a very marked rise in locally-celebrated marriages throughout the country. From Wrigley and Schofield's corrected totals of marriages it can be seen that the year 1695 saw the biggest percentage increase in locally-celebrated marriages over the previous year since the first full year of civil marriage in 1654.[28] In comparison, the immediate national impact of the much better known Hardwicke Marriage Act of 1753 was negligible. Using this measure the effect of the Marriage Duty Act was comparable with the recovery of marriages following the Restoration of the Anglican Church between 1661 and 1663.[29] Despite this apparent success however the Duty Act, even before it lapsed in 1706, did not totally eradicate all centres of clandestine marriage, nor did it prevent the continuing widespread abuse of the marriage licence system. Clandestine centres of one type or another continued to operate in certain areas in the eighteenth century and were not all closed down until the Hardwicke Act placed marriage on a new statutory footing.[30] Although its success was only partial, the Duty Act may well have played an important part in causing the decline of clandestine marriage in rural areas. By the time of the Hardwicke Act it was noted in parliamentary debates that in the country 'they have very few clandestine marriages'.[31] In effect the Hardwicke Act was designed to close down the notorious clandestine marriage centres in London.

27 7 and 8 Wm. III c.35, ss.1,2 and 3.

28 Between 1694 and 1695 the number of marriages increased by 33.9 per cent compared to a 45.3 per cent jump 1653-4. The totals have been corrected to account for defective registration and missing Quaker marriages: Wrigley and Schofield, *Population History*, pp.556-7. The measure adopted here is a crude one and is only designed to illustrate the possible short term effects of legislation on recorded events.

29 Between 1661 and 1663 the number of recorded marriages increased by 37.6 per cent compared to 33.9 per cent in the single year 1694-5: Wrigley and Schofield, *Population history*, p.556. There was no significant increase in recorded marriages in the national sample 1753-4, p.558.

30 Wrigley and Schofield, *Population History*, pp.28-30, 65; Cox, *Parish Registers*, pp.92-5; Brown, 'Fleet marriages', pp.117-8.

31 Cobbett, *Parliamentary History*, vol. 15, p.47.

The Marriage Duty Act was concerned to widen the scope of parochial registration of births and deaths as well as of marriages so that all events, and not merely Anglican ceremonies, could be properly taxed. It is important to bear in mind, however, that the ultimate aim of the legislation was to help the collector of the tax to make accurate and complete returns. Consequently, as noted above, ministers were enjoined to 'take an exact and true account' of all persons married, buried, 'christened or borne' and allow the local collectors to have free access to this register. Parents should, within five days, have given notices of births of all children to the collectors. Similarly stillbirths were to be certified.[32] In essence, therefore, the original Act envisaged two systems of vital registration, that operated by the collector in association with, and in addition to, improved parochial registration. If parents had notified the collectors of all children born, then England would have had two registration systems. In reality, however, both subsequent legislation and the evidence from London discussed below suggests that the collectors came to depend heavily on the incumbents' ability to record all vital events in the parish register.

Recognising this, the amending Act which had placed firmer restrictions on clandestine marriage centres went further in tightening up the system of registration. In particular, a clause was introduced to remedy a deficiency in the original Act, namely that although parents had been ordered to notify the collectors of births, they were not so ordered to notify ministers which made the latters' task of keeping a comprehensive register extremely difficult.[33] This represented a tacit admission that parents had been neglecting to notify local collectors of births and that, in future, they would depend heavily on the 'distinct' register kept by the minister. This is an important point since, as we shall see, the extent to which the collectors' returns were independent registration systems has a bearing on how they can be used to measure the accuracy of Anglican parochial registration.[34] In fact

32 6 and 7 Wm. and M. c.6, ss.20-21. However, children of paupers were exempt from the tax on births (s.3), while, although the members of families in receipt of poor relief were exempt from all charges, the parish was responsible for paying their burial duties (ss.44-5). For the responsibility of heirs for the burial payment of their relations, see chapter 8.

33 7 and 8 Wm. III c.35, s.4.

34 Glass, 'Inhabitants', pp. xxxvi-xxxvii; Glass, 'Notes', pp.282-5. The fact that these two registration systems were very unlikely to have been independent was conceded by Glass, 'Notes', p.284.

the dependence of the collectors on incumbents was further underlined by the terms of a later amending Act which ordered each minister to expand his parish register entries still further to include 'together with the Name of every Person so married buried christened or born sett down and express...the respective Degree Condition or Quality according to which His Majesties Duty ought to be paid for every such Burial Birth or Marriage'. The same clause ordered that those liable to pay the duty on burials were also to be listed.[35] This clause suggests that in some places adequate listings of inhabitants were not being maintained by collectors.

As has been shown in Table 1, at a national level Wrigley and Schofield estimated that the Marriage Duty Act reduced the percentage of defectively-kept registers, but had no impact on the numbers of persons estimated to have been under-registered.[36] The Marriage Duty Act did not have the effect, either, of increasing the estimated number of births significantly.[37] The number of recorded deaths also showed no significant increase in 1694-5.[38] Yet at the local level parish registers occasionally leave traces of the Duty Act legislation. For example, a few registers are known to have survived which complied with an amending Act ordering the recording of payments liable on vital events under the original Act.[39] The commonest effect of the Act was that some registers sometimes contain references to the births of dissenters' children during the period when the Act was in

35 9 Wm. III c.32, s.3.

36 Wrigley and Schofield, *Population History*, p.153.

37 Although the number of estimated births increased by 14.3 per cent between 1694 and 1695 this large increase was really due to a recovery from the exceptional fall in the birth rate that had occurred in the previous year. The years 1693-4 showed the thirteenth biggest fall in births, 1541-1871; Wrigley and Schofield, *Population History*, pp.324, 541.

38 Wrigley and Schofield, *Population History*, p.549.

39 See for example, Nevill, *Denchworth*, pp.47, 71, 78-9: 'Note that Joseph Belcher, a Day Labourer, of our parish, and Sarah Baker of the parish of Marcham were married since Lady Day last past but not in our parish. The tax to the King, 2s. 6d.', dated 1697 (p.71). Between April 1698 and April 1704 the parish register of Morden, Surrey, records sporadically the payment of duties, including the burial of paupers paid for by the Overseers of the Poor. 6 and 7 Wm. and M. c.6, ss.44-5, imposed the burden of paying tax on pauper burials on churchwardens; Clayton, *Registers of Morden*, pp.34-9. This register also lists heirs paying duty, thus the entry dated 1699, 'Hugh Dollet labourer was buried the fiveteenth day of October... The King's dues to be payd by his son Richard Dollet of Coleman Street.' [in London], (p.36).

operation.[40] In many cases it is clear that separate lists of children born in the parish but not baptised in the local church were drawn up.[41] Such lists, if compared to the parish registers, can be used to test the accuracy of the registration system and, given appropriate evaluation, can be used to compare the probable level of under-registration with that estimated by Wrigley and Schofield in the *Population History of England*.

The Marriage Duty Act and marriage registration in London

London's marriage pattern represents a particularly dramatic example of the local effects of the Marriage Duty legislation. Figure 1 shows simple aggregatives of the number of marriages celebrated annually in the large suburban parish of St Botolph Bishopsgate and in the clandestine marriage centre of St James Duke Place.[42] There are good grounds for supposing that the experience of St Botolph was typical of many London parishes in the later seventeenth century.[43] Following the Restoration increasing numbers of Londoners chose to marry in clandestine marriage centres without banns or licence. Before 1695 the two most important centres were St James Duke Place and Holy Trinity Minories. As a consequence the number of marriages in many local churches fell to extremely low levels, much lower than those experienced by many rural parishes. The success of the

[40] Krause, 'Changing adequacy', p.383; Wrigley, 'Births and baptisms', p.281, fn 1. Although the occasional appearance of dissenters' births in Anglican parish registers has sometimes been noted, it has not always been connected to the operation of the Duty Act; see *Local Population Studies* 13 (1974), p.47. The baptism register of Tetbury also occasionally notes the births of Quakers.

[41] The minister of North Wingfield, Derbyshire, recorded the births of nine Quaker children between 1698 and 1705 on the flyleaf of his register book. The minister of Atworth, Wiltshire, kept a separate book of Anabaptists and Quakers born in his parish; Cox, *Parish Registers*, p.256. A separate list of births 'chrisings not chrisened in the church' has also survived for Eglingham, Northumberland, which lists no less than 68 unbaptised children between 1696 and 1702; Cox, *Parish Registers*, p.255.

[42] These aggregatives were taken from printed parish registers; see Phillimore and Cokayne, *London Parish Registers*; and Hallen, *Registers of St Botolph*.

[43] Roger Brown found very similar patterns in other London parishes; see Brown, 'Clandestine marriages', pp.257-8. The same patterns are to be found in the Southwark parishes of St Saviour and St Olave, in St Dunstan, Stepney and in other large parishes in the suburbs. Gregory King noted that a similar fall-off in the inner city parish of St Benet Paul's Wharf had taken place in the later 1680s and early 1690s, 'the marriages of these later 7 years seem to be under the Comon Proportion'; *Burns Journal*, p.97.

Figure 1 Frequency of marriages in St Botolph, Bishopsgate and St James, Duke Place, 1660-1720

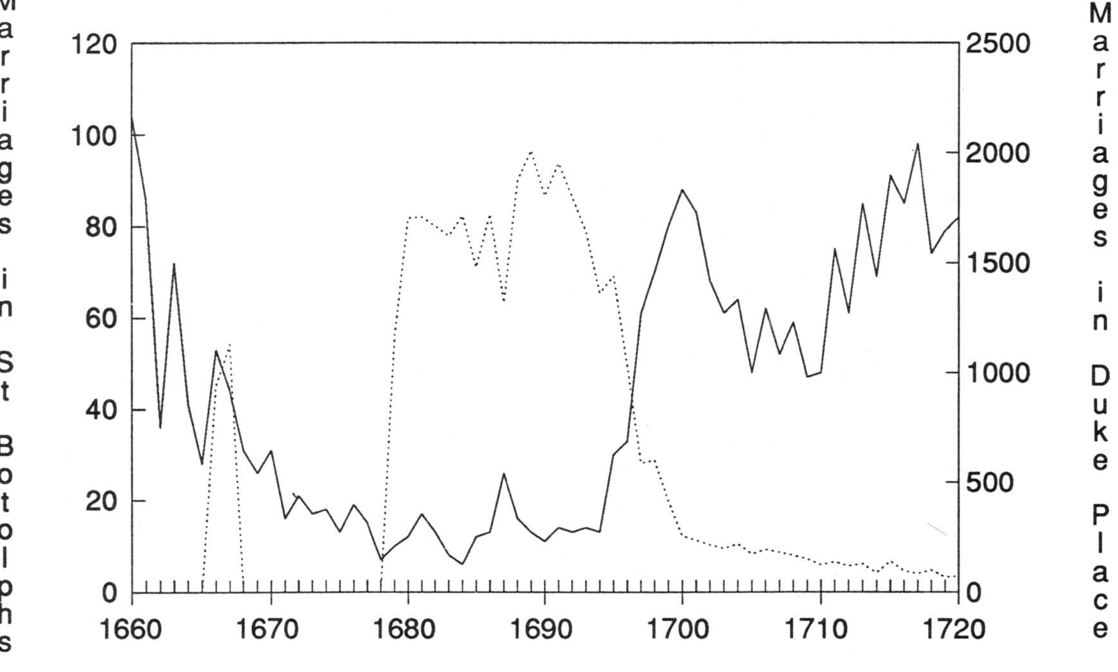

Duty Act, and the more rigorous amending Act in force from 24 June 1696, in reducing the number of irregular marriages in Duke Place (and in the other centres) resulted in a sudden, and to some extent a lasting, recovery in local parish marriage in this large suburban parish. Whilst the marriages in St Botolph increased by 367 per cent, the number of unions celebrated in Duke Place slumped from 1,689 per annum in 1691-4 to 535 per annum by 1696-9. Within a few more years the number of marriages in Duke Place had fallen to exceptionally low levels. In London, however, unlike in rural areas, the Duty Act's relative success in closing down clandestine centres merely handed the chapels located in the Fleet Prison and its 'Rules' a virtual monopoly of irregular marriage in London. As a consequence, couples from St Botolph gradually deserted their parish church for this new centre, as can be seen by comparing the two curves of Figure 1. By the 1730s clandestine marriage in London had reached levels comparable to the immediate post-Restoration period and did not recover until the Hardwicke Act put an end to the Fleet marriages and their like in 1753.

The Marriage Duty Act and registration of births and deaths in London

Table 2 sets out information for the births and baptisms recorded in the parish register and 'notices of births' kept by the minister of St Vedast Foster Lane and St Michael le Querne under the terms of the original Act of 1695.[44] St Vedast and St Michael were small and rather well-off parishes located inside the city walls of the capital, and at the end of the seventeenth century probably contained about 550 and 440 persons respectively.[45]

A number of points stand out from this table. The first is that the extent to which Anglican baptisms under-record births was very much higher than the national levels of under-registration estimated by Wrigley and Schofield (see above Table 1). Under-registration ran at 20.4 per cent for St Vedast, while in St Michael under-registration ran at 18.5 per cent during the first quinquennium of the Act but dropped to only 7.1 per cent between 1701 and 1706. It seems probable that the reason for this was a

[44] The registers of St Vedast and St Michael have been printed; Littledale, *Registers of St Vedast*, pp.124-37, 230-42, 248-57, 303-10.

[45] Estimated from figures given in the 1638, 1695 and 1801 survey and censuses; see Jones and Judges, 'London Population', pp.60-1; Finlay, *Population and Metropolis*, pp.170-1.

Table 2 Births and baptisms in St Vedast Foster Lane (1695-1704) and St Michael le Querne (1695-1706)

	St Vedast Foster Lane				St Michael le Querne			
	Baptisms in register (n)	Unrecorded births (n)	Total births (n)	Under-registration (%)	Baptisms in register (n)	Unrecorded births (n)	Total births (n)	Under-registration (%)
1695* *	27	8	35	22.9	9	5	14	35.7
1696	24	5	29	17.2	20	3	23	13.0
1697	35	6	41	14.6	13	3	16	18.8
1698	20	5	25	20.0	17	2	19	10.5
1699	23	8	31	25.8	16	3	19	15.8
1700	24	8	32	25.0	22	6	28	21.4
1701	20	8	28	28.6	17	1	18	5.6
1702	25	6	31	19.4	15	1	16	6.3
1703	26	8	34	23.5	18	2	20	10.0
1704	33	4	37	10.8	13	1	14	7.1
1705					18	1	19	5.3
1706					11	1	12	8.3
Total	257*	66	323	20.4	189	29	218	13.3

Source: Littledale, **Registers of St Vedast**, pp. 124-37, 230-42, 248-57, 303-10.
Notes: * * = The figures for 1695 are from May onwards only.
* = Includes three adult baptisms.

failure to record unbaptised children in the second quinquennium. It was not reflected in any compensatory increase in the number of baptisms recorded. Given that the latter quinquennium is an aberration, the notices of birth suggest that in inner London Anglican baptism registers under-registered births from between 17 and 20 per cent. Under-registration on this level was not reached nationally until the last decades of the eighteenth century.

There are important reasons why the foregoing analysis should be taken further. Firstly, as discussed previously, there were three separate components of birth under-registration, yet it is not known what is included in the above figure. Secondly, an assessment needs to be made of the part played by the administration of the Duty Act. Thirdly, given such high rates of under-registration, is it appropriate to undertake detailed demographic analysis using such parish registers? As has been noted, there were in theory two systems of vital registration provided for under the original 1695 Act. The surviving returns for London compiled under that Act have previously been used by Glass and others to make estimates of the completeness of Anglican registration in the 1690s.[46] The purpose of what follows is to take Glass's classic study further in order to gain a fuller understanding of the complex realities of registration procedures in the capital and the way in which the collectors' returns compiled under the Marriage Duty Act shed light on them.

Glass's estimates, unlike those detailed in Table 2, included an extra-statistical component derived from the application of the Chandrasekar-Deming test which was used to make statistical allowance for events that escaped from both the parish register and the collectors' returns. As Glass knew very well, and others have subsequently pointed out, this procedure could well have been invalid since the two sets of records were in all probability not generated independently. As we have seen, the terms of the original Act and subsequent amending legislation show that the collectors were expected to rely heavily on the notices of births and parish registers kept by ministers. As the amending Act of 1696 admitted, without an accurately kept notice of births 'many Persons...do thereby escape the Payment of the several sums'.[47] It is of peculiar interest, therefore, that the parish registers, notices of birth and the collectors' returns all survive for St Vedast and St Michael le Querne in London. By comparing all three records it should be possible to tell the extent to which the collectors in these two parishes compiled their returns independently of the registration system operated by Anglican ministers. If the collectors' returns did not rely totally on the church records one would expect to find some individuals appearing only in the returns. Moreover, one might expect to find the form and detail of such entries to be substantially different.[48]

As a check the first three complete returns, namely the years 1696-9, were compared to the appropiate periods in the register and notice of births (running from May to April each year). The

[46] Glass, 'Introduction', pp. xxxvi-xxxvii; Glass, 'Notes', pp.282-5; Jones and Judges, 'London Population', pp.49-51; Finlay, *Population and Metropolis*, p.34.

[47] 7 and 8 Wm. III c.35, s.4. Both St Vedast and St Michael also began to enter memoranda on their registers recording duties and rates under the Act from February 1699 under the terms of 9 Wm. III c.32, s.3; Littledale, *Registers of St Vedast*, pp.233, 212, 304.

[48] For the collectors' returns, see Corporation of London Record Office (CLRO), Assessments Box 28, 30, 39 for the years 1697-8, 1698-9 and 1696-7 respectively.

results of this simple exercise suggest very strongly that, in London, the collectors relied exclusively on the notices of birth to compile their own returns. In neither St Michael le Querne nor St Vedast did a collector ever record a birth not listed in the notice of births or in the parish register. In both parishes the format of the collectors' returns were identical to that of the notices of births. In all but a few cases the order in which the entries were listed in the notices of birth and the returns was identical, and the few mismatches were probably due to transcription errors made by the collectors. Two children in St Vedast and one child in St Michael were apparently listed in the parish registers and the collectors' returns only, possibly due to an accidental omission from the notices of birth perpetrated by the editor of the Harleian Society.[49] The collectors omitted three children listed in the notices of birth. These could have been simple errors, the deliberate omission of pauper children or children of parents not thought to be liable for tax in the parish in question. Foundlings were not included in notices of birth (although their baptisms were listed in the parish register) possibly because their dates of birth were unknown, or more probably to save parish expense. They were also omitted from the collectors' returns.

This suggests that the collectors' main task was to use the notices of births as a basis for their returns, checking off each entry against their assessment list to ascertain the correct duty. Therefore, if all collectors followed the same procedure, their returns are merely more or less accurate copies of the notices of birth compiled by incumbents. Consequently, Glass's use of the Chandrasekar-Deming test was not valid since the lists of births were, in effect, compiled by the same authority. Recalculating his figures to exclude this element gives under-registration estimates for Anglican registration as shown in Table 3.

The surprising element first discovered by Glass and depicted in Table 3 is that, seemingly, under-registration of births was much more serious in the small relatively well-off inner city parishes than it was in the larger and poorer extra-mural parishes. This is odd since one might expect more births to escape notice in the larger and more difficult-to-administer parishes, and it suggests that, for some reason, the collectors' returns might have been

49 Unfortunately the original registers of St Vedast and St Michael are no longer extant, having been destroyed in the Blitz.

Table 3 Estimates of birth under-registration in London, 1695-1706

	Baptisms in parish register	Total births	Missing births	Percent under-registration
London 1696-9[1]				
38 inner city parishes	3094	3873	779	20.1
2 suburban	283	317	34	10.7
St Mathew Friday St[2]	26	34	8	23.5
St Mildred Poultry[2]	37	46	9	19.6
St Botolph Bishopsgate[3]	372	442	70	15.8
St Vedast 1695-1704	257	323	66	20.4
St Michael 1695-1700	97	119	22	18.5

Source: 1 = Glass,' Demography of London', p. 283.
2 = Glass, 'Introduction', p. xxxvi.
3 = M.F. and T.H. Hollingsworth, 'Plague mortality rates', p. 139.

compiled less efficiently in these districts.[50] By matching births (and also deaths) in his thirty-eight inner city sample to those throughout the city, Glass seemed able to demonstrate that the reason for differential omission did not lie in significant numbers of individuals recording vital events in parishes other than their own.[51]

It is possible that under-registration of births was more extensive than appears from Tables 2 and 3. If the notices of birth and/or collectors' returns record all births which were not followed by a baptism, they should include the children of known religious dissenters, a related element for 'residual non-registration' and also numbers of children who died before baptism had taken place, that is who died very shortly after birth. In the event, however, an exercise in linking the names of the omitted children

50 It is certainly the case that the extra-mural parishes contained larger numbers of poor. In 1698-9 6.8 per cent of births escaped taxation on grounds of poverty within the city walls, but outside no less than 30 per cent did so; Jones and Judges, 'London Population', p.48, n.4.

51 'In the city of London vital events were very largely recorded in the parish of residence'; Glass, 'Notes', p.285, n.15. It should be noted that Glass was never able, as promised, to publish the 'detailed findings' of this matching exercise. Although the weight of the evidence suggests that baptisms *did* usually take place in the parish of residence, the same cannot be said of burials in inner city parishes where in some decades in the later seventeenth and early eighteenth centuries as many as 10-14 per cent of persons dying were buried, and frequently registered, elsewhere.

to the burial register demonstrated that few had died immediately after their birth. Since there is some evidence that various London parish registers failed to record infants who died within a few days of being born, it is very probable that the levels of under-registration reported here should be inflated. Wrigley and Schofield estimated that between 1690 and 1699 about half the under-registration of births nationally, about 4 per cent, was caused by death before baptism. Making a similar allowance for London would raise birth under-registration in the city from around 18 to 20 per cent to about 22 to 24 per cent.[52] Some surviving notices of birth make it explicitly clear that the lists were intended to register births of religious dissenters.[53] That this should be the case is hardly surprising; after all the 1696 amending Act had specified that it was children 'not christened according to the Rites and Ceremonies of the Church of England' or those baptised privately that were escaping notice. In this context a note by Gregory King deserves a wider audience. Describing the parish registers of late seventeenth-century Tiverton, Devon, or possibly Shrewsbury, he recorded that an informant (a parish clerk) writing on 29 January 1675 'says that the dissenters children were generally Registred heretofore, but not now'.[54]

A closer look at the 180 families who were included in the notice of births and the baptism register also suggests that religious dissent, rather than children dying before baptism, was responsible for the under-registration detected in St Vedast. The

[52] The fall in rates of under-baptism derived from identifiable and explicit burial entries of the order of 'X Y an unbaptised child of Z Y', led Roger Finlay to conclude that this was 'in itself strong grounds for believing that registration was deteriorating - indicating that the number of infant deaths which occurred before baptism was not known' in later seventeenth-century London; Finlay, *Population and metropolis*, p.35.

[53] Cox, *Parish Registers*, pp.255-6. The list compiled by the minister of Eglingham, Northumberland, headed at one point 'crisings not crisened in the church', also contains a heading 'children of dissenters'. The register of Eglingham demonstrates the striking density of religous dissent that might exist in some rural areas. Between September 1696 and March 1702 the register and separate list record 133 baptisms and no less than 64 dissenters, an under-registration rate of 32.5 per cent; Northumberland Record Office, EP 156/1. See also a list of 'children borne and not chrisen according to the Church of England', 1698-1701, for St Nicholas Cole Abbey; London, Guildhall Library, MS. 5686.

[54] For the relevant Act see, 7 and 8 Wm. III c. 35, s.4. For King see his *Burns Journal*, p.98. It is not clear to which area the note referred, although it is probably Tiverton.

key point here is to estimate the extent to which families appearing in one register also appeared in the other. Of the sixty-seven families to whom two or more children were born only twelve appeared in both registration systems, each family having one child unbaptised. There was no convincing link between very early death and the failure to baptise these twelve children.[55] Ten families having two or more children only appeared in the notice of births and the remainder appeared only in the baptisms. Most of the children, therefore, appearing in the notice of births in St Vedast, fifty-four out of sixty-six, came from families who do not appear in the baptism register. A disproportionate number came from families appearing more than once.[56] Many of the families, therefore, who appear in the notices of birth must have been religious dissenters, who deliberately opted out of Anglican ceremonial. This is particularly the case of certain families who appear regularly.[57]

This implies that the size of the dissenting groups in London might well have been more substantial than recent estimates have suggested. It is clearly difficult in such cases to disentangle religious allegiance from the effects of indifference or apathy; but recent estimates of the extent to which dissent throve in London have produced much reduced figures. Calculations of Protestant dissent based on a list drawn up in 1715 suggest a figure of only 5.7 per cent for London and Middlesex.[58] Individual dissenters, being clearly identifiable members of Protestant dissenting sects, were persons who 'esteem the Discipline, Rites and Ceremonies of the present established Church no better than Popery and Popish innovation'.[59] The levels of under-registration found here, however, fit more comfortably with the estimates of those who find that

55 Seven of the twelve are not recorded as dying, four died aged between 8 and 17 days and one at about 8 months old. Children dying younger than this in these families were also baptised.

56 Thus families appearing twice or more recorded thirty-two out of sixty-six entries or 48.5 per cent of all births, but only 36.4 per cent of all baptisms (figures exclude families of two appearing in both systems).

57 One man, a certain Samuel Bourne, a goldsmith living in Gutter Lane, appeared seven times in the notices of births between May 1696 and September 1704. Another, Nathaniell Markes, a glover living at the sign of the glove in Cheapside, had five children between December 1697 and June 1703. Five families alone produced 22 of the 66 children (33 per cent) found in the notice of births.

58 Port, *Commissions for building*, p.ix, fn.3, quoting Watts, *Dissenters*, p.509.

59 Quoted in Harris, 'Politics', chapter 3.

religious dissenters formed between 15 and 20 per cent of the population of Greater London in the early eighteenth century.[60]

A close relationship between dissent and under-registration suggests another possible reason for the differential rates of birth/baptism shortfall found by Glass in the inner city and its extra-mural areas. It suggests that the comprehensiveness of the collectors' returns might be linked in some way to the size and visibility of the dissenting group. Thus, if the number of dissenters was small and highly visible, more of their births would be noticed. In the larger parishes deliberate concealment or evasion might be more possible.

The effects of dissent noted above may be compared to the bias in reporting of dissenters found in the Compton census. In this survey, as in other surveys and reports of religious dissent, the numbers returned may not so much reflect actual spatial or numerical incidence as the vigour of the reporting and/or the problem posed by partial conformity. Although it might well have been the case that dissent was numerically strongest in the suburbs and densely-populated outer parishes of London, the Compton census seems to tell a different story. Within the archdeaconry of London the census records 64,321 conformists, 131 papists and 1,736 nonconformists in eighty-seven parishes: an overall figure of 2.6 per cent. Within the city walls, however, in seventy-four parishes there were 24,522 conformists, 75 papists and 1,039 dissenters or 4.1 per cent of the population. In the outer parishes in the archdeaconry there were only 753 dissenters and 39,799 conformists or 1.9 per cent.[61] Reporting of dissent varied wildly. For example, St Giles Cripplegate, a large extra-mural parish in the peculiar jurisdiction of the Dean and Chapter of St Pauls, returned no less than 8,140 dissenters and 20 papists out of a total population of only 24,550 – a figure of 33.2 per cent! St Sepulchre, a large extra-mural parish, returned no dissenters at all out of a total of 7,042 conformists and 4 papists. It seems likely that one reason for such unreliable reporting was the effect of religious division on London neighbourhoods. In some parts of the capital in the later seventeenth century parishioners refused to operate laws against dissenters, often placing 'loyalty to their

[60] De Krey, *Fractured Society*, p.75.

[61] Whiteman, *Critical edition*, pp. 57-60. Whiteman has also suggested, in her chapter above, that the dissenters were recorded most erratically in the large urban parishes.

neighbours above loyalty to the government'.[62] The other possibility, equally interesting, is that the numerical proportion of dissenters was, in reality, higher in the wealthier districts of seventeenth-century London than in its poorer suburbs. If this was the case, it would fit rather neatly with those who believe that religious dissent 'was especially strong among the "middling sort"' in London and other provincial towns.[63]

The type of under-registration of births detected from the records generated by the Marriage Duty Act should not discourage attempts to use later seventeenth-century London parish registers for demographic work based on family reconstitution. This is because, since most of the missing births were due to religious dissent, there was only a small overlap between the two registering groups. Thus a reconstitution using entries in the baptism register of St Vedast alone would only omit twelve births belonging to families using the Anglican registration system.[64] Instead, a much more serious obstacle to successful family reconstitution in Restoration London is represented by the growth of clandestine marriage in the capital as discussed above.[65]

The Marriage Duty Act and registration of deaths in London

The actual extent to which the records generated by the Marriage Duty Act also allow us to make an estimate of the under-registration of deaths in the parish registers of the capital leaves open more questions than it answers. Glass's use of the collectors' returns seems to show that parish registers seriously under-

62 Harris, 'Politics', chapter 3.

63 De Krey, *Fractured Society*, p.75. Baptists, whose impact on baptism practices would presumably have been greatest, were 'probably the largest sect outside the walls'. Presbyterianism seems to have been numerically dominant within the city proper (pp.85-7).

64 Reincorporating these missing children only raises the infant mortality rate for this parish from 257 to 264 per 1,000 which is not a very large margin of error.

65 Amanda Copley's tragic death interrupted what would have been a first-class study of London's population history. She had largely overcome the problem of clandestine marriage by recovering 'missing' marriages for Clerkenwell, her study area, from all available clandestine marriage centres. She recovered no less than 2,564 marriages from the eighteenth-century Fleet registers alone. The unpublished results from her sadly unfinished Ph.D. research are held at the Cambridge Group for the History of Population and Social Structure.

recorded burials.[66] However, an examination of the surviving collectors' returns, two notices of burial and the parish registers of St Vedast and St Michael le Querne for 1696-9 show a completely different picture. There were no entries in the collectors' returns not included in either the parish register or the notices of burial. In this case it seems likely that the collectors used the parish register as a source since the returns record detail not listed in the notices of burial that were listed in the parish register.[67] The collectors then merely added the appropriate assessment. Unlike the notices of birth, the notices of burial do not record any events that escaped the parish register.[68] The collectors' returns do omit a few entries from the parish register, presumably because no tax was due or from transcription errors, but as noted above do not record any individuals not listed in the parish register. This is very odd because Glass's use of the records shows a very considerable mismatch and very significant under-registration, ranging (if the double exclusion estimate is ignored) from 5.1 per cent in the two outer London parishes to 15.6 per cent in the thirty-eight inner city ones.[69] A check on Glass's workings for the two parishes which he identified by name, St Mathew Friday Street and St Mildred Poultry, reveals that there are, in fact, a number of names appearing in the collectors' returns which do not appear in the relevant sections of the parish registers. How can the different results of comparing the collectors' returns and parish registers for St Michael le Querne and St Vedast Foster Lane be explained?

Table 4 shows a comparison between Glass's original figures and the reworked set. This still reveals an omission rate of between 13 and 19 per cent for parish register burials. A closer look at the process of linkage, however, is revealing. Six of the eleven entries omitted from the burial register of St Mathew Friday Street occur in one year, 1696-7, a year in which the number of burials is

66 Glass, 'Introduction', pp. xxxvi-xxxvii; Glass, 'Notes', p.282.

67 For example the collectors' returns for St Vedast list on 28 November 1696 'Elizabeth Ridley sister to Coll. John Adams 4s'. The notice of burial records only 'Mrs Elizabeth Ridley' on that day, but the parish register records 'Mrs Elizabeth Ridley sister to Coll. John Adams...'.

68 In fact since some events, such as stillbirths, were not taxable and because the burials of individuals not liable for the duty in that parish were not listed, the notices of burials record *fewer* events than the parish register.

69 Glass also found under-registration running at 12.2 per cent and 17.9 per cent in St Mathew Friday Street and St Mildred Poultry. See Glass, 'Introduction', p.xxxvi.

Table 4 Burial registration in St Mathew Friday Street and St Mildred Poultry, 1696-9.

	St Mathew Friday Street		St Mildred Poultry	
	(Figures in brackets refer to those published by Glass)			
Parish register	47[1]	(46)[2]	65[3]	(65)[4]
collectors' returns	33[5]	(33)	44	(42)
In both parish register and collectors' returns	22	(23)	34	(33)
In collectors' returns only	11[5]	(10)	10	(9)
In parish register only	25[1]	(23)	31[3]	(32)

Notes: **1** = Excludes five outsiders and one abortive; **2** = Excludes individuals stated as not being parishioners; **3** = Excludes thirteen prisoners; **4** = Excludes ten prisoners; **5** = Includes one erased entry.

suspiciously low and which suggests, therefore, that the register was defective in that year.[70] Moreover, four out of the ten burials omitted from the register of St Mildred Poultry occur in a single block between March and April 1699. This coincides exactly with the insertion at this point of a list of 'Prisoners buryed out of the comter 1698'. The insertion of this list may have been at the expense of the intervening burial entries. Nearly half of all the burials omitted from these parish registers may have been due to poorly preserved registers. Registers not suffering from such defects might well demonstrate more comprehensive coverage. If Glass's much larger exercise included such defective registers the results may give an unnecessarily pessimistic picture of the comprehensiveness of well-kept London burial registers.

If gaps explain some of the mismatch, there still remain entries in the collectors' returns not included in the parish registers. The Glass explanation would be, of course, that since the returns and parish register were to some extent compiled independently, missing entries represent events of which the one registration system was notified but not the other. There is, however, as we have seen, strong evidence that in some parishes the returns were based exclusively on the records kept by the incumbent. Moreover,

[70] The annual totals recorded in the Friday Street register are (from May to end of April): 1694-5 - 12; 1695-6 - 17; 1696-7 - 11; 1697-8 - 23; 1698-9 - 19; 1699-1700 - 12; 1700-01 - 6. Burials in the latter year also suggest defective registration.

for the alternative to be correct, it would have to be envisaged that some individuals were dying without using the ceremonies of the Anglican church at burial. The true explanation for the mismatch between collectors' returns and parish registers resolves these questions, yet in so doing, however, it is argued that omissions from each system were deliberate and logical. Moreover it is also argued that, as a consequence, few if any burials escaped Anglican registration in at least one parish in the 1690s in London.

One reason why the collectors' returns contain entries not listed in the parish register lies in the actual nature of the former. It has not been fully understood that the returns are accounts and were designed first and foremost to record money received. They were not necessarily intended as a register of names; a common title for a return often began 'An account of money collected...'. Sometimes the title promised more but ultimately implied the same thing; for example, 'A list of all the names of all persons buried borne and married...with the severall and respective sums of money collected and received'.[71] The obvious problem here is the extent to which the collectors may not have included those persons who did not pay the tax due at all. In some inner city returns, but by no means all, separate lists of those failing to pay were appended. Even when drawn up, such lists were often written on fragile and presumably easily mislaid bits of paper.[72] Other collectors were clearly more aware of the confusion; a few were entitled 'An account of what money hath been and Aught to be receaved'.[73] It seems likely that in parishes where the aggregate number of non-payers was very large the collectors took greater pains to record all those owing duty. Thus in St Sepulchre, St Botolph Bishopsgate and St Botolph Aldersgate the returns make detailed provision for those in arrears.[74] In the first division of Bishopsgate no less than 78 (40.8 per cent) of the 191

71 CLRO, Assessments Box 39, St Mary Abchurch.

72 CLRO, Assessments Box 39, St Mary Abchurch lists four names owing for births described as 'gone', St Mary le Bow lists five individuals owing for three burials and three births for the same reason.

73 CLRO, Assessments Box 39, St Nicholas Acon and St Sepulchre.

74 For 1696-7 St Botolph Aldersgate sent in two sets of collectors' returns, listing money collected and also uncollected. In this parish 20 out of 132 births (15.2 per cent) went unrecorded in the main return and 32 out of 146 (21.9 per cent) of all burials. In this case when taken together, no burial listed in the collectors' return was not also listed in the parish register. The explanation for this latter comprehensive coverage is given below.

births had 'not paid' as well as 141 (48.6 per cent) of the 290 burials. This indication of poverty or evasion is all the more impressive since the burials of twenty-seven paupers and foundlings were included in the paid category. The returns for the Smithfield Quarter of St Sepulchre included separate lists of 'Returns of those that I cannot collekt' which dealt with those too poor to pay or those who had 'gone quite away'.[75] Failure to report those in arrears in the returns may well explain why some of the inner city returns were so deficient compared to the parish registers.[76] Other marginalia also reinforce the possibility that the collectors' returns within the walls omitted those who failed to pay. In St Martin Orgar, for example, one Thomas Uphold was added to the returns after the list had been drawn up with this note: 'Thomas Uphold charged 12s. for a birth and refuses to pay but 2s. - he lives in Nicholas Lane'. Against this entry is the significant comment, 'return his name it is now paid'.[77]

Although the fact that the collectors' returns were not always intended to be comprehensive records of names partly explains how they were sometimes extremely deficient in reporting burials, it still leaves a significant number of burials recorded in the collectors' returns but not in the parish register. A further reason for omissions and mismatches stems from this feature of the returns because, since they were accounts, the returns sometimes returned not the name of the deceased (or for that matter those born) but the person responsible for paying the duty. Obviously those liable for the payment of duty on births were normally parents, and their names were often put down on the returns rather than the name of the child.[78] The most likely possibility is

[75] See also the Old Bailey Division; Holborn Cross; Church precinct of St Sepulchre. The title of the last arrears list was 'Returns...which are charged by mistake and are poore and which refuse to pay'.

[76] Glass found that in two outer parishes 33 (10.5 per cent) of the 314 burials were in the parish register but not in the returns, compared to a massive 1,058 (27 per cent) of the 3,922 in 38 parishes within the walls. In addition to under-recording of arrears the remaining mismatch was probably caused by the inclusion in the parish register of individuals not liable to duty, such as stillbirths, imported burials and prisoners who were not so labelled in the register.

[77] CLRO, Assessments Box 39, St Martin Orgar.

[78] That is entries of the form 'X's child'. This can make linkage difficult and of course opens up the possibility that a few step-children and grandchildren may not have been linked. It seems unlikely, however, that this would prove a serious obstacle in the case of births. The collectors' return of St Nicholas Acon 1696-7 does contain under-payments for births, 'John Green for his grandson 2s', an entry that cannot be linked to the parish register.

that those paying for burials would be far more difficult to link to the actual burial in those cases where the returns only listed the liable next of kin. Thus when the collectors in St Nicholas Acon listed Mary Dobbins paying 4s. 'for a cosen' in 1696-7, the entry produces a spurious 'unique event' in both the returns and the parish register.[79] Only very detailed family reconstructions, using evidence of wills to recover executors, might shed light on such practices. There are still other good reasons why the collectors' returns might contain entries not recorded in the Anglican burial registers.

An important reason for the collectors' returns containing entries not appearing in the parish registers seems to have derived from the different purposes for which each document was required. Anglican parish registers were intended to record burial ceremonies whilst the principal concern of the collectors' returns was to record all individuals dying in a parish liable to pay duty there, irrespective of their subsequent place of burial. Put simply, Anglican parish registers may often have deliberately omitted the names of persons who died, but were not buried locally. In practice, some registers recorded all deaths and others only burials. It is the registers containing all deaths, irrespective of subsequent place of interment, which show no omissions when compared to the collectors' returns.

The taxation problem represented by the traffic in corpses was noted in the Marriage Duty Act. The amending Act which mentioned both religious dissent and private baptism in connection with birth under-registration also made an important addition to the original legislation in respect of burials. Noting that 'whereas diverse Persons are buried in other Parishes than where they lived or resided by reason whereof the Duties payable upon the Burial of such Person or persons are not answered to His Majesty', a clause ordered incumbents to notify the collector

[79] Some of Glass's links in St Mathew Friday Street and St Mildred Poultry seem to have been of the parent to deceased child variety. For example, the appearance of Joshua Gee, paying 14s. for a burial in Friday Street seems to have been linked to the burial of William Gee in the same year in the parish register. Joshua headed a household in St Mathew Friday Street in 1695; Glass, *London inhabitants*, p.117. In St Mathew too, Sarah Chandle appears only in the returns 1696-7 but might be the person responsible for paying the duty on the burial of Margaret Chandler recorded in the parish register for 22 July 1696. In this case, since the surnames were slightly different, no link was made.

of such a person's residence.[80] This latter clause seems to have been referring to a considerable traffic in corpses in the later seventeenth century as individuals were shipped back to 'home' parishes for burial, perhaps to lie in family vaults near their spouse or parents. There is some evidence that this traffic may have been on the increase from the Restoration. In particular, in relation to poorer social groups, Snell has argued that the practice of sending the elderly poor back to their home parishes may have increased following the Settlement Acts of 1662 and 1685.[81]

Marginalia in the collectors' returns for London enable us to pin down the procedure adopted under the Act to deal with burials sent in from elsewhere. The second collectors' return of St Botolph Aldersgate for 1696-7, which recorded 'uncollected' money, also contained a separate list entitled 'The names of Persons of whom I have Satifecates for'. This list is revealing; seven individuals were named, six of them from other London parishes. All these incoming burials were omitted from the collectors' returns proper but were included in the parish register of Aldersgate. Although recorded in the parish register they were not labelled as incoming burials, so that without the extra material supplied by the returns it would be assumed that they were parishioners.[82] The seventh entry recorded the burial of Benjamin Alport at Shoreditch. In this case the burial was also recorded in the collectors' return proper (presumably because the executors had chosen to pay tax in Aldersgate) and in the parish register (which again failed to label the burial as an export). Deaths as well as burials were being recorded in Aldersgate at this time. It is no coincidence, therefore, that all the burials listed in both sets of collectors' returns for 1696-7 appear in the parish register. Since there were very large numbers of burials per year in Aldersgate the proportion of burials imported and exported must have been

[80] 7 and 8 Wm. III, c. 35, s.6. The following amending Act ordered that place of residence should be included in each burial entry; 9 Wm. III, c.32, s.3.

[81] Snell, 'Parish registration', pp.33-8. In the late eighteenth century 28 per cent of all burials in Barming, Kent, were of 'imported corpses', 12 per cent of which came from London; Schofield, 'Traffic in corpses', pp.49-53.

[82] The six incoming burials were 9/7/96 Alice Wether from St Paul Shadwell; 7/9/96 Mary Pain from Deptford; 9/9/96 Doctor Luke Rodgley from St Giles-in-the-fields; 29/10/96 Jane Lewis from Clerkenwell; 17/1/97 The Lady Sarah Herington from St Benet Gracechurch; 12/4/97 John Jennings from St Mary Islington; CLRO, Assessments Box 39. For the parish register see, Guildhall Library MS. 3854/2.

small.[83] The fact that the collectors' returns contain details not recorded in the parish register does not, by itself, indicate independent notification since such detail may have been available in separate memoranda kept by the parish clerk or the incumbent. Indeed other marginalia, in addition to the evidence from St Michael le Querne and St Vedast Foster Lane, also suggests that the collectors were heavily dependent on records kept by the incumbent.[84]

Normally the collectors' returns supply evidence of the reason for omitting incoming burials rather than the inclusion of those carried away to other parishes for burial. When the collectors of the Church Precinct of St Sepulchre listed separately those 'which are charged by mistake and are poore and which refuse to pay' they included 'Hester Boutell buried from St Andrew Holborn to be their paid', but also James, son of James Wells 'a child buried in St Clements to be their paid'. The latter entry was also correctly listed in the collectors' return proper because a certificate from the collectors of St Clement had been received. Certified burials of those sent in from outside were not normally recorded in the collectors' returns proper; when they were it would have been because, as in the case of James Wells, duty was paid in the place of burial rather than that of death. The collectors of St Mary Woolnoth listed three individuals paying duty locally who were in fact buried in St Swithin, London, Surrey and Cambridgeshire and one individual brought from Peckham paying in Woolnoth.[85] Other certificates emphasise the fact that place of death rather than burial was often the place of assessment. In this case the only evidence of independent registration is that those transporting corpses needed to satisfy local collectors that tax had been paid. A plausible scenario would be that the collectors learned of deaths and burials from local church authorities and then asked for either payment of the appropriate duty or a certificate of payment. On payment a

83 The Bills of Mortality show an average of 188 burials in Aldersgate 1696-7, so that only 3.2 per cent were imported. Totals from the bills as listed in Marshall, *Mortality*, p.72.

84 For surviving parish clerks' memoranda books see Forbes, *Chronicle from Aldgate*, and Boulton, *Neighbourhood*, p.67. When the collectors' returns of St Dunstan in the West were being compiled in 1696-7, a stray paper (unsigned) noted that 'The minister is now out of Towne and will bee so for four months so that wee cann[ot] Give a particular of the places of abode of the above mentioned persons' (referring to a list of marriages).

85 CLRO, Assessments Box 39, St Mary Woolnoth.

receipt would presumably be issued.[86] The traffic in corpses could therefore cause omissions from both collectors' returns and parish registers.

In London, parish registers almost invariably record burial ceremonies but often (in perhaps two out of three cases) did not record deaths which involved interment in foreign parishes.[87] Even when corpses were brought in or sent out this fact was not necessarily recorded in the register, even if the burial itself was recorded. When the parish register is known to record both burial and also deaths resulting in a burial export, there are no burials listed in the collectors' returns not also listed in the parish register.[88]

Summary and conclusion

This chapter has argued that the impact of the Marriage Duty Act of 1695 and its subsequent amending legislation may have been neglected by demographic and social historians. Where the records which it generated exist, they can tell us much about local registration practice and something about local patterns of religious dissent. The Act's impact on recorded marriages was of particular significance, exceeding that of the much better known

86 Kept by the collectors of St Katherine Coleman Street, the certificate ran as follows, 'This is to satisfie whome itt may Concerne Whareas William Cust Clothdrawer in the Parish of St Katherine Coleman London: Dying att Westerham in Kent The Tax According to Act of Parlament for the Dead is Dewley satisfied'. The collectors of St Michael Bassishaw noted, separately, three names of individuals, one a Mrs Philipps from Hackney, 'these persons were buried in this parish But were not rated here, and the Certificates, wee cannot gett'. See the parish returns in CLRO, Assessments Box 39. A study of exceptionally detailed burial registers for three city parishes demonstrated that between 8 and 14 per cent of individuals dying were exported to other parishes.

87 This *excludes* the case of burial in extra-parochial burying grounds such as Bethlem churchyard, Bunhill fields or various dissenting cemeteries. Copley's work referred to in footnote 65 sheds important light on the deteriorating quality of Anglican parish registration in the second decade of the eighteenth century caused by burial in such cemeteries. This work showed that parish registers began to omit such burials in large numbers from about 1720, her figures being as follows: percentage of Bunhill fields burials registered in Clerkenwell, 1713-9, 86.9 per cent; 1720-9, 38.8 per cent; 1730-9, 2.9 per cent.

88 This statement receives further support from a matching exercise carried out on the collectors' returns and parish burial register of St Dionis Backchurch. The comprehensiveness of this register, recording deaths not merely burials, meant that all the 23 burials listed in the collectors' returns were listed in the parish register.

Hardwicke Marriage Act of 1753, and causing dramatic increases in celebrated weddings in the capital.

This study has also produced further information as to the meaning of the collectors' returns and their relationship to late seventeenth-century parochial registration. It seems very likely that the collectors' returns were totally dependent on the parish register and other ancillary records kept by the incumbent or parish clerk for information about vital events in their parishes. Events missing from one or other set of records are not, in fact, evidence that each registration system operated independently.[89] Events were omitted deliberately by the record keepers for quite logical reasons. Births and burial ceremonies that did not take place locally were often not recorded in parish registers, but there is evidence that separate lists of births and (to a lesser extent) deaths might be kept, to which the collectors had access. Where the collectors listed a death not recorded in the parish register they were often listing an individual who died and paid duty locally but whose burial took place elsewhere. Since such burial ceremonies were usually recorded most deaths would have been recorded at least once. The collectors might not list burials or births because individuals other than the natural parents paid the duty (thus causing insoluble linkage problems), because burials were imported from outside the parish (the duty having been paid at place of death) or because they were stillbirths. In some cases, too, the collectors may also have omitted individuals in arrears from what were, in reality, accounts of money received.

The national estimates of birth under-registration made by Wrigley and Schofield may be particularly vulnerable in the light of the levels of omission found in the wealthier parts of London. This is made the more likely by the fact that other urban areas may have exhibited similar rates. The 'by-register' of babies not baptised in the Anglican church has survived for the parish of St Mary, Reading. Between 1697 and 1706, 105 births were listed in this 'by-register' alone, and 502 baptisms in the parish register, an under-registration rate of 17.3 per cent.[90] This estimate does not include any allowance made for children dying shortly after birth, before registration was possible. If it is assumed that the parish of St Mary was representative of the whole town, and

[89] Glass, 'Notes', p.284.

[90] See Crawfurd, *Registers of St Mary*.

given that Reading's population was about 5,000 in 1700, then the following line of argument suggests itself. It has been estimated recently that 17 per cent of England's population lived in urban areas exceeding 5,000 inhabitants in 1700.[91] If one makes the assumption that 17.5 per cent of all births were omitted from Anglican parish registers in such settlements in the later seventeenth century then this would cast some doubt on Wrigley and Schofield's estimates that only around 9 per cent were omitted nationally at this date, since registration in all rural areas would need to be better than they estimated to offset such poor urban registration.

The lessons for London historians from this modest exercise might also be considerable. Few individuals would have escaped burial registration in the capital at the end of the seventeenth century.[92] The aggregate effect of those bodies exported out of the London area would have been countered both by the element of double counting (where parish registers recorded all deaths and not merely all burials) and by the small number of bodies brought to the capital for burial. Birth under-registration, on the other hand, caused by religious dissent, may have been running at about 17 per cent in the late seventeenth century. If this was so, as Glass pointed out sometime ago, 'the balance of births and deaths appears more favourable than is often assumed to have been the case for London'.[93] This statement carries particular weight since these allowances include no estimate for children dying before baptism. In summary, in future historians may need to be especially wary of applying Wrigley and Schofield's correction figures to local research.

91 For estimates of England's urban population, see Wrigley, 'Urban Growth', p.688. Reading's population was 'under 5,500' in the 1670s, but had grown to around 7,000 by 1750; Goose, 'Decay and regeneration', p.66; de Vries, *European Urbanization*, p.270. Reading is not in Wrigley's urban population. Glass stated that calculations of under-registration could also be made for Shrewsbury (population c.6,000 in 1700) from the Marriage Duty Act material, but, as far as I am aware, never published them; Glass, 'Notes', p.285, fn.14. See above for Gregory King's comments on the effects of dissent on registration in Tiverton.

92 A study of the destination of exported corpses in one city parish revealed that 61 out of 104 bodies were transported within the capital Bills of Mortality. Of those imported, 77 out of 87 came from other parishes within the Bills.

93 Glass, 'Notes', p.284.

12

Variations in household structure in the late seventeenth century: toward a regional analysis

KEVIN SCHURER

Introduction

> 'The basic structure of English households in the pre-industrial era is now well known. Households were small. The majority contained fewer than five persons, and membership was customarily confined to parents and their unmarried children. If the family was sufficiently wealthy, or involved in farming or trade, then the household might well contain servants, but there were remarkably few complex households containing grandparents, parents, and grandchildren'.[1]

Since the publication in 1972 of *Household and Family in Past Time*,[2] the seminal work on the subject, much research has been undertaken on the structure of English households, most of which confirms, to a greater or lesser extent, this summary statement made by Richard Wall a decade later. However, despite the volume of research analysing patterns in household structure, the regional dimension, in terms of a systematic comparison between different geographical areas of the country at the same time, has been virtually absent. In one of the first publications to present a 'national' examination of historical household structures, its author, Peter Laslett, promised a second complimentary article to appear later in the same journal which would 'describe and analyse variations in mean household size by region and by period'.[3] Indeed, the original article was even subtitled Part I. This was in 1969, and the fated 'Part II' has still to appear.

1 Wall, 'The household', p.493. In writing this chapter a great debt is owed to Richard Wall. Not only is this analysis an expansion of work previously undertaken by him (see Wall, 'Household structure from 1650') but in commenting on an initial draft he provided many useful suggestions.

2 Laslett and Wall, *Household and Family*.

3 Laslett, 'Size and Structure', p.199. A regional analysis of mean household size was, however, presented in Wall, 'Mean household size', pp.191-5.

The general failure to produce a picture of regional diversity, or the lack thereof, in the study of historical demography and social structure has been noted in a recent review of research in this field. In his survey of work undertaken in historical demography Ogden concluded that 'perhaps the greatest research challenge lies in the discovery and interpretation of geographical variations'.[4] In the case of household and family structures, an investigation of regional patterns in the past may indeed prove most rewarding and instructive. For example, taking a simple, straightforward proxy measure of kin complexity within households from the published returns of the 1981 census shows that in England and Wales as a whole only 0.87 per cent of households contained two or more families living together.[5] However, as one might expect, quite a large degree of regional variation occurred around this 'average' national figure. In particular, based on the Standard Regions of England and Wales by which the census data are tabulated, it is possible to see a dividing line running from the Bristol Channel, eastwards along the Cotswolds, then northwards to join the spine of the Pennines. To the south and east of this line the proportion of two-family households is relatively low, while to the west it is relatively high. The East Anglian region recorded a low of 0.61 per cent two-family households; the South West 0.76 per cent; North region 0.69 per cent;[6] the East Midlands 0.78 per cent and Yorkshire and

4 Ogden, 'Historical demography', p.240. It is also interesting to note that in his re-examination of Wrigley and Schofield's *Population History*, Goldstone proposed that 'a complete theory of England's demographic revolution is most likely to emerge from a regional mapping of real wages, industrialisation, agricultural change, and shifts in nuptiality and fertility'; Goldstone, 'The Demographic Revolution', p.31. Recent research has illustrated the apparent geographic homogeneity of mortality and fertility in England compared with the experience of the countries on the continent, especially France; for example see Wrigley and Schofield, 'Summary results', p.183, and Wrigley, 'The fall of marital fertility', pp.142-61. Such findings have prompted Laslett to describe the demographic experience of the English like 'the red coats on parade in front of Buckingham Palace, every unit in step with every other, and all changing direction at the same time'; Laslett, 'Review of Teitelbaum', p.537. Yet see also Anderson, 'Historical demography', pp.600-5 and Woods and Hinde, 'Nuptiality'.

5 In the published tables from the 1981 census a family is defined as i) a married couple with or without never married children; ii) a lone (single) parent with or without his or her never married children; or iii) grandparent(s) with grandchild(ren) if there are no apparent parents of the grandchild(ren) usually resident in the household. *OPCS Census 1981. Household and family composition*, pp.ix-x.

6 Using the definitions of the 1981 census the North region consists of Northumberland, Tyne and Wear, Cleveland, Durham and Cumbria.

Humberside 0.80 per cent. To the west, Wales recorded 1.09 per cent; the West Midlands region 1.04 per cent, and within this the West Midlands Metropolitan County (Birmingham) 1.35 per cent; the North West region 0.93 per cent, again within which the Merseyside region recorded 1.07 per cent.[7] Of course, there are exceptions to this general regional pattern. Most notable is the South East region which returned an overall mid-way figure of 0.89 per cent, while within this region the highest proportion of all, 1.1 per cent, was recorded for the Greater London area.[8] These figures not only point to the possible existence of a general rural-urban dichotomy operating within a regional context, but also suggest that the stereotyped north-south divide is not as straightforward as is sometimes portrayed.

Although it is possible to identify regional patterns of household structure and complexity in the present, as Richard Wall has demonstrated, such patterns are not necessarily constant over time.[9] Despite the fact that the picture for 1981 is broadly similar to that of 1971 or even 1951, Wall has shown that in 1851 the household complexity map of Britain was somewhat different. Then Wales and the South West were the areas with the least complex households, the East occupied a middle position, while the North recorded the highest proportions of household complexity.[10] Such variation in the regional patterns of household structure over the past 150 years suggests that an evaluation of trends in pre-industrial England would be of particular value.

7 *OPCS Census 1981. Household and family composition*, Table 1, pp.2-13.

8 *OPCS Census 1981. Household and family composition*, Table 1, pp.7-8.

9 R. Wall, 'Regional and temporal variations'.

10 R. Wall, 'Regional and temporal variations'; see especially Figure 3 (p.78) and Figure 6 (p.82). Interestingly Scotland stands out as having amongst the highest degree of complexity in both the modern period and the mid-nineteenth century, yet in 1951 was one of the areas in which households with kin were relatively infrequent; Wall, 'Regional and temporal variations', pp.81, 83. It should also be noted that despite the temporal comparisons that have been made the 'measuring stick' is not consistent over time. In his analysis of the published census data for 1951-71, Wall used the proportion of households with resident relatives. Due to the classification employed in the tabulations on household structure for 1981 it is not possible to obtain such a measure for this year. Instead, the proportions of households containing two or more families was used. Although a proxy measure of variations in household structure, this is clearly not the same as the proportion of households with relatives since the majority of relatives attached to households do not form secondary conjugal family units. In his analysis of the 1851 two per cent national sample, prepared by Michael Anderson, Wall took the mean number of relatives per household as the

Variations in household structure in the past

Despite the need for an examination of regional variation in household structure for a pre-industrial period, as in many areas of historical research, this is easier said than done. The basic obstacle preventing a full-scale regional analysis of household structure in pre-nineteenth century England and Wales is the lack of adequate source material. In order to gain an insight into the residential composition of households prior to the introduction of enumeration books with the national census of 1841, one has to resort to the use of such census schedules as survive from the censuses of 1801-1831 or the unofficial, *ad hoc* local listings of inhabitants, often drawn up by a local clergyman or other parish official in order to help monitor the population under their jurisdiction. The precise motivation which prompted the creation of such documents is, unfortunately, not always known. Some may have been compiled for pastoral or other religious reasons, while others clearly may have resulted from a deep concern regarding social welfare and the relief of the poor. Others, though, can only be described as idiosyncratic, such as the listing for the parish of Ardleigh in Essex, made by the Rev John Kelly in 1796. Concerned by the 'intention of the French to make a descent upon this coast' he undertook 'a domicilary visitation; that in the event of an actual Invasion, such a list may be useful, either to assemble us in order to make a resistance, or in case of dispersion, to enable us, upon our return, to discover and ascertain our respective claims and settlements.'[11]

Although interesting, this random and *ad hoc* nature of pre-nineteenth century listings of inhabitants is clearly a significant handicap when it comes to producing any systematic regional analysis. Without the complete geographical coverage offered by a national census taken at a single point in time, and without common, standard criteria, it is difficult if not impossible to present a cohesive regional picture of differences in household structure. In the absence of such a standard base, any attempt at a regional analysis of groups of local listings of inhabitants is

measure of regional household complexity; see Wall, 'Regional and temporal variations', p.83. Lastly, in comparing any census data over time, whether published or not, one must be aware that the most basic of measuring units such as the household may itself have undergone various changes of definition; see Wall, 'Regional and temporal variations', pp.62-5, and Higgs, *Making sense of the Census*, pp.58-62.

11 Erith, *Ardleigh in 1796*, p.106.

hampered by the fact that any differences may be due to the varying nature, quality or temporal range of the listings included in the 'regional' groupings, rather than any significant geographical effect. For example, the listings available for one region may relate primarily to small agricultural parishes enumerated in the seventeenth century, while for a second region, the 'sample' may consist of a late eighteenth-century mix of small towns with developing proto-industrial sectors and large parishes with an agricultural base. With this dilemma in mind, the records generated under the provisions of the Marriage Duty legislation for the period 1695 to 1706 may prove particularly valuable in throwing a shaft of light on the regional framework of household structure in late seventeenth-century England, if not actually illuminating the entire picture.

The availability of sources

The legislative and administrative background to the enforcement of the Marriage Duty Act of 1695 has been fully documented elsewhere in this book, and in this respect there is little point in duplicating this information.[12] In theory, if not in practice, the Marriage Duty Act, like the censuses of the nineteenth and twentieth centuries, was applicable at a national level: each city, town, village and hamlet was liable to pay the tax and consequently to draw up the assessment lists of inhabitants giving details of liability. Although important, in relation to the analysis of household structure, it is not, however, the coverage of the tax *per se* that is our main concern but rather the actual survival of the documents generated, the range of information that they contain, and the way in which this information was organised. Again, a detailed discussion of the format and scope of these documents is contained elsewhere in this volume and it is not proposed to replicate this here.[13]

In all, some 150 or so listings of inhabitants resulting from the Marriage Duty Act are known to have survived.[14] From time to

12 See both chapter 8 by Tom Arkell above and the valuable work of Glass, 'Introduction', especially pp.ix-xviii.

13 See 'Introducing the documents, part II'.

14 Copies of many of these are housed in the library of the Cambridge Group for the History of Population and Social Structure. Summary details of the greater part of this collection have been given in the 'List of Listings' published on a county basis in *Local Population Studies* 20, 1978 to 37, 1986. See also the list in Vialls, 'The duty on marriages'.

time new listings are discovered and it is hoped that many more survive in various archival repositories and await the attention of local researchers.[15] Yet even so it must be made clear that the coverage of the entire stock that survives will not in any way equate to a representative national sample along the lines of census enumeration. Furthermore, even of those that do survive, many are of limited value for the purposes of analysing household structure. Some lists may fail to make adequate distinction between the end of one household and the beginning of another. Others, although perhaps with households clearly delineated, may simply list the household members other than the head without any indication of relationship to the head, perhaps even as a straightforward count of individuals in each tax category. A third category of lists, despite indicating the boundaries of most households, may enumerate those subject to special attention separately, typically bachelors over the age of twenty-five, and widowers without children, perhaps as a long list of individuals at the end of the document.

Despite these words of reservation, the returns of the Marriage Duty Act still offer the historian of the household the best opportunity to investigate household structure in a geographical context prior to the mid-nineteenth century. For the purpose of illustration, the examination that follows focuses on just six relatively small areas, chosen because for each several Marriage Duty returns appropriate for the study of household structure have survived for a number of parishes in close geographic proximity, if not actually contiguous. Five of these areas have already been examined elsewhere, yet this analysis both elaborates and extends this initial study.[16]

A complete list of the six areas selected for investigation and their constituent parts, invariably parishes or tithings except in the case of Shrewsbury, is given in Table 1, together with the size of the population covered, the number of households and the date of the enumeration. The dates of the enumerations range between 1695 and 1705, covering the entire period of the Marriage Duty assessments. In only three of the areas is the timing of the enumerations internally consistent, and each of these is different:

15 See, for example, Medlycott, 'Survey'.

16 See Wall, 'Household structure from 1650', pp.100-8. Wall's article excludes Bristol from its analysis. Copies of the Marriage Duty documents used in this chapter are held in the Cambridge Group library.

Table 1 Marriage Duty assessments selected for study

Parish or Ward	Population (n)	Households (n)	Date
Bristol			
Castle Precinct	1274	282	1698
Christchurch	653	179	1697
St Augustine	1526	411	1695
St Leonard	314	80	1697
St Michael	982	235	1697
St Stephen	1649	439	1698
St Werburgh	287	72	1697
Totals	6685	1698	
East Kent			
Adisham	125	22	1705
Ash Chilton	728	150	1705
Ash Overland	454	95	1705
Barfreston	50	12	1705
Buckland	107	19	1705
Froghamborough	100	27	1705
Guston	80	20	1705
Little Mongeham and Ashley Borrow	162	36	1705
Shepherdswell	160	32	1705
Womenswold	107	23	1705
Wotton	85	20	1705
Totals	2158	456	
London			
All Hallows Staining	847	148	1695
*St Anne Blackfriars	667	85	1695
**St Botolph Without Bishopsgate	1005	176	1695
St Ethelburga	664	131	1695
St Mary Bothaw	324	56	1695
St Mary le Bow	693	106	1695
St Mary Woolchurch	483	69	1695
Totals	4673	771	
Shrewsbury			
Castle Ward 2	769	161	1698
Castle Ward 3	297	55	1698
Castle Ward 4	424	107	1698
Castle Ward 5	509	119	1698
Stone Ward 1	645	143	1698
Stone Ward 2	433	86	1698
Stone Ward 3	392	94	1698
Welsh Ward 1	198	344	1698
Welsh Ward 2	450	95	1698
Welsh Ward 3	353	80	1698
Welsh Ward 4	226	56	1698
Welsh Ward 5	346	72	1698
Totals	5041	1112	

Table 1 Contd.

Parish or Ward	Population (n)	Households (n)	Date
Southampton			
All Saints Without Bar	376	101	1697
Holyrood	730	185	1697
St John	147	40	1696
St Lawrence	300	62	1696
St Mary	192	45	1695
Totals	1745	433	
East Wiltshire			
Chiseldon	160	41	1705
Elcombe	63	12	1701
Liddington	230	61	1705
Uffcott	91	20	1701
Westlecott	111	24	1701
Wroughton	478	134	1700
Totals	1133	292	

Notes: * = one in five sample; ** = one in ten sample.
The parish population and household count given in this table refer to the number analysed. In some cases households were left out of the analysis due to illegibility.

London, 1695; East Kent, 1705; Shrewsbury, 1698. Of the remaining three – East Wiltshire, Bristol and Southampton – a variety of enumerations have been selected, due to the better quality of the lists for some years over others or the differential survival of the assessments.

Each area also exhibits a wide distribution in the size of the composite units. All include assessments with less than 50 households alongside assessments with 150 households or more, except East Wiltshire where the parish of Wroughton, with its enumerated population of 478 and 134 households, stands out in comparison with the other parishes included in the group. The range of population recorded in each area is clearly of central importance, especially when, in searching for geographical variation, the 'mean' experience of one area is compared with that of another. It is possible that many such aggregated figures may hide significant differences within any area, caused perhaps by local social or occupational characteristics.

Differences in social class are perhaps most acute in the parishes selected to represent London. Clearly, these seven parishes, with a total population of 4,683, are little more than a drop in what was at the time one of the largest and fastest growing cities in Europe, with a total population numbering some 490,000.[17] Firstly, the parishes selected are drawn only from the City of London (both within and without the walls) since Marriage Duty assessments have not survived for the intra-metropolitan parts of Middlesex and Surrey. Secondly, the size of two of the parishes chosen, St Anne Blackfriars and St Botolph Without Bishopsgate, necessitated a further sample to be made, analysing every fifth page in the case of St Anne and every tenth in the case of St Botolph.[18] London clearly experienced wide variations in the wealth of its inhabitants,[19] a factor which one might well expect to influence the structure of households. Consequently, in order to represent an appropriate social mix, the sample for London was selected to ensure that a full range of wealthy and poorer parishes was included, using the proportion of 'substantial households' in each parish as the criteria for measurement.[20]

17 Finlay and Shearer, 'Population growth', pp.48-9.

18 For St Botolph Without Bishopsgate the sample of 1,005 relates, according to Jones and Judges's estimation of the population at 9,753, to 10.3 per cent of the total. In the case of St Anne, the sampled population of 667 accounts for 24.0 per cent of Jones and Judges's estimate of the total; see Jones and Judges, 'London population', pp.59, 62. It should be noted, however, that Glass's population estimate for St Botolph differs slightly from that of Jones and Judges, being 2,829, as opposed to 2,782, making the sample a 23.6 per cent representation; Glass, 'Introduction', pp.xxiv (fn.1), xxvi. Recalculating various figures given by Glass for the whole parish of St Anne Blackfriars, the proportion of the population recorded as servants is 9.3 per cent, the proportion of households containing kin is 6.8 per cent and the proportion of households headed by a married couple is 85.8 per cent. Respectively, these figures compare with the one-in-five sample used in this chapter as follows: 7.8, 4.7 and 81.2; Glass, 'Introduction', pp.xxvi, xxxiii.

19 For details see the chapter by Alexander above (chapter 9). See also Glass, 'Introduction', pp.xix-xxv, and Power, 'Social topography'.

20 'Substantial households' are defined as those with individuals liable to additional surtax on the flat Marriage Duty rate, that is of persons with a personal estate worth not less than £600 or real estate worth not less than £50 per annum, plus persons of a certain status or occupation. See chapter 8 by Tom Arkell; also Glass, 'Introduction', p.xx, and Jones and Judges, 'London population', pp.59, 62. The proportion of substantial households in each of the selected parishes is as follows: All Hallows Staining, 16.1 per cent; St Anne Blackfriars, 1.1 per cent; St Botolph Without Bishopsgate, Division 1, 4.1 per cent; Division 2, 7.7 per cent; St Ethelburga, 20.3 per cent; St Mary Bothaw, 43.4 per cent; St Mary le Bow, 53.8 per cent; St Mary Woolchurch, 33.3 per cent; see Jones and Judges, 'London population', Table III, pp.58-62.

In the case of the remaining five areas chosen for study, the problem of sampling does not arise since the selection was made entirely according to the survival of assessments and their suitability for household analysis. In the case of Shrewsbury and Southampton, with respective populations of around 6,000 and 3,000 at the turn of the century, the coverage is virtually complete.[21] The former includes all of the central area but lacks some of its suburbs,[22] while only the parish of St Michael and part of All Saints is excluded from Southampton. For the City of Bristol, although a complete set of Marriage Duty assessments has survived for 1696[23] as well as for subsequent years in some instances, the delineation of households is often inadequate. However, those selected for analysis still provide the largest population base of the six areas, the 6,685 representing some 33 per cent of the total population of 20,000 estimated for the entire urban area at the end of the seventeenth century.[24] In short, all three were quite substantial-sized towns by late seventeenth-century standards.

Clearly, with data available for only six areas, what follows can hardly be considered to be a regional analysis on a national scale. Although certain geographical comparisons can be made, attention will inevitably be focused on drawing contrasts or noting similarities between the four urban areas (Bristol, London, Shrewsbury and Southampton) and the two rural ones (Wiltshire and Kent), as well as making some comparisons between the two rural areas or between one urban area and another. Yet at the same time, one must avoid drawing too sharp a dichotomy between the areas that have been identified here as either 'urban' or 'rural'. Perhaps with the exception of Bristol and London, each area contains a mix of settlement type. Shrewsbury and Southampton include suburban or less-densely populated parishes or sub-districts, while in the two rural groups the workforce was clearly not exclusively involved in agricultural activities. The occupation details recorded in the Marriage Duty assessments of the Kentish parish of Ash show that the settlement supported five

21 Corfield, *English towns*, p.40; Hindson, 'The Marriage Duty Acts', p.21.

22 The suburbs of Castle Ward are included, namely Castle Foregate, Old Heath, Cotton Hill and Gravel Hill, while the suburbs of Frankwell, Coleham and Abbey Foregate are excluded.

23 These have been transcribed and published by the Bristol Record Society with an introduction by Ralph and Williams.

24 Corfield, *English towns*, p.35.

victuallers, three maltsters, a tallow chandler and a glazier. It is also highly likely that the relatively populous parish of Wroughton in the Wiltshire group displayed a more varied occupational structure than its neighbours.

In addition to possible variations in the economy of these areas, one must also take account of differences in social class, since one would expect that this too would exert an influence on the composition of households. The social class component of the selected London parishes has already been mentioned and one would also expect to find some social segregation in Southampton, Shrewsbury and Bristol. Consequently, in the analyses that follow, when comparing one area with another, the lack of internal homogeneity must always be borne in mind. For example, a particular parish in London may have had more in common, in terms of household structure, with one in Bristol or Shrewsbury rather than with its immediate neighbours. In short, the whole range of experience exhibited within the six selected areas must be taken into account.

Residential kin

In examining the characteristics of, and variations in, household structure in the past attention has focused on the kin composition of households, especially the extent to which households contained relatives in addition to the immediate family of the head.[25] Since,

25 The standard schema by which households are classified is that devised by Hammel and Laslett. The building block of this classification is the conjugal family unit (cfu), such units being formed by a married couple, a married couple with never-married child(ren) (of any age), or a lone parent (unmarried, widowed or separated) with never-married child(ren). Once a person marries (or has a child) they automatically exit their parents cfu to form one of their own, and once having exited cannot return. Therefore, by definition no individual can be in more than one cfu at the same time. Relatives (or kin) of the head are consequently usually defined as any related person residing in the same household but not in the head's cfu. Hammel and Laslett, 'Comparing household structure'; Knodel, 'Household composition' and Laslett, 'Introduction', pp.28-34, 41-4. See also Cooper's contribution to this volume (chapter 10). Since the Marriage Duty assessments do not record marital status consistently, particularly the marital status of the children of the head of the household, in this study it was necessary to adopt a more elementary definition of kin. Consequently, as rule of thumb, unless the register suggests otherwise, all sons and daughters have been assumed to be unmarried, residential kin or relatives have been taken as being any person related to the household head other than their spouse and supposedly unmarried children, regardless of age or marital status. Therefore, some married and widowed sons and daughters may be included in the count of children rather than relatives.

Figure 1 Characteristics of household structure: six areas, 1695-1705

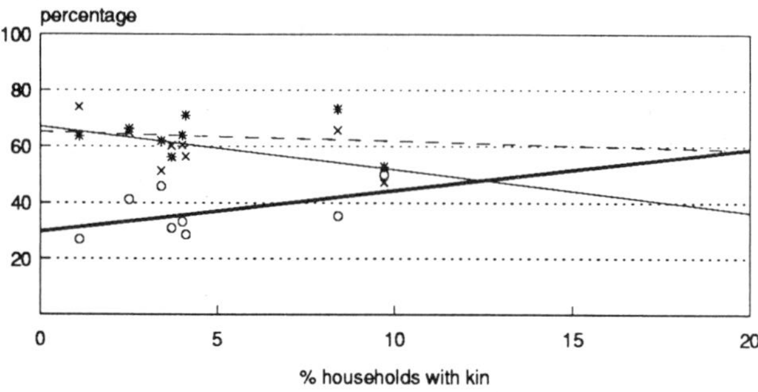

Kent

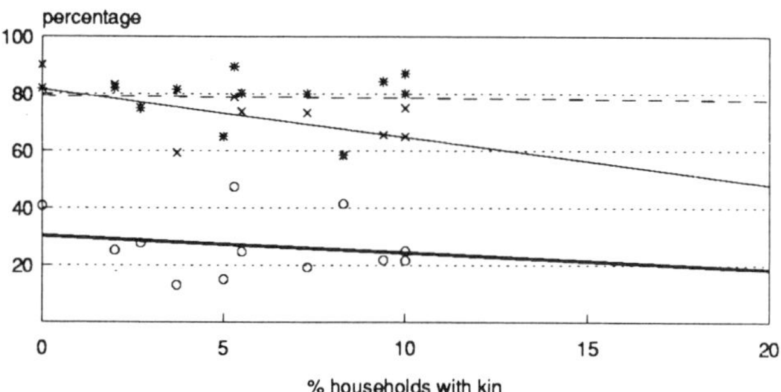

London

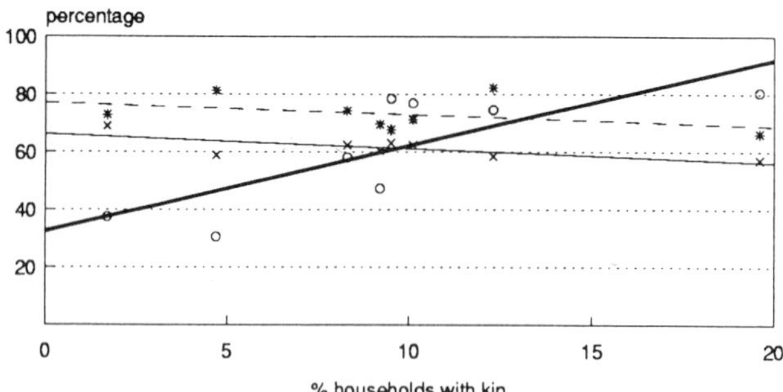

% households with children
% households with servants
% households headed by married couples

Figure 1 Contd.

Shrewsbury

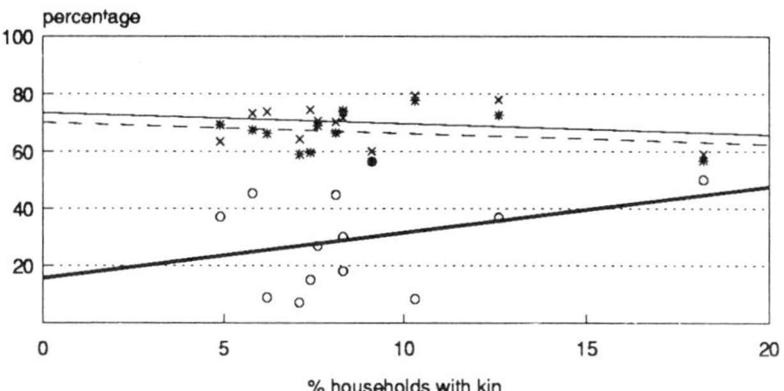

Southampton

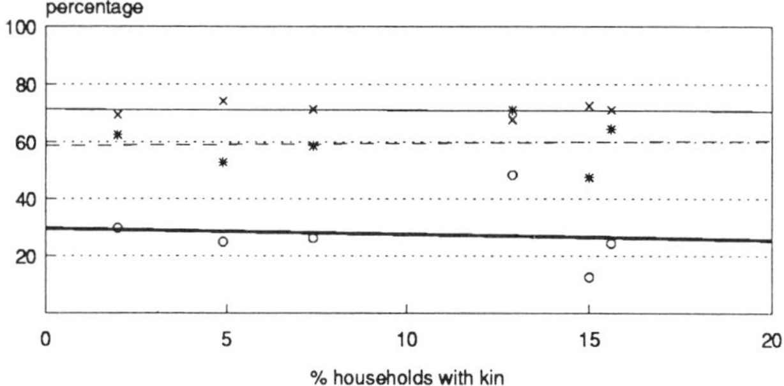

Wiltshire

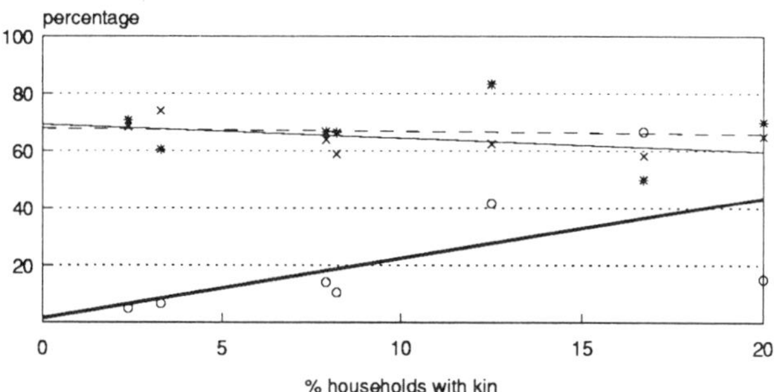

% households with children

% households with servants

% households headed by married couples

Table 2 Residential characteristics in six areas, 1695-1705

Proportions (%), sex ratios and mean sizes	Bristol	Kent	London	Shrewsbury	Southampton	Wiltshire
Households with kin	4.0	5.5	8.3	8.3	7.4	7.9
Kin in population	1.3	1.6	2.2	2.6	3.0	3.4
Sex ratio of kin	35.4	30.8	65.1	52.9	52.9	81.0
Households headed by married couple	63.9	80.2	74.1	67.5	58.6	66.7
Households headed by lone male	9.2	9.3	11.4	11.3	13.7	17.0
Households headed by lone female	26.9	10.5	14.5	21.3	27.7	16.3
Households with children	60.4	73.8	62.3	71.6	71.3	64.0
Children in population	35.3	41.8	26.0	40.6	43.4	45.7
Children in single person group	15.5	31.8	46.0	33.6	28.7	27.4
Mean size of child group	2.3	2.6	1.9	2.4	2.4	2.7
Households with servants	33.2	24.8	58.0	30.0	26.2	14.0
Servants in population	14.6	16.6	20.0	10.9	12.1	7.6
Sex ratio of servants	69.3	226.5	84.8	70.6	91.6	100.0
Servants in single person group	14.6	7.2	20.9	10.9	32.7	19.8
Mean size of servant group	1.7	3.2	2.1	1.6	1.7	2.1
Households (n)	1698	456	771	1112	433	292
Individuals (n)	6685	2158	4673	5041	1745	1133

Notes: In the case of servants in Kent sex is specified only for the parishes of Adisham, Buckland, Fronghamborough, Shepherdswell and Womenswold, plus thirteen servants in the joint parish of Ash.
Sex ratios measure the number of males per 100 females.

as the opening quotation of this chapter stressed, few households in the past contained relatives, this might be seen as placing undue emphasis on the kin component of the household. However, regardless of this problem the proportion of households containing kin has become the conventional benchmark of household complexity and has been used in the composite graphs of Figure 1. Concentrating initially on the horizontal axes of the graphs which measure the residential kin component of households, it can be seen that all six areas display quite a range of experience. This is particularly true of the Southampton, Wiltshire and London groups, the latter two displaying rates of less than 5 per cent alongside rates of 20 per cent or just under. The remaining three areas, however, show a tighter clustering in the proportion of households with relatives. Of these, the proportions recorded for Shrewsbury appear somewhat higher than the other two, being clustered mainly in the band between 5 and 10 per cent, and with an overall mean figure of 8.3 per cent is, together with London, the highest mean figure recorded. The parishes of Kent display greater variation, ranging from 0 (in the case of Adisham) to 10 per cent, but most fall between 2 and 7 per cent, giving an overall mean of 5.5 per cent. The lowest rates, however, are recorded in Bristol. If the figures for the central district of Castle Precinct (8.4 per cent) and parish of St Werburgh (9.7 per cent) are considered separately, all of the remaining parishes record levels of less than 5 per cent, giving an overall mean of 4 per cent (Table 2).

Clearly then, Bristol stands out as exhibiting the least complex household structure in terms of residential kin. Even the more complex district of Castle Precinct and parish of St Werburgh record relatively low proportions in relation to other areas, especially London and Shrewsbury. The rates for Bristol are less than half the mean figure of 10 per cent produced by Laslett from his sample of one hundred English pre-industrial communities.[26] Indeed, all six of the chosen areas fall short of this figure. However, this pre-industrial mean does of course relate to a range of experience over some two and a half centuries.[27] Following Bristol, the Kent group also displays comparatively low rates of complexity, yet the overwhelming picture is one of widespread variation within areas. Little evidence can be found to support an urban-rural dichotomy of residential kinship, and it is also difficult to account for any difference according to regional geographical factors. Rather, it seems that any difference that does occur – and overall it must be remembered that this is quite wide, from no households containing relatives to one in every five doing so – must be accounted for by micro-level factors.

26 Laslett, 'The household over three centuries', p.149. However, one must realise that some children in the Marriage Duty assessments who have been assumed to be unmarried may in fact be married, thus increasing the population of households with kin (see previous fn.). Yet even so the numbers of married/widowed children living with their parents in Laslett's sample is very low and consequently the failure of the Marriage Duty assessments to record marital status consistently would not dramatically increase the proportion of households with kin.

27 In this respect it is important to note that Wall has shown residential kinship to have increased in importance by the late eighteenth and early nineteenth centuries compared with the late seventeenth and early eighteenth centuries; see Wall, 'The household', pp.497-9.

Table 3 Mean composition of households and housefuls in six areas, 1695-1705

Household membership	Bristol*	Kent	London	Shrewsbury	Southampton	Wiltshire
Head and/or spouse	1.6	1.8	1.8	1.6	1.6	1.7
Children	1.4	2.0	1.2	1.7	1.6	1.7
Kin	0.1	0.1	0.1	0.2	0.1	0.1
Servants	0.6	0.7	1.3	0.5	0.5	0.3
Mean household size	3.7	4.6	4.4	4.0	3.8	3.8
Attached lodgers	0.2	0.1	1.7	0.5	0.2	0.1
Mean houseful size	3.9	4.7	6.1	4.5	4.0	3.9
Total houseful (n)	1698	456	771	1112	433	292
Total individuals (n)	6685	2158	4673	5041	1745	1133

Notes: * The Marriage Duty assessments of Bristol include 111 individuals who are deemed as living in institutions rather than households; these are mostly schoolchildren.
The houseful is a term which relates to all household members plus all additional persons (boarders, lodgers or secondary households) attached to the household. See Laslett, 'Introduction', pp.34-7.

Headship

Mention has already been made of the over-emphasis placed upon the presence or otherwise of residential relatives in assessing household structure. With this in mind, let us now consider the various categories plotted on the vertical axes of the graphs of Figure 1, beginning with the population of households headed by a married couple. Whereas, in all six areas combined, residential kin accounted for only 2.1 per cent of the population, heads of households (where married) and their spouses comprised over a third of the entire population (37.6 per cent). Likewise, as Table 3 shows, the mean number of relatives per household ranged from just 0.1 to 0.2 persons, while the household head and his spouse, where present, accounted on average for between 1.6 and 1.8 persons in every household. Obviously, not all household heads were married; the proportion of households headed by a married couple ranged from 50 to 90 per cent – the minimum in Elcombe, Wiltshire and the maximum in Buckland, Kent. Inspecting the trend-lines drawn on figure 1[28] which show the association

[28] The lines plotted on these graphs are the result of regressing the distribution of the individual parishes; see Bradley, *A Glossary for Local Population Studies*, pp.36-8, 53-4.

between the proportion of households headed by a married couple and the proportion of households with kin (plotted on the graphs as broken lines), it is immediately noticeable that in each case these run almost horizontally with little or no slope. Interestingly, what slope there is suggests a negative correlation with the proportion of households with kin. In other words, those parishes which recorded a high proportion of households headed by a married couple were less likely to record a high percentage of households with kin. This seems to suggest that the absence of a spouse encouraged the presence of a relative, either as a spouse-substitute, maybe to help pay household expenses, or perhaps due to the greater availability of accommodation.

By contrast, unlike the proportion of households with kin, reference to the proportion of households headed by a married couple does point to potential structural differences between the six areas. The Kent group of parishes stand apart from the rest in generally having high proportions, eight of the eleven parishes recording at least 80 per cent of households being headed by a married couple. At the other end of the scale, Southampton and Bristol record rates of nearer 60 per cent, obviously pointing to the fact that in these places there was a greater tendency for widowed, single or separated persons to head households. Indeed, Table 2 shows that these two areas recorded significantly higher numbers of households headed by females. The fact that London and Shrewsbury returned rates in the upper sixties and low seventies would suggest that this is not a feature associated purely with urban areas. Equally the fact that Wiltshire was on a par with London and Shrewsbury, if not slightly lower in some cases, implies that a high proportion of households headed by married couples is not necessarily a feature of rural areas. Rather, the low rates of Bristol and Southampton may be explained by their position as maritime ports.[29] At the end of the seventeenth century Bristol was the most important port outside London, especially for overseas shipments. Although Southampton's trade was significantly smaller *pro rata* to the population size of the town and had declined in importance by this time, the port still played an important function in the life of

[29] London was the largest port in the country at this time yet none of the seven parishes selected for the City were dock areas.

the town.[30] It may be that the relative high levels of mortality at sea, plus a possible greater tendency amongst maritime folk toward marital separation, were both generally reflected in the marital status of household heads.[31] However, the relatively high numbers of widows and 'single' persons found in the mid-nineteenth century maritime village of Appledore in north Devonshire was also accompanied by a high proportion of households with resident kin.[32] This was certainly not the case for Bristol. It is also of interest that the two Bristol parishes with the lowest proportion of households headed by a married couple, St Augustine and St Werburgh, were also those which were home to many of the wealthiest inhabitants of the city.[33] Yet in London the wealthiest parish of the sample, St Mary le Bow, returned a figure of 82.2 per cent of households headed by a married couple, the highest figure for any of the urban areas. Clearly, although some regional variation in the marital status of household heads can be identified, it is difficult to interpret the differences that occur.[34]

Children in households and non-family members

Although heads and their spouses, where present, were the most numerous group in the population, almost as numerous were children, sons and daughters of the head of household,[35] who overall accounted for 36.4 per cent of the entire population and on average contributed between 1.2 and 2.0 members of each household (Table 3). Interestingly, when the proportion of

30 The amount of shipping carried in Bristol in 1709 had a total tonnage of 15,500 compared to that of 1,600 for Southampton. However, at this time the population of Bristol was probably over 20,000, whilst that of Southampton was a little under 3,000; see Corfield, *English Towns*, pp.35-6, 40, and 'Urban Development', pp.226-7. On her excursion through the country in the 1690s, Celia Fiennes recorded of Southampton that 'Now the trade has failed and the Town [is] almost forsooke and neglected'; quoted in Corfield, *English Towns*, p.43.

31 See Wrigley and Schofield, *Population History*, p.221, especially fn.41; Kent, 'Gone for a Soldier' and Sharpe, 'Marital separation'.

32 Howlett, 'Family and households', pp.42-4.

33 Ralph and Williams, 'Introduction', p.xxii.

34 It is of course the case that differences in the Marriage Duty assessments in recording surcharges is a significant factor. Clearly, in some cases surcharges were not always recorded; see, for example, 'Introducing the documents' at the beginning of this part of the volume. However, the assessment lists used in this chapter were specifically selected on the basis that they appeared to be accurate and complete.

35 For the definition of children, see fn.25 above.

households containing children is used as a measure of household structure, as in the case of married couples, both Kent and Bristol stand out as the extreme areas. Relative to the others, Kent records a quite high number of children, ranging from an absolute high of 90.1 per cent households with children (Adisham) to the high sixties. Yet Kent is the only area which resembles the pre-industrial 'mean' calculated by Wall, who estimated that children accounted for 39.9 per cent of the population.[36] Consequently, at the other end of the spectrum, the number of children recorded for Bristol appears as being very low indeed, from the mid-sixties to an overall low of 47.2 per cent of households with children (St Werburgh).[37] However, both of these areas show quite a marked inverse correlation with the proportion of households containing kin, suggesting that a uniform trend towards the presence of children precluded the presence of kin (and/or vice versa). Yet equally, it must be noted that the range of experience regarding the proportion of households with children was greatest in these two areas.

The fact that London, like Bristol, also records quite low rates of households with children may suggest a lack of children was essentially an urban, as opposed to a rural, phenomenon. However, given the low proportion of households with children in the Wiltshire group, the exact relationship is unclear. For the parishes of London and Wiltshire it would seem that servants rather than kin are, if anything, the substitute for children. It is not too misleading, after all, to view servants as children resident in the household of an employer rather than that of their parent.

[36] Wall, 'The household', Table 16.3, p.498. This calculation relates to the period 1650-1749 and in line with the definition adopted in this chapter includes as children all apparently unmarried (never-married) offspring resident with parent(s), regardless of age. This differs from the definitions of children given in chapter 5 in discussing the Compton census returns in which children are taken as those aged under sixteen. Laslett has estimated a pre-industrial mean for children being present in 74.6 per cent of households and accounting for 42.6 per cent of the population. These figures, however, include not only never-married offspring but all never-married descending residential kin, i.e grandchildren, nephews, etc.; Laslett, 'Introduction', p.87 and 'The household over three centuries', p.148.

[37] It must be remembered, however, that Laslett's 'mean' figure covers the entire period 1574-1821 and, in this respect, the late eighteenth and early nineteenth centuries witnessed higher numbers of children in households compared with the late seventeenth and early eighteenth centuries, due mainly to an increase in fertility plus other structural changes. See Wall, 'The household', pp.495-505; Wrigley and Schofield, *Population history*, pp.228-36 and Smith, 'Fertility, economy and household formation', pp.596-602.

In summary, therefore, as with the marital status of heads, differences between areas can be detected, yet little in the way of regional variation or urban-rural patterns can be found.

In addition to the members of the heads' family there were large numbers of servants and lodgers living in, or attached to, the household.[38] Reference to Table 3 illustrates that as far as these two groups of individuals were concerned, London clearly stands out as being distinct from the other five areas. Not only was it the sole place to house lodgers in any number, but it also had almost twice as many servants per household than any other area. Although not matching the rates of London, it is interesting to note that lodgers were relatively more important in the other three urban areas than in Kent and Wiltshire. This, of course, probably reflects the greater pressures on housing and accommodation to be found in central urban areas, although one must not underestimate the problems of overcrowding in rural areas. However, by this account, the ability to maintain one's own household would appear to have been rather easier in rural areas.[39]

As with lodgers, the incidence of service also displays a marked urban-rural difference. The overall proportion of households with servants was not only high in London – at 58 per cent some 25 per cent higher than in any other area (Table 2) – but also relatively high in the other three urban areas; around a third in Bristol and Shrewsbury and a quarter in Southampton. Despite the fact that Kent also recorded some one in four households as having servants, the character of service in this area was quite distinct from the experience of the urban areas. Not only was the mean size of the servant group somewhat larger than in the other areas, but the proportion of servants resident in households with just a single servant was significantly lower than in all the other

38 By convention, residential servants in the employ of the household head or a member of his family are deemed to be members of the household. Attached inmates (i.e. lodgers and boarders) are not counted as part of the household but are included in what is termed the houseful which embraces both the household and any individuals attached to the household; see Laslett, 'Introduction', pp.36-7, 87.

39 The tendency for inmates to form an important component of urban societies continued through the eighteenth century and indeed intensified in the nineteenth century; see Anderson, 'Social implications', p.64. Yet it must be stressed that the definition of what constituted a household is critical in this respect. Any apparent changes over time or between places may be due to a different definition rather than any significant change.

areas, especially those that were urban. In addition, in both rural areas the sex ratio of servants[40] was quite high. In all four urban areas female servants predominated, especially in Bristol and Shrewsbury, while in Wiltshire there were equal numbers of male and female servants, and in Kent of the 271 servants with sex specified in the Marriage Duty assessments 188 were male against only 83 females.[41] This basic gender differentiation would suggest that in urban areas service was predominantly characterised by female domestics, while in the countryside it included relatively large numbers of males working as farm servants and servants in husbandry.[42] However, female domestics did also feature in rural areas and, clearly, female domestic servants were not the only type of servants in urban areas. As one might expect, those learning a craft or trade, sometimes listed as apprentices or journeymen, invariably young unmarried males resident within the household of a master, were important in some urban parishes, especially in London and Southampton.

Social class and household structure

The social mix within particular areas has already been mentioned, especially in London. As has been made clear elsewhere in this volume, higher rates of duty were chargeable for certain categories of individuals, essentially those with a personal estate worth at least £600 or real estate worth at least £50 per annum, plus those of noble or gentlemanly status. In the case of those parishes analyzed for London and Bristol these extra surcharges appear to have been recorded comprehensively and accurately.[43] Thus, by calculating the proportion of households in

40 The sex ratio is calculated by dividing the number of males by the number of females and multiplying the result by 100.

41 Obviously many of those with sex unspecified could have been females; indeed, given that the majority of servants in pre-industrial England were young and unmarried (see Laslett, *Family life*, p.34 and Laslett, 'Service', p.57), one might suspect that there was a tendency to register bachelors more accurately than spinsters since if aged over twenty-five they were subject to a special rate. However, even if all of the 88 servants in Kent with sex unspecified were female, this would still only result in a total number of 171 female servants, producing a sex ratio of 110, higher than in any of the other five areas.

42 See Kussmaul, *Servants in husbandry*; Wright, 'Churmaids, huswyfes and hucksters' and Earle, 'The female labour market'. However, as Earle makes clear, it is wrong to see domesticity as being the only form of female employment in urban areas. See also Prior, 'Women and the urban economy'.

43 See chapter 8 for details of surcharges. In Bristol fifty-seven appeals were heard on 4th November, 1695, the majority of which (28) were to protest

Figure 2 Household characteristics by social class: Bristol and London

London

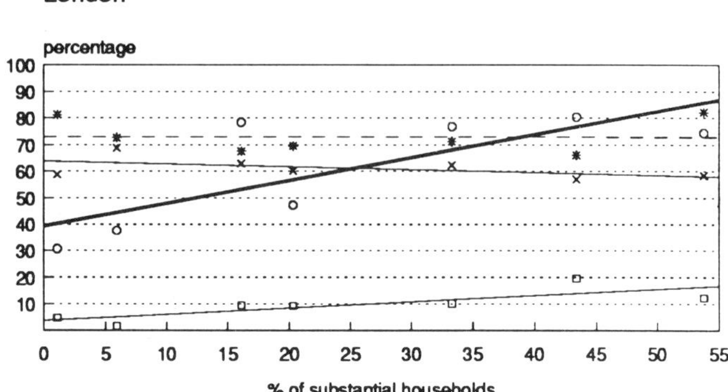

Bristol

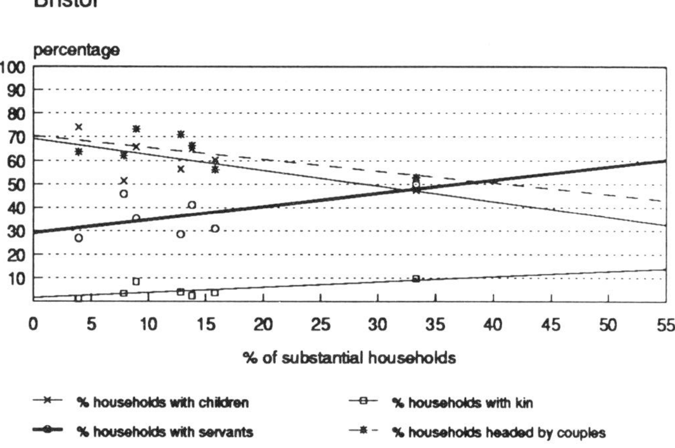

the parish classified as 'substantial', these surcharges can be used as a surrogate measure of wealth and indirectly as an indication of the social class composition of individual parishes.

against being charged as having £600 in personal wealth in order to have this altered to £50 per annum. Although this did not affect their rating under the Marriage Duty Act it would have affected their liability to other taxes such as the 4s. Aid (see chapter 9 by Alexander). Many of the remaining contesters appealed against their alleged bachelor status, with the result that very few of the 'substantial' householders were reassessed downwards; see Ralph and Williams, 'Introduction', pp.xi-xiv. It also appears that very few reassessments were made in London; see Glass, 'Introduction', p.xvi. However, one must equally be aware of the possibility of omissions; few would appeal against the fact that their liability to pay surcharges had been overlooked.

For London and Bristol, Figure 2 plots the variables already discussed – proportion of households with kin, children, servants and the proportion headed by a married couple – against the substantial household index of social class. As one might expect, this exercise shows that in both areas the presence of kin and/or servants in a household was positively related to social class. The wealthier the parish was, the more households it had with kin and servants and vice versa, with the relationship for servants being especially marked in the case of London. The central streets of Shrewsbury also displayed high proportions of both substantial households and servants.[44] Not surprisingly, this confirms the earlier finding of Laslett, who in his subsample of one hundred English communities, 1574-1821, discovered that the gentry were more likely to live with relatives and servants than were labourers, recording percentages of 27.6 and 84.1 respectively, against 7.9 and 2.2. In turn, the proportion of households with kin rose steadily throughout the whole social hierarchy of occupations – yeoman, tradesman and craftsman.[45]

It is perhaps more interesting to note that the relationship between substantial households and the proportions of households with children displays the reverse tendencies, being negatively correlated in both Bristol and London. Rather than any social class fertility differential, this is probably a feature of the life-cycle, with the wealthier households tending to be headed by older individuals whose children were more likely to have left home. Yet London, unlike Bristol, has no corresponding downturn in the proportion of households headed by married couples, which is what one might expect if substantial households were headed by older persons. Clearly one can only speculate, but such a pattern may point to wealth being accumulated at relatively earlier ages in London, and if this were so the wealthier classes displayed signs of reduced fertility, higher infant or child mortality or a greater propensity for children to leave the

44 Hindson, 'Marriage Duty Acts', Maps 2 and 5, pp.26-7.

45 Laslett, 'The household over three centuries', pp.152-4. The classification used by Laslett for this analysis of household variation by social class is based on that of Gregory King; see Laslett's chapter in this volume. This relationship between social class, servants and kin also held true for the nineteenth century, although not in the case of paupers. See Schurer, 'Migration, population and social structure' and Sokoll, 'The pauper household'.

parental home at a relatively early age.[46] Alternatively, and perhaps more plausibly, the wealthier householders of London experienced relatively favourable levels of mortality in middle and later life, or higher levels of remarriage, with the result that they were more likely to be living with a spouse than those further down the social scale. Whatever the situation, it seems that the experience was not shared by their counterparts in the wealthier parishes of Bristol.

Conclusion

The original purpose of this chapter was to examine the possibility of regional variation in household structure as depicted by the assessments generated by the Marriage Duty Act. With the exception of some broad indicators, more illustrative of possible rural-urban differences rather than regional disparity and the suggestion of the uniqueness of London, very little evidence of geographic specificness could be found. Indeed, the evidence throughout has pointed to disparities within, rather than homogeneity across, the six areas studied. In order to test the uniformity of the geographical areas, a cluster analysis was performed, treating each of the composite parishes (or districts) as an independent unit. As indicated above, the summary indicators selected for the purposes of classification were the proportion of households with kin, children, servants and the percentage headed by married couples.[47] The result is represented in graphical form as Figure 3 and, by way of conclusion, is most instructive.

In an attempt to mimic the geographical divisions of the six areas, a statistical model was specified to group or cluster the forty-eight individual parishes into six categories, according to the 'likeness' of the household characteristics of each parish, yet disregarding geography. Figure 3 shows that rather than being grouped by areal definition, in each case the composite parishes are clustered with those from another area. In no case are all the composite parishes of a single area retained within the same

[46] See Finlay, *Population and the metropolis*, especially chapters 5 and 7, and Landers, 'London mortality' which suggest that infant and child mortality levels were higher in the capital compared with the national average. See also Fildes, *Wet nursing*, pp.79-83, for evidence of the placing of children from the capital to its surrounding villages for the purposes of wet nursing.

[47] The statistical routine was carried out using the FASTCLUS procedure in the SAS software system; Ray, *SAS User's Guide: Statistics*, pp.433-47.

Figure 3 A cluster analysis of the component parishes

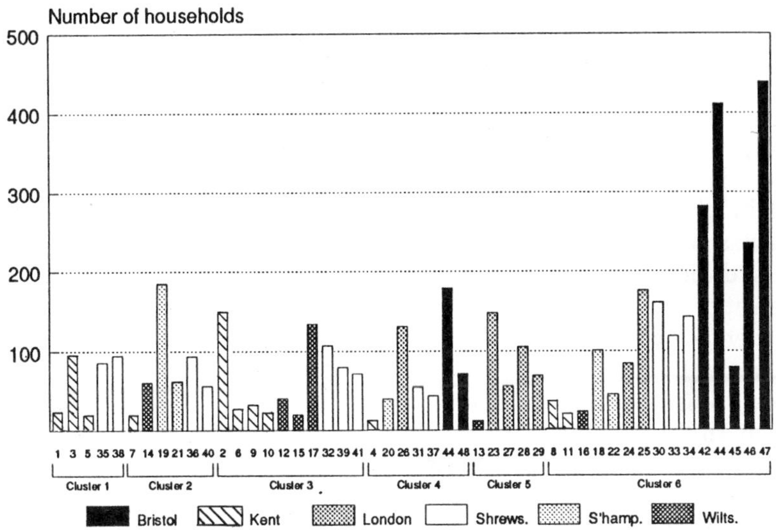

cluster. Thus, in many cases an individual parish from a given geographical area displays more in common with a parish from another area than with its neighbours. In particular, the twelve districts of Shrewsbury are split across five of the six clusters. However, the parishes selected for London again stand out as being relatively distinct, with the fifth cluster containing four of the seven London parishes. Interestingly, these parishes are four of the five wealthiest parishes of the London sample. Bristol also appears as a relatively homogeneous area because its parishes are split across just two clusters, with five of its seven parishes grouped together in the sixth cluster. The two poorest London parishes in the sample, St Botolph Without Bishopsgate and St Anne Blackfriars, are also found in the same cluster (the sixth), which, with thirteen other parishes, is the largest cluster of all. Although it includes some Wiltshire and Kent components, this cluster appears to be principally urban, including the three most heavily populated districts of the Shrewsbury sample and the majority of the Bristol parishes. However, it should be pointed out that the two parishes of Southampton placed in this cluster, All Saints and St Mary, were both located on the suburban fringe and had the lowest population densities of the Southampton area.[48] The rural parishes of Kent are chiefly split between clusters one and three, the latter of which also contains three of the six Wiltshire parishes together with three Shrewsbury districts. Because cluster one is composed entirely of Kent and Shrewsbury components, this may perhaps suggest that, with the exception of a central core, Shrewsbury was essentially rural in character rather than urban.

All in all the cluster analysis exercise, together with the earlier discussion of household characteristics, clearly demonstrates that it is difficult to make any case for distinct patterns of regional identity at the close of the seventeenth century as far as household composition is concerned. It is true that in many respects London stands out as being distinct from the rest – something that would have hardly surprised a contemporary, given that it was one of the largest and fastest growing urban centres in the world.[49] Bristol also appears to have been a relatively uniform urban area, yet with the exception of these two cases no sharp divisions along geographical lines can be drawn. Basic urban-rural differences there may have been, but even these are difficult to detect with any certainty. From the evidence available one is inclined to conclude that the regional variations that can be seen in household structure from the nineteenth century onwards were less a product of underlying geographical factors than of the processes of industrialization and de-industrialization that took place in the two and a half centuries following the compilation of the Marriage Duty assessments.

48 James, 'History of Southampton', Figure 4, between pp.12-3.

49 It is not just total population size that set London apart, for example the population densities of the sampled parishes were much higher than those of Bristol, the third largest city in the country. The density of the seven parishes selected for London ranged from 172 to 248 persons per acre, while those of Bristol (including only built-up areas) ranged from just 35 to 136 persons per acre, all except one (St Augustine) having fewer than 100 persons per acre; see Jones and Judges, 'London population', Table III, pp.58-62 and Ralph and Williams, 'Introduction', p.xxii. Equally, sheer weight of numbers was not the only distinguishing feature of London; the capital also acted as the driving force in many aspects of economic and social development; see Wrigley, 'London's importance' and McKendrick, 'The consumer revolution'.

Accumulated Bibliography

J. Alexander, 'The economic and social structure of the City of London, c.1700', unpublished Ph.D. Thesis, University of London, 1989.

— 'The economic structure of the City of London at the end of the seventeenth century', *Urban History Yearbook*, 1989.

N. Alldridge, 'Hearth and home: a three-dimensional reconstruction', in N. Alldridge (ed), *The Hearth tax: problems and possibilities*, Hull, 1984.

— (ed), *The Hearth tax: problems and possibilities*, Hull, 1984.

— 'House and household in Restoration Chester', *Urban History Yearbook*, 1983.

R.A. Ambler (ed), *Lincolnshire Returns of the Census of Religious Worship 1851*, Lincoln Record Society, 70, 1979.

M. Anderson, *Family structure in nineteenth century Lancashire*, Cambridge, 1971.

— 'Historical demography after *The Population History of England*', *Journal of Interdisciplinary History*, 15, 1985.

— 'The social implications of demographic change', in F.M.L. Thompson (ed), *The Cambridge social history of Britain 1750-1950*, volume 2, Cambridge, 1990.

K.R. Andrews, 'The Elizabethan seaman', *Mariner's Mirror*, 68, 1982.

T. Arkell, 'Assessing the reliability of the Warwickshire hearth tax returns of 1662-1674', *Warwickshire History*, 6, 1986-7.

— 'The incidence of poverty in England in the later seventeenth century', *Social History*, 12, 1987.

— 'Multiplying factors for estimating population totals from the hearth tax', *Local Population Studies*, 28, 1982.

— 'A student's guide to the hearth tax: some truths, half-truths and untruths', in N. Alldridge (ed), *The Hearth tax: problems and possibilities*, Hull, 1984.

A.B. Atkinson, *The economics of inequality*, Oxford, 1975.

M.W. Barley, 'Farmhouses and cottages', *Economic History Review*, second series, 7, 1954-5.

— 'Rural housing in England', in J. Thirsk (ed), *The agrarian history of England and Wales, Volume IV, 1500-1640*, Cambridge, 1967.

J.V. Beckett, 'Land tax or excise: the levying of taxation in seventeenth and eighteenth-century England', *English Historical Review*, 100, 1985.

— 'Origins of the land tax' in J. Gibson and D. Mills (eds), *Land tax assessments, c.1690-c.1950*, Federation of Family History Societies, Plymouth, 1983.

J.V. Beckett with M.W. Barley and S.C. Wallwork, 'Introduction: the administration and collection of the Hearth Tax in Nottinghamshire', in W.F. Webster (ed), *Nottinghamshire Hearth Tax 1664:1674*, Thoroton Society Record Series, 38, Nottingham, 1988.

A.L. Beier and R. Finlay (eds), *London 1500-1700: the making of the metropolis*, London, 1986.

T.M. Blagg (ed), *Nottinghamshire Parish Registers. Marriages,* 18, London, 1913.

T.M. Blagg and G.P. Proctor (eds), *Nottinghamshire Parish Registers. Marriages*, 20, London, 1915.

C.B. Bolam, *et al.*, *The English Presbyterians from Elizabethan Puritanism to modern Unitarianism*, London, 1968.

D. Bond, 'The Compton Census - Peterborough', *Local Population Studies*, 10, 1973.

L. Bonfield, R. Smith and K. Wrightson (eds), *The world we have gained: histories of population and social structure*, Oxford, 1986.

P. Borsay, 'The English urban renaissance: the development of a provincial urban culture, c.1690-c.1760', *Social History*, 5, 1977.

J. Boulton, *Neighbourhood and Society: a London suburb in the seventeenth century*, Cambridge, 1987.

L. Bradley, *A Glossary for Local Population Studies*, Local Population Studies, Supplement no.1, 2nd edition, Matlock, 1978.

P. Brandon, *The Sussex landscape*, London, 1974.

J. Brewer and J. Styles, *An ungovernable people*, London, 1980.

C. Brooks, 'Projecting, political arithmetic and the act of 1695', *English Historical Review*, 47, 1982.

—— 'Public finance and political stability: the administration of the land tax, 1688-1720', *Historical Journal*, 17, 1974.

R.L. Brown, 'Clandestine marriages in London, especially within the Fleet Prison, and their effects on Hardwicke's Act, 1753', unpublished MA Thesis, University of London, 1974.

—— 'The Days before Somerset House', *Local Population Studies*, 29, 1982.

—— 'The Rise and Fall of the Fleet Marriages', in R.B. Outhwaite (ed), *Marriage and Society*, London, 1981.

A. Browning (ed), *English historical documents 1660-1714*, London, 1953.

—— *Thomas Osborne, Earl of Danby* (3 vols), Glasgow, 1944-51.

R.W. Brunskill, *Traditional farm buildings*, London, 1981.

R. Burn, *The ecclesiastical law* (2 vols), London, 1773.

E. Calamy, *An Account of the Ministers, Lecturers, Masters and Fellows of Colleges and Schoolmasters, who were ejected or silenced after the Restoration in 1660*, 2nd edition, London, 1713.

E. Cardwell, *Documentary annals of the reformed church*, volume 2, 1839.

C.W. Chalklin, 'The Compton Census of 1676: the dioceses of Canterbury and Rochester', *Kent Records*, 17, 1960.

— *Seventeenth-century Kent*, London, 1963.

C.W. Chalklin and M.A. Havinden (eds), *Rural change and urban growth: essays in English regional history in honour of W.G. Hoskins*, London, 1974.

G. Chalmers, *An estimate of the comparative strength of Great Britain, to which is now annexed Gregory King's celebrated State of England*, 1804. The appendix of this is reprinted in Laslett, *Earliest classics*.

C.D. Chandaman, *The English public revenue, 1660-1688*, Oxford, 1975.

M. Clapinson (ed), *Bishop Fell and Nonconformity: Visitation Documents from the Oxford Diocese 1682-83*, Oxfordshire Record Society, 52, 1980.

G.N. Clark, *The wealth of England from 1496 to 1760*, Oxford, 1946.

P. Clark (ed), *Country towns in pre-industrial England*, Leicester, 1981.

— (ed), *The Transformation of English Provincial Towns*, London, 1984.

P. Clark and P. Slack, *English towns in transition, 1500-1700*, London, 1976.

L.A. Clarkson, *The pre-industrial economy in England*, London, 1971.

F. Clayton (ed), *The Registers of Morden, Surrey 1634-1812*, Parish Register Society, 37-8, 1901.

A. Clifton-Taylor, *The patterns of English building*, London, 1962.

W. Cobbett (ed), *The Parliamentary History of England from the earliest period to the year 1803*, volume 15 (1753-65), 1813.

A.M. Coleby, *Central government and the localities: Hampshire 1649-1689*, Cambridge, 1987.

S. Cooper, 'Family, household, and occupation in pre-industrial England: social structure in King's Lynn, 1689-1702', unpublished Ph.D. Thesis, Indiana University, 1985.

P.J. Corfield, *The impact of English towns 1700-1800*, Oxford, 1982.

— 'Urban development in England and Wales in the sixteenth and seventeenth centuries', in D.C. Coleman and A.H. John (eds), *Trade, government and economy in pre-industrial England*, London, 1976.

J.C. Cox, *The parish registers of England*, London, 1910.

G.P. Crawfurd (ed), *The Registers of St Mary, Reading, Berks, 1538-1812*, Reading, 1891.

D. Cressy, *Literacy and the social order: reading and writing in Tudor and Stuart England*, Cambridge, 1980.

C. Davenant, *Discourse upon the public revenues and trade of England*, London, 1699.

— *An essay upon the probable methods of making a people gainers in the balance of trade*, London, 1699.

—— 'An Essay upon Ways and Means', in C. Whitworth (ed), *The political and commercial works of Charles D'Avenant*, volume 1, London, 1771.

G.S. De Krey, *A fractured society: the politics of London in the First Age of Party, 1688-1715*, Oxford, 1985.

J. de Vries, *European Urbanization 1500-1800*, London, 1984.

P.G.M. Dickson, *The financial revolution in England, 1688-1756*, London, 1967.

R.A. Dodgshon and R.A. Butlin (eds), *An historical geography of England and Wales*, London, 1978.

S. Dowell, *A history of taxation and taxes in England*, volumes 2 and 3, 2nd edition, 1988.

E. Dwelly, 'Somerset hearth tax 1664-5', in *Dwelly's national records*, volume 1, 1916.

A.D. Dyer, 'Urban housing: a documentary study of four Midland towns, 1530-1700', *Post-Medieval Archaeology*, 15, 1981.

P. Earle, 'The female labour market in London in the late seventeenth and early eighteenth century', *Economic History Review*, 42, 1989.

D.G. Edwards (ed), *Derbyshire hearth tax assessments 1662-70*, Derbyshire Record Society, 7, 1982.

—— 'Population in Derbyshire in the reign of King Charles II: the use of hearth tax assessments and the Compton census', *Derbyshire Archaeological Journal*, 102, 1982.

F.G. Emmison, 'Jacobean household inventories, 1617-1619', *Bedfordshire Historical Record Society*, 20, 1938.

F.H. Erith, *Ardleigh in 1796*, East Bergholt, 1978.

A.M. Everitt, 'The Banburys of England', *Urban History Yearbook*, 1973.

—— *Change in the provinces: the seventeenth century*, Occasional Papers in Local History, University of Leicester, 1970.

M.A. Faraday, 'The Ludlow poll-tax return of 1667', *Transactions of the Shropshire Archaeological Society*, 61, 1971-2.

V. Fildes, *Wet nursing: a history from antiquity to the present*, Oxford, 1988.

R. Finlay, *Population and metropolis: the demography of London 1580-1650*, Cambridge, 1981.

R. Finlay and B. Shearer, 'Population growth and suburban expansion', in A.L. Beier and R. Finlay (eds), *London 1500-1700: the making of the metropolis*, London, 1986.

J-L. Flandrin, *Families in former times: kinship, household and sexuality*, Cambridge, 1979.

A. Fletcher, 'The enforcement of the Conventicle Acts 1664-1679', in W.J. Sheils (ed), *Persecution and toleration*, Studies in Church History, volume 21, Oxford, 1984.

T.R. Forbes, *Chronicle from Aldgate*, London, 1971.

D. Foster, 'The Hearth Tax and settlement studies', *Local Historian*, 11, 1974-5.

P.J. Fowler, 'The Royal Commission on Historical Monuments (England)', *Antiquity*, 55, 1981.

C. Fox and Lord Raglan, *Monmouthshire houses: a study of smaller building techniques and smaller house plans in the fifteenth to seventeenth centuries* (3 vols), Cardiff, 1954.

M.S. Frankel and P.J. Seaman, 'Norfolk hearth tax assessment, Michaelmas 1664', *Norfolk Genealogy*, 15, 1983.

M.D. George, *England in transition*, London, 1931.

J.S.W. Gibson, *The Hearth tax and other later Stuart tax lists and the association oath rolls* Federation of Family History Societies, Plymouth, 1985.

J. Gibson and D. Mills (eds), *Land tax assessments, c.1690-c.1950*, Federation of Family History Societies, Plymouth, 1983.

H. Gill and E.L. Guilford (eds), *The Rector's book, Clayworth Nottinghamshire*, Nottingham, 1910.

D.V. Glass, 'Introduction', in D.V. Glass (ed), *London inhabitants within the walls, 1695*, London Record Society, 2, 1966.

— 'John Graunt and his 'Natural and political observations', *Proceedings of the Royal Society*, Series B, 1963.

— (ed), *London inhabitants within the walls, 1695*, London Record Society, 2, 1966.

— 'Notes', in D.V. Glass and R. Revelle (eds), *Population and social change*, London, 1972.

— 'Socio-economic status and occupations in the City of London at the end of the seventeenth century', in A.B. Hollaender and W. Kellaway (eds), *Studies in London history*, London, 1969.

— 'Two papers on Gregory King', in D.V. Glass and D.E.C. Eversley (eds), *Population in History*, London, 1965

D.V. Glass and D.E.C. Eversley (eds), *Population in history*, London, 1965.

J.A. Goldstone, 'The demographic revolution in England: a re-examination', *Population Studies*, 40, 1986.

J. Goody, *Development of the family and marriage in Europe*, Cambridge, 1983.

N.R. Goose, 'Decay and regeneration in seventeenth-century Reading: a study in a changing economy', *Southern History*, 6, 1984.

— 'Household size and structure in early Stuart Cambridge', *Social History*, 5, 1980.

J. Graunt, *Natural and political observations made upon the bills of mortality*, 1662, reprinted in Laslett, *Earliest classics*.

R.L. Greaves, *Deliver us from Evil*, New York, 1986.

M. Greenwood, *Medical statistics from Graunt to Farr*, Cambridge, 1948.

A.W. Hallen (ed), *The Registers of St Botolph Bishopsgate*, volume 1,

London, 1889.

E. Hammel and P. Laslett, 'Comparing household structure over time and between cultures', *Comparative Studies in Society and History*, 16, 1974.

T.J.G. Harris, 'Politics of the London crowd in the reign of Charles II', unpublished Ph.D. Thesis, University of Cambridge, 1984.

H. Hartopp, *Roll of the freemen of the City of Leicester, 1193-1936*, Leicester, 1936.

— *Roll of the Mayors of the Borough and Lord Mayors of the City of Leicester with biographical heraldic and historical details*, Leicester, 1936.

M.A. Havinden, *Household and farming inventories of Oxfordshire, 1550-1590*, Oxfordshire Record Society, 69, 1965.

L. Henry, *Manual de démographie historique*, Paris, 1967.

S.H.A. Hervey (ed), *Suffolk in 1674*, Suffolk Green Books, 1905.

D. Hibberd, 'Data-linkage and the hearth tax: the case of seventeenth-century York', in N. Alldridge (ed), *The hearth tax: problems and possibilities*, Hull, 1984.

E. Higgs, *Making sense of the Census: the manuscript returns for England and Wales 1801-1901*, London, 1989.

J. Hindson, 'The Marriage Duty Acts and the social topography of the early modern town: Shrewsbury, 1695-8', *Local Population Studies*, 31, 1983.

A.B. Hollaender and W. Kellaway (eds), *Studies in London History*, London, 1969.

G.S. Holmes, 'Gregory King and the social structure of pre-industrial England', *Transactions of the Royal Historical Society*, 27, 1977

W.G. Hoskins, 'Exeter in the seventeenth century: tax and rate assessments, 1602-1699', *Devon and Cornwall Record Society*, N.S. 2, 1957.

— *Industry, trade and people in Exeter, 1688-1800*, Exeter, 1935.

— *Local history in England*, 2nd edition, London, 1972.

— *The Midland peasant: the economic and social history of a Leicestershire village - Wigston Magna*, London, 1957.

— *Provincial England*, London, 1963.

— 'The rebuilding of rural England', in W.G. Hoskins, *Provincial England*, London, 1963.

F. Howell, *The hearth tax*, Historical Association, Short Guide to Records, 1971.

N.M. Howlett, 'Family and household in a nineteenth-century Devon village', *Local Population Studies*, 30, 1983.

C. Hull (ed), *The economic writings of Sir William Petty* (2 vols), Cambridge, 1899.

J.J. Hurwich, 'Nonconformists in Warwickshire 1660-1720', unpublished Ph.D. Thesis, Princeton University, 1970.

C. Husbands, 'The hearth tax and the structure of the English economy', unpublished Ph.D. Thesis, University of Cambridge, 1985.

— 'Regional change in a pre-industrial economy: wealth and population in England in the sixteenth and seventeenth centuries', *Journal of Historical Geography*, 13, 1987.

M. Ingram, 'Spousals litigation in the English ecclesiastical courts c.1350-1640', in R.B. Outhwaite (ed), *Marriage and society*, London, 1981.

C.F. Innocent, *The development of English building construction*, London, 1916.

P.W. Jackson, 'Nonconformists and society in Devon, 1660-1689', unpublished Ph.D. Thesis, University of Exeter, 1986.

T.B. James, 'A handbook of demographic, quantitative and nominal records for the history of Southampton 1450 to 1850', unpublished Ph.D. Thesis, University of Southampton, 1975.

P.E. Jones and A.V. Judges, 'London population in the late seventeenth century', *Economic History Review*, 6, 1935.

W. Kennedy, *English taxation 1640-1799: an essay on policy and opinion*, London, 1913.

D.A. Kent, 'Gone for a soldier: family breakdown and the demography of desertion in a London parish, 1750-91', *Local Population Studies*, 45, 1990.

G. King, *The LCC Burns Journal*, a manuscript notebook containing workings for several projected works, composed c.1695-1700, reprinted in Laslett, *Earliest classics*.

— *Natural and political observations and conclusions upon the state and condition of England*, published as an appendix to G. Chalmers, *An estimate of the comparative strength*, and reprinted in Laslett, *Earliest classics*.

J.E. Knodel, 'An exercise on household composition for use in courses in historical demography', *Local Population Studies*, 23, 1979.

J.T. Krause, 'The changing adequacy of English registration', in D.V. Glass and D.E.C. Eversley (eds), *Population in history*, London, 1965.

P. Kreager, 'New light on Graunt', Department of Population Studies, London School of Economics, unpublished typescript for the European Population Conference, Jyvaskyla, Finland, June 1987.

A. Kussmaul, *Servants in husbandry in early modern England*, Cambridge, 1981.

J. Langton, 'Industry and towns 1500-1730', in R.A. Dodgshon and R.A. Butlin (eds), *An historical geography of England and Wales*, London, 1978.

Marquis of Lansdowne, *The Petty-Southwell correspondence*, London, 1928.

P. Laslett, 'The character of familial history, its limitations and the conditions for its proper pursuit', *Journal of Family History*, 12, 1987.

— (ed), *The earliest classics: Graunt and King*, London, 1973.

— *Family life and illicit love in earlier generations*, Cambridge, 1977.

— 'Gregory King, Robert Malthus and the origins of English social realism', *Population Studies*, 39, 1985.

— 'The institution of service', *Local Population Studies*, 40, 1988.

— 'Introduction', in P. Laslett and R. Wall (eds), *Household and family in past time*, Cambridge, 1972.

— 'Mean household size', in P. Laslett and R. Wall (eds), *Household and family in past time*, Cambridge, 1972.

— Review of M.S. Teitelbaum, 'The British fertility decline: demographic transition in the crucible of the Industrial Revolution', *Population and Development Review*, 11, 1985.

— 'Size and structure of the household in England over three centuries', *Population Studies*, 23, 1969.

— *The World we have lost*, 1st edition, 1965, 2nd edition, London, 1971.

— *The World we have lost – further explored*, 3rd edition, London, 1983.

P. Laslett and R. Wall (eds), *Household and family in past time*, Cambridge, 1972.

R.C. Latham and W. Matthews (eds), *The Diary of Samuel Pepys*, volumes 1 and 8, London, 1970 and 1974.

Le Roy Ladurie, E. 'Les comptes fantastiques de Gregory King', in *Annales, Economies, Sociétés, Civilisations*, 5, 1968.

D. Levine, 'The reliability of parochial registration and the representativeness of family reconstitution', *Population Studies*, 30, 1976.

P.H. Lindert and J.G. Williamson, 'Reinterpreting Britain's social tables', *Explorations in Economic History*, 20, 1983.

— 'Revising England's social tables 1688-1867', Working paper no.176, Department of Economics, University of California.

W.A. Littledale (ed), *The Registers of St Vedast, Foster Lane, and of St Michael le Querne, London, vol 1: Christenings,* Harleian Society Registers, 29, 1902.

A. Macfarlane, 'Studies in poverty and poor relief in London at the end of the seventeenth century', unpublished Ph.D. Thesis, University of Oxford, 1983.

R.A. Machin, 'The great rebuilding: a re-assessment', *Past and Present*, 77, 1977.

C.B. Macpherson, *Political theory of possessive individualism*, Oxford, 1963.

J. Marshall, *Mortality in the Metropolis*, London, 1832.

L.M. Marshall, 'The rural population of Bedfordshire, 1671-1921', *Bedfordshire Historical Record Society*, 16, 1934.

A.G. Matthews (ed), *Calamy revised*, Oxford, 1934.

N. McKendrick, 'The consumer revolution of eighteenth-century England', in N. McKendrick, J. Brewer and J.H. Plumb (eds), *The birth of a consumer society: the commercialization of eighteenth-century England*, London, 1982.

M. Medlycott, 'A survey and guide of listings of inhabitants', *Local Population Studies*, 46, 1991.

C.A.F. Meekings, *Dorset hearth tax assessments, 1662-1664*, Dorchester, 1951.

— *The hearth tax, 1662-1689, exhibition of records*, Public Record Office, London, 1962.

C.A.F. Meekings, S. Porter and I. Roy, 'The hearth tax collectors' book for Worcester, 1678-1680', *Worcestershire Historical Society*, N.S. 11, 1983.

P. Millican, *Freemen of Lynn*, Norwich, 1913.

E.R. Nevill (ed), *Denchworth, Berkshire*, Parish Register Society 73-5, 1914.

P.E. Ogden, 'Historical demography', in M. Pacione (ed), *Historical geography: progress and prospect*, London, 1987.

R.B. Outhwaite (ed), *Marriage and society*, London, 1981.

M. Overton, 'Estimating crop yields from probate inventories: the case of East Anglia', *Journal of Economic History*, 39, 1979.

J. Patten, *English towns, 1500-1700*, Newton Abbott, 1978.

— 'The hearth taxes, 1662-1689', *Local Population Studies*, 7, 1971.

— 'Population distribution in Norfolk and Suffolk during the sixteenth and seventeenth centuries', *Transactions, Institute of British Geographers*, 65, 1975.

A.T. Patterson, *History of Southampton, 1700-1914*, volume 1, Southampton, 1966.

A. Percival, 'Gloucestershire village populations', *Local Population Studies*, 8, 1972.

P. Pett, *The Happy Future State of England*, 1688.

W. Petty, *A discourse of taxes and contributions*, 1689.

S.A. Peyton, 'Religious census of 1676', *English Historical Review*, 48, 1933.

W.P.W. Phillimore (ed), *Gloucestershire Parish Registers: Marriages*, 9, London, 1905.

— (ed), *Nottinghamshire Parish Registers: Marriages*, 19, London, 1913.

W.P.W. Phillimore and T.M. Blagg (eds), *Nottinghamshire Parish Registers: Marriages*, 3, London, 1900.

W.P.W. Phillimore and G.G. Bonser (eds), *Nottinghamshire Parish Registers: Marriages*, 11, London, 1907.

W.P.W. Phillimore and G.E. Cokayne (eds), *London Parish Registers: Marriages at St James Duke Place 1668-1837* (4 vols), London, 1900-2.

L. Pollock, *Forgotten children: parent-child relations from 1500 to 1900*, Cambridge, 1983.

M.H. Port (ed), *The Commissions for building Fifty New Churches*, London Record Society, 23, 1986.

D. Portman, 'Vernacular building in the Oxford region in the sixteenth and seventeenth centuries' in C.W. Chalklin and M.A. Havinden (eds), *Rural change and urban growth: essays in English regional history in honour of W.G. Hoskins*, London, 1974.

J.F. Pound, *The Norwich census of the poor, 1570*, Norfolk Record Society, 40, 1971.

M.J. Power, 'The social topography of Restoration London', in A.L. Beier and Roger Finlay (eds), *London 1500-1700: the making of the metropolis*, London, 1986.

M. Prior, 'Women and the urban economy: Oxford 1500-1800', in M. Prior (ed), *Women in English society 1500-1800*, London, 1985.

E. Ralph and M.E. Williams, 'Introduction', in *The inhabitants of Bristol in 1696*, Bristol Record Society, 25, 1968.

A.A. Ray (ed), *SAS User's Guide: Statistics*, Cary, North Carolina, 1982.

M. Reed, 'Economic structure and change in seventeenth-century Ipswich', in P. Clark (ed), *Country towns in pre-industrial England*, Leicester, 1981.

T. Richards, 'The Religious census of 1676', *The Transactions of the Honourable Society of Cymmrodorion*, 1925-6.

A. Rogers, *Approaches to local history*, 2nd edition, London, 1977.

P.D.D. Russell, 'Hearth tax returns for the Isle of Wight, 1664 to 1674', *Isle of Wight Records Series*, 1, 1981.

G.V. Scammell, 'Manning the merchant service in the sixteenth century', *The Mariner's Mirror*, 56, 1970.

R.S. Schofield, 'English Marriage Patterns revisited', *Journal of Family History*, 10, 1985.

— 'Traffic in corpses: some evidence from Barming, Kent (1788-1812)', *Local Population Studies*, 33, 1984.

K. Schurer, 'Migration, population and social structure: a comparative study based on rural Essex, 1850-1900', unpublished Ph.D. Thesis, University of London, 1988.

M. Segalen, 'Family cycle and household structure: five generations in a French village', *Journal of Family History*, 2, 1977.

P. Sharpe, 'Marital separation in the eighteenth and early nineteenth centuries', *Local Population Studies*, 45, 1990.

W.J. Sheils (ed), *Persecution and toleration*, Studies in Church History, volume 21, Oxford, 1984.

J.A. Sheppard, 'Vernacular building in England and Wales: a survey of recent work by architects, archaeologists and social historians', *Transactions, Institute of British Geographers*, 40, 1966.

V. Skipp, *Crisis and development: an ecological case study of the Forest of Arden, 1570-1674*, Cambridge, 1978.

C.T. Smith, 'Population', in *The County of Leicestershire*, volume 3, Victoria County Histories of England, Oxford, 1955.

R.M. Smith, 'Fertility, economy, and household formation in England over three centuries', *Population and Development Review*, 7, 1981.

— *Land, kinship and life-cycle*, Cambridge, 1984.

— 'Population and its geography in England 1500-1730', in R.A. Dodgshon and R.A. Butlin (eds), *An historical geography of England and Wales*, London, 1978.

K.D.M. Snell, 'Parish registration and the study of labour mobility', *Local Population Studies*, 33, 1984.

T. Sokoll, 'The pauper household small and simple? The evidence from listings of inhabitants and pauper lists of early modern England reassessed', *Ethnologia Europaea*, 17, 1987.

D. Souden, 'Migrants and the population structure of later seventeenth-century provincial cities and market towns', in P. Clark (ed), *The transformation of English provincial towns*, London, 1984.

— 'Pre-industrial English local migration fields', Unpublished Ph.D. Thesis, University of Cambridge 1981.

M. Spufford, 'The dissenting churches in Cambridgeshire from 1660 to 1700', *Proceedings of the Cambridge Antiquarian Society*, 61, 1968.

— 'The significance of the Cambridgeshire hearth tax', *Proceedings of the Cambridge Antiquarian Society*, 55, 1962.

T.L. Stoate, *Cornwall hearth and poll taxes 1660-1664*, Bristol 1981.

— *Devon hearth tax return, Lady Day 1674*, Bristol, 1982.

R. Stone, 'Some British empiricists in the social sciences 1650-1900', Raffaele Mattiolo Lectures, Milan, October 1986.

— 'When will the war end?', *Cambridge Journal of Economics*, 12, 1988.

P. Styles, 'Introduction to the Warwickshire hearth tax records', *Warwick County Records: Hearth Tax Returns*, 1, 1957.

— 'The social structure of Kineton Hundred in the reign of Charles II', *Transactions of the Birmingham Archaeological Society, supplement: Essays in Honour of Philip B. Chatwin*, 1962, reprinted in Styles, *Studies in seventeenth-century West Midlands History*, Kineton, 1978.

— *Studies in seventeenth-century West Midlands History*, Kineton, 1978.

I. Sutherland, 'John Graunt, a tercentenary tribute', *Journal of the Royal Statistical Society*, 1963.

A.J. Tennant, 'Brailes, 1550-1800', unpublished M.Phil. Thesis, University of Leicester, 1977.

J. Thirsk (ed), *The agrarian history of England and Wales, Volume IV, 1500-1640*, Cambridge, 1967.

J. Thirsk and J.P. Cooper (eds), *Seventeenth century economic documents*, Oxford, 1972.

K. Thomas, 'Numeracy in early modern England', *Transactions of the Royal Historical Society*, 37, 1987.

J.E. Thorold Rogers, *A history of agriculture and prices in England* (6 vols), Oxford, 1866-1900.

K. Tiller (ed), *Church and chapel in Oxfordshire 1851*, Oxfordshire Record Society, 55, 1987.

A. Tindal Hart, *Clergy and society 1600-1800*, London, 1968.

G. Trosse, *The life of the Reverend Mr George Trosse*, 1714.

G. Lyon Turner, *Original Records of Early Nonconformity* (3 vols), 1911-4.

T. Unwin, *Late seventeenth-century taxation and population: the Nottinghamshire hearth taxes and Compton Census*, Historical Geography Research Series, 16, Norwich, 1985.

C. Vialls, 'The Duty on Marriages, Births and Burials, 1695-1706', unpublished dissertation submitted to Institute of Heraldic and Genealogical Studies for diploma in Heraldic and General Studies, 1987.

K. Wachter, E.A. Hammel, and P. Laslett, *Statistical studies of historical social structure*, London, 1978.

T.C. Wales, 'Poverty and parish relief in seventeenth-century Norfolk', in R. Smith (ed), *Land, kinship and life cycle*, Cambridge, 1984.

R. Wall, 'The household, demographic and economic change in England, 1650-1970', in R. Wall (edited in collaboration with J. Robin and P. Laslett), *Family forms in historic Europe*, Cambridge, 1983.

— 'Regional and temporal variations in household structure from 1650', in T. Hobcraft and P. Rees (eds), *Regional demographic development*, London, 1977.

— 'Regional and temporal variations in the structure of the British household since 1851', in T. Barker and M. Drake (eds), *Population and society in Britain 1850-1980*, London, 1982.

— 'Women alone in English society' *Annales de Démographie Historique*, 1981.

R. Wall (edited in collaboration with J. Robin and P. Laslett), *Family forms in historic Europe*, Cambridge, 1983.

W.R. Ward, *The English Land tax in the eighteenth century*, Oxford, 1953.

M.R. Watts, *The Dissenters from the Reformation to the French Revolution*, Oxford, 1978.

L. Weatherill, *Consumer behaviour and material culture in Britain 1660-1760*, London, 1988.

W.F. Webster (ed), 'Nottinghamshire Hearth tax 1664:1674', *Thoroton Society Record Series*, 38, Nottingham, 1988.

M.M.B. Weinstock, 'Oxfordshire hearth tax returns, 1665', *Oxfordshire Record Society*, 21, 1940.

J. West, *Village records*, London, 1962.

A. Whiteman, 'The census that never was: a problem in authorship and dating', in A. Whiteman, J.S. Bromley and P.G.M. Dickson (eds), *Statesmen, scholars and merchants: essays in eighteenth-century history presented to Dame Lucy Sutherland*, Oxford, 1973.

— 'The Episcopate of Dr Seth Ward Bishop of Exeter, 1662-1667, and Salisbury, 1667-1689', unpublished D.Phil Thesis, University of Oxford, 1951.

— (ed. with the assistance of Mary Clapinson), *The Compton Census of 1676: a critical edition*, British Academy: Records of Social and Economic History, N.S. 10, London, 1986.

C.E. Whiting, *Studies in English Puritanism from the Restoration to the Revolution, 1660-1688*, London, 1931.

C. Whitworth, *The political and commercial works of Charles D'Avenant* (8 vols), London, 1771.

W.F. Willcox (ed), *Natural and Political Observations ... by John Graunt*, Baltimore, 1939.

J.G. Williamson, *Did Britain's capitalism breed inequality?*, Boston, 1983.

C. Wilson, *England's apprenticeship 1603-1673*, London, 1965.

R.B. Wood-Jones, *Traditional domestic architecture of the Banbury region*, Manchester, 1963.

R.I. Woods and P.R.A. Hinde, 'Nuptiality and age at marriage in nineteenth- century England', *Journal of Family History*, 10, 1985.

S. Wright, 'Catechism, confirmation and communion', in S. Wright (ed), *Parish, church and people*, 1988.

— 'Churmaids, Huswyfes and Hucksters', in L. Charles and L. Duffin (eds), *Women and work in pre-industrial England*, London, 1985.

— 'Easter books and parish rate books: a new source for the urban historian', *Urban History Yearbook*, 1985.

— 'A guide to Easter Books and related parish listings', *Local Population Studies*, Part I, 42, Part II, 43, 1989.

— (ed), *Parish, church and people: local studies in lay religion*, London, 1988.

K. Wrightson, 'The social order of early modern England: three approaches', in L. Bonfield, R. Smith and K. Wrightson (eds), *The world we have gained: histories of population and social structure*, Oxford, 1986.

— 'Two concepts of order', in J. Brewer and J. Styles (eds), *An ungovernable people*, London, 1980.

E.A. Wrigley, 'Births and baptisms: the use of Anglican Baptism registers as a source of information about the numbers of Births in England before the Beginning of Civil Registration', *Population Studies*, 31, 1977.

— 'Clandestine marriage in Tetbury in the late seventeenth century', *Local Population Studies*, 10, 1973.

— 'The fall of marital fertility in nineteenth-century France: Examplar or exception?' (Part II), *European Journal of Population*, 1, 1985.

E.A. Wrigley, (ed), *An introduction to English historical demography: from the sixteenth to the nineteenth century*, London, 1966.

—— 'Marital fertility in seventeenth-century Colyton: a note', *Economic History Review*, 2nd series, 31, 1978.

—— 'Mortality in pre-industrial England: the example of Colyton, Devon, over three centuries', *Daedelus*, 97, 1968.

—— 'Urban growth and agricultural change: England and the continent in the early modern period', in *Journal of Interdisciplinary History*, 15, 1985.

E.A. Wrigley and R.S. Schofield, 'English population history from family reconstitution: summary results 1600-1799', *Population Studies*, 38, 1983.

—— *The population history of England, 1541-1871: a reconstruction*, London, 1981; 2nd edition, Cambridge, 1989.

D. Wykes, 'A reappraisal of the reliability of the 1676 Compton Census with respect to Leicestershire', *Leicestershire Archaeological and Historical Society, Transactions*, 60, 1980.

Official publications

British Parliamentary Papers, *Abstract of the Answers and Returns made pursuant to an Act...Intituled An Act for taking an Account of the Population of Great Britain*, 1801.

British Parliamentary Papers, *Second Report of the Committee on Municipal Corporations in England and Wales*, 1837.

Calendar of Treasury Books, III, VII.

Calendar of State Papers (Domestic), 1671-72, 1672, 1672-3.

Journal of the House of Commons, VIII.

Journal of the House of Lords, XI.

OPCS Census 1981, Household and family composition, England and Wales, (CEN 81 HFC), HMSO, 1984.

Royal Commission on the distribution of income and wealth, HMSO, 1980.

Index

Three separate indexes are provided, arranged by name, subject and place. For each, page numbers given in *italics* refer to illustrations, figures or tables.

NAME INDEX

SUBJECT INDEX

PLACE INDEX